BELFAST SHIPBUILDERS

A Titanic Tale

STEPHEN CAMERON is a co-founder and past Chairman of the Belfast Titanic Society, which was formerly called The Ulster Titanic Society. He has researched the *Titanic* since 1992. He was a Station Commander with the Northern Ireland Fire Brigade. He lives in Bangor, Co. Down with his wife. He continues to research the subject and has lectured widely on his research.

For my granddaughters Grace and Rebekah

BELFAST
SHIPBUILDERS
A Titanic Tale

STEPHEN CAMERON

Published 2011 by
Colourpoint Books
Colourpoint House, Jubilee Business Park
Jubilee Road, Newtownards, BT23 4YH
Tel: 028 9182 6339
Fax: 028 9182 1900
E-mail: info@colourpoint.co.uk
Web: www.colourpoint.co.uk

First Edition
First Impression

A catalogue record for this book is available from the British Library.

Designed by April Sky Design, Newtownards
Tel: 028 9182 7195
Web: www.aprilsky.co.uk

Printed by W&G Baird, Antrim

ISBN 978-1-906578-78-7

Front cover: 'Titanic Leaving Belfast for Sea Trials' by E.D. Walker

Contents

Acknowledgements

To undertake this quite lengthy historical view of the history of the shipbuilding in Belfast has proved to be both extremely difficult and immensely interesting. It would have been so much harder without the valuable help and assistance given by many people. I should particularly like to thank the following people who have helped me throughout my research:

Mary Bradley and the staff at the South Eastern Education and Library Board Headquarters;

Stephen Hanson and the staff at Bangor Library, for their continuing support and assistance;

The Staff at the Public Record Office for Northern Ireland;

The Staff at the Belfast Central Library, Irish Section and the Newspaper Section;

Sally Skillen at the Ulster Folk and Transport Museum;

Vincent Dargan and family for information regarding William Dargan;

Anthony Hickson, for information regarding Robert Hickson;

The late John Parkinson, President of the Belfast Titanic Society;

George McAllister who gave so much of his time and his wealth of information on how things were done in the Harland and Wolff shipyard;

David Mann for information relating to Gustav Schwabe;

Charlie Hass and Jack P. Eaton;

Mr Tom O'Connor of the Belfast Harbour Commissioners;

Christine McKenna for her detctive work in New York;

The Editor and staff of the *Belfast Newsletter*;

Titanic Quarter Limited;

Nomadic Charitable Trust.

I especially want to thank Una Reilly and Alastair Walker for their comments and analysis of my original manuscript, and also to thank Una Reilly for doing me the honour of writing the Foreword to this book.

Foreword

I was very honoured to have been asked to write this foreword to my friend Stephen Cameron's latest book. Shipbuilding brought us together as we first met at the fledging meeting to discuss the formation of a *Titanic* Society in the city of her birth. Stephen and I went on to become the co-Founders of the Belfast Titanic Society which seeks, and in my mind has succeeded, to set Belfast in its correct place in the worldwide *Titanic* story. I'm afraid I'm a bit of a one-ship girl but Stephen, over the years since that meeting in the early 1990s, has developed a passion for the history of the city and the men who built ships from wood, iron and then steel. Ships of which Belfast can be so proud. A Belfast built ship was a worthy addition to any Shipping line and was created by the dedication, skill and craftsmanship of the workforce of the various yards involved.

Until I got interested in the Belfast *Titanic* story, I, born and bred in the city, was totally unaware of our proud maritime history. Unless involved with 'the Yard' directly, shipbuilding was a hidden world, locked behind those famous green gates, under the imposing yellow cranes Samson and Goliath. The book sets the history of shipbuilding here in context and makes fascinating reading.

Stephen sets the scene for readers and goes a long way to answering that question – Why Belfast? How come a small town – not a city until relatively late in the nineteenth century, with no port to talk of, with a contorted and very difficult waterway, no raw materials to mention and nobody of skilled workforce – came to rule the world's shipbuilding industry?

Stories and characters abound, beginning with the building of the wooden ship *Eagle Wing* in 1630 and ending in 1924 with the death of William Pirrie, Chairman of Harland and Wolff. Thousands of ships have been built and sailed away from Belfast. The history shows the development of 'the family business' with names that resonate down the years ... the great and the good. But there is also the story of the men who actually built the ships, the harsh conditions involved with building ships practically by hand.

In the 20 years I have known Stephen, I have seen him develop his interest in Belfast and its maritime history along with his commitment to the Belfast Titanic Society which would not be where it is today without his input and enthusiasm. Stephen is highly sought after as a speaker on Belfast and all things and people involved with shipbuilding. I know this latest book will be as well received as his previous ones.

The book is not only a great read for all but will be a must for students of the topic and the era. It opens our eyes to the vision of those first merchants of Belfast, who saw the potential of Belfast when others didn't, who had the courage to fight for what they wanted and to whom we all owe a great deal of gratitude for setting in motion what was to become the Belfast we know today. I cannot recommend this book highly enough and I congratulate Stephen on the fruits of his prodigious research.

Una Reilly
Chairman and Co-founder Belfast Titanic Society

Introduction

Belfast, the capital of Northern Ireland sits astride the river Lagan as it makes its way towards Belfast Lough and the Irish Sea.

The city is a bit of a strange place. You both love and hate it, a place where the locals just about tolerate each other, but yet strangely reach out a hand of friendship to a visitor. At times Belfast can also seem a very drab and dirty place, but it has so much to offer, not only to the locals but to those visitors who care to come to our City. Belfast is buzzing! Just look around at the investment and building work that has been going on in just the past few years, at the Cathedral Quarter and the new Titanic Quarter.

Sadly, however, over recent years the industrial heart of the city has diminished from its former glory. Today in Belfast heavy industry is the exception rather than the rule. Yet this city and its hard working citizens have, over the years, placed Belfast at the top of the industrial league. At one time it boasted having the largest rope works in the world, there was a massive glass works and, maybe not that politically correct in today's health conscious society, the Gallaher Tobacco Company was at the forefront for smokers, with its Blues, Greens and Condor brands. Firms like Mackies, Davison's Sirocco works, airplane manufacturers Short Brothers and Harland, and even the short lived Delorean car plant were all testaments to Belfast build and quality.

What Belfast did have and what was to make it world famous was shipbuilding. It could proudly boast to have the largest shipyard in the world, that of the massive East Belfast shipyard of Harland and Wolff. It was in this yard that the work force continually constructed and launched bigger and bigger ships, practically each one of them becoming the largest ship in the world at its respective launch. It was here in 1912 that probably the most famous or infamous ship, the *Titanic*, departed from the Lough and into the realms of the history books. Belfast shipyards also have the unique distinction of giving the world not one ship named *Titanic* but two. In 1888 the shipbuilding firm of McIlwaine and McColl, launched a 1,608 ton, schooner with a triple expansion steam engine and named the vessel *Titanic*.

The earliest records of this fledgling industry date back to around the year 1630, when King Charles I was on the throne, Urban VIII was Pope and, in Belfast, local Presbyterian ministers commissioned the building of a ship, The

An aerial view of the Belfast port and Queen's Island.
(Courtesy of Titanic Quarter Ltd.)

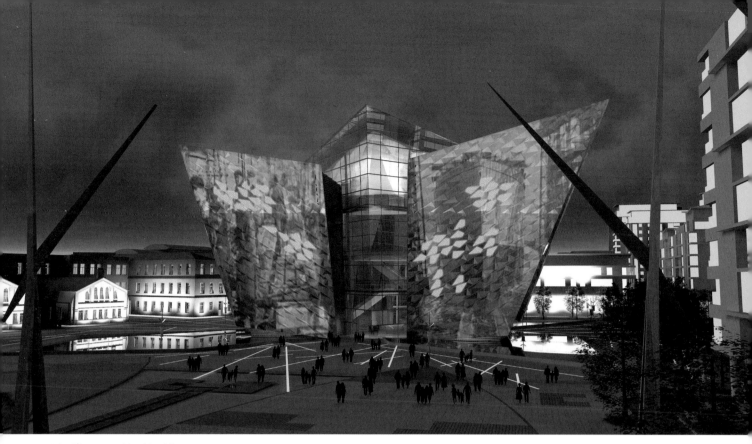

The 'Titanic Belfast' building, Titanic Quarter.

(Courtesy of Titanic Quarter Ltd.)

Eagle Wing, that was unsuccessfully to transport them away from these shores.

Shipbuilding was formally established on the shores of the river Lagan in 1791 when a Scot by the name of William Ritchie, having been invited by local businessmen to advise them about the possibility of setting up a shipbuilding yard, saw the potential himself and set up his own firm, becoming the founding father of that trade in Belfast. From that date shipbuilding was to grow to such levels that Belfast became the envy of the world. Individuals were to make their mark in the passage of time but mostly the growth was to be attributed to families and their connections.

Douglas Carson, the well known and respected Belfast historian and public speaker, begins his talk entitled 'The Family Tree of *Titanic*' by informing his audience, "that the beginnings of what was to become the giant shipyard of Harland and Wolff in East Belfast was a family firm and it grew out of a family with a larger family growing around it." This is quite correct. One of the first families was that of the previously mentioned William Ritchie. They were to be the instigators and pioneers of shipbuilding from those early days. Following mergers with Ritchie's own family and others there is a direct connection to another major Belfast shipyard, that of Workman Clark, this yard being bought over eventually by Harland and Wolff and absorbed into his own shipyard.

The Pirrie family, starting with Captain William Pirrie around 1820 and finishing with his grandson William Pirrie, who became Viscount Pirrie of Belfast, were to shape the port of Belfast and produce the finest ships in the world. Included in the Pirrie family were Alexander Carlisle, brother in law of Pirrie junior, who was a Managing Director and Chief Naval Architect in the shipyard and Thomas Andrews, a nephew of the young Pirrie who would take over the designing reins from Carlisle and ultimately lose his life while representing Harland and Wolff on the maiden voyage of the *Titanic*.

The Hickson family of Tralee, Ireland, were to produce a son, Robert, who would first be involved in the family lumber and shipping business, before moving north to Belfast to take over a struggling Iron Foundry. He would unsuccessfully try his hand at shipbuilding and eventually be forced to sell his small yard for £4,900 to an Englishman, Edward Harland. Harland's family connections were to see him take his distant cousin Gustav Wolff as a Partner with financial assistance from another relative Gustav Schwabe, who was the uncle of Wolff.

The Wilson's were another family that would become involved in the story of shipbuilding when Walter and his brother Alexander became pupils at the Harland and Wolff yard and eventually Walter, who was the first pupil of Hickson, would become a Partner in the firm of Harland and Wolff.

Others who would shape the destiny of Harland and Wolff were the Bibby family, owners of the Bibby Line. They were to place the very first order with Edward Harland for the *Venetian*, which was launched in 1859. The Bibby Line were also part of a consortium which had the *Anvil Point* constructed, probably the last ship built at the yard. The Ismays too played an important role, with the father Thomas and son Bruce deciding to build practically every ship in their White Star Line in Belfast.

In my first book, *Titanic Belfast's Own*, I looked specifically at the construction of the *Titanic* and the local people who both worked and sailed on her. I have to stress that this book is not meant to be an in-depth history of Harland and Wolff. That has been fully detailed and recorded in the very well researched and written *Shipbuilders to the World* by Michael Moss and John D. Hume. Rather, in this book, I wish to explore how shipbuilding first started and expanded here in this 'wee town', the city of my birth, that with no natural resources, neither any deposits of coal or iron ore, but yet gifted individuals and workmen, would produce some of the most beautiful and graceful ships that were ever to be launched. Ships built here included the *Oceanic, Majestic, Teutonic,* the three Olympic class liners and even the proposed 1928 *Oceanic III*, a 1,000 ft, 60,000 ton monster of a ship that would never get off the drawing board.

In researching this subject, much was drawn from the company records of Harland and Wolff, which are held at the Public Record Office in Belfast. In those priceless records however, there are several large gaps, which were the result of a disastrous fire at the Record Office in Dublin in the 1920s. This blaze destroyed many invaluable records including census returns. Also many of Harland and Wolff's records were destroyed when the shipyard was targeted and very heavily damaged as a result of the air raids in the Belfast Blitz on the 15 April 1941. If all of that wasn't bad enough, William Pirrie, the Chairman of the Belfast

12

shipyard, in late 1902, decided that the growing mountains of paperwork and official books accumulating in the yard should be reduced and he introduced a system of document disposal. He sent a memorandum dated January 1903 to the senior Managers ordering the destruction of old books and papers held by their respective departments. This practice is something that today is widely carried out by larger companies.

I feel that it would be fitting to end this exploration of the contribution that Belfast shipbuilders and workmen made, with the demise of those family connections, on the death of William James Pirrie, first Viscount Pirrie of Belfast in June 1924.

Stephen Cameron
Bangor

CHAPTER 1

Early Shipbuilding in Belfast

To take a stroll around the harbour area of Belfast today, reveals an area that is bustling with new developments. New apartment blocks, office space and entertainment areas such as new bars, the Waterfront Hall and the massive Odyssey Arena with its cinemas, W5 centre, bars, restaurants and full size ice rink, illustrate how the City has progressed. The port of the City has a regular High Speed Ferry that links it with Stranraer in Scotland, container ships berth continuously bringing goods and materials in while taking finished goods away. Over the last few years cruise ships have placed Belfast on their itinerary making the city a must see place.

Stenna Line H.S.S. in the Musgrave Channel with the Samson and Goliath cranes in the background.

(Donna Marijne)

However, if you take a closer look in that area there is little sign of the former industrial glory of Belfast. Gone are the glass works, the rope works, the heavy industrial trade of firms like Davidson and Company with their Sirocco Works, which was built on the site of the earlier glass works. Gone also are the shipyards that made the town famous, the 'wee yard' of Workman Clark and the 'bigger yard' of Harland and Wolff.

Certainly, Harland and Wolff are still there today, their presence imprinted on the sky line of Belfast with the two massive yellow cranes, Samson and Goliath. However, in reality the days of shipbuilding in Belfast are now gone and most probably will never return. Between these two shipyards, in their heyday, they would be responsible for a massive output of ships. To give an example of this, in the years 1901 to 1909 the two yards would be accountable for a combined output of over 1.2 million tons of shipping, which was 50% more that the output of the shipyard of Swan Hunter on the Tyne.

However, Belfast wasn't always the main maritime centre of this area of Ireland. In the early 1600s the population of the town, if it could even be described as such, was less than 500 people, and was situated in the area now know as Custom

House Square, where the river Farset discharged into the Lagan. The conditions of the river at Belfast quayside were so poor that when the tide was out, ships could virtually be stranded at the quayside until the next high tide. Early maps of the area show Carrickfergus on the northern shoreline of the lough as being of more importance. The lough that we know today as Belfast Lough was in those early days referred to as Carrickfergus Lough. Vessels would be able to come and go reasonably freely into Carrickfergus without the hindrance of waiting for the right tidal conditions. Carrickfergus also benefited financially with the town being able to retain one third of all customs duties on goods both entering and leaving the town.

The situation for Carrickfergus was about to change and for them it would be for the worse as they were about to lose their position as the main port on the shores of the lough.

Many years earlier in 1538, Sir John Perrot, a Lord Deputy for Queen Elizabeth I, reported to the Monarch that Belfast seemed like a suitable location for shipbuilding. Around the banks of the river were large wooded areas of Irish oak and in Cromac Wood (now the Cromac Street area) wild deer were in abundance. This report from Perrot was not acted upon initially, but finally on 27 April 1613, Belfast was granted its Charter of Incorporation by King James I. Among other things, this Charter allowed the newly constituted Town of Belfast to elect a Sovereign (First Citizen or Chief Magistrate) and 12 Burgesses to govern the town, and also to return two members to Parliament. Mr John Vesey was to be the first Sovereign, with Sir John Blennerhasset and George Trevillian being the first two men to represent Belfast at the Westminster Parliament. More importantly, this new Charter allowed the town to construct "one wharf or quay, in any convenient place on the banks of the river of Belfast aforesaid", and custom dues could be collected.

This new wharf was constructed at the point where the river Farset flowed into the Lagan, this today is around the area where the Albert Memorial Clock is situated. (The river remained open until around 1770. It was then that a decision was taken to cover it over. However the area around the new High Street was prone to flooding. In January 1796, floodwater was over a foot deep.) Several years later in 1637 the town of Carrickfergus finally was to lose its premier position on the shores of the Lough when their local Corporation was forced to sell its maritime and custom rights for the sum of £3,000 to the town of Belfast.

John Vesey, the newly appointed Belfast Sovereign, was permitted to hold a Court of Petty Offences for the recovery of sums not exceeding £20 and with the Burgesses they were granted the right to make different laws and regulations for the prosperity of the town and to dispose of merchandise within the town or a three mile radius of it. He was also permitted to make regulations regarding the Town's market. The Sovereign was requested to compile a list of all men in the town of Belfast and make arrangements for them to be trained as soldiers. Two

An early engraved image of High Street in Belfast with sailing ship docked at quayside on left.

(From paintings held in the collection of the Belfast Harbour Commissioners.)

years later a new law was passed ordering that all persons over the age of 13 years were to attend the High Street Corporation Church upon the Sabbath or at any other prayer meeting. Failure to attend was punished by fine of up to five shillings.

The first major record of ship building in Belfast was around 1636, regarding the sailing vessel *Eagle Wing*. This 150 ton sailing ship had been built in Belfast having been commissioned by local Presbyterian ministers who felt that they were being persecuted for their faith. This ship was intended to take them and their followers to a new life in America. At that time there was no organised shipbuilding in the town. However, there were several carpenters and joiners who would undertake repair work and most probably this group would have been approached with a request to construct the vessel out of the local oak. The ship, with 140 passengers and four Presbyterian Ministers, left Belfast on the morning of the 9 September 1636 heading for a new life in America. Just after departing from Belfast the ship encountered heavy seas and had to seek shelter in Loch Ryan across the North Channel in Scotland. The vessel then set sail for the new world and initially made very good progress with following winds. It was almost 800 miles from the coast of the Americas when very heavy seas and horrendous gales pounded the ship. The rudder was torn off its hinges. A shipwright on board managed to repair the rudder, but the Reverend John Livingstone, who was the leading Minister on the ship, declared that the storm was a warning from God and that it was His way of telling them that they should return home. This they did and the *Eagle Wing* limped back into Carrickfergus Lough (prior to it being called Belfast Lough) where they made land on 3 November at Groomsport on the County Down coast. What later became of the ministers and their flock is uncertain but the event is commemorated each year in the village of Groomsport with the 'Eagle Wing Festival'.

There is no direct documented evidence that the *Eagle Wing* was in fact built anywhere in Belfast, or Carrickfergus Lough. Over the years it has been assumed that the ship was built there. It does seem strange that prior to the *Eagle Wing* there had been no other mention of ships being built. It also seems strange, bearing that in mind, that Belfast would even be able to construct a complex vessel fit to attempt an Atlantic crossing. However, the Reverend Thomas Hamilton, a Past President of Queen's University, in his *History of the Presbyterian Church* comments that here may have been seen the construction of a small ship. Professor John M. Barkley, past Principal of Union Theological College in Belfast, in a paper *To America by the Eagle Wing* states that during his research he was given a document entitled *The Girvan Family* which states that one member of that family, David, was involved with the construction of the *Eagle Wing* in Carrickfergus. The name of the ship is taken from the Book of Exodus where the Lord, referring to how He brought the Israelites out of Egypt, tells Moses "how I carried you as an eagle carries her young on her wings and brought you here to me."[1]

Over the next years the trade in and out of the new quay at Belfast was to increase, with the enterprise of some of the local merchants and business people. In 1658 a consortium of locals including Michael Bigger, William Smith and Hugh Eccles (who would in 1674 be elected Sovereign) purchased a sailing vessel called the *Unicorn* for the substantial sum of £618. The vessel was engaged in trading between Belfast and Amsterdam. Later the same group, but now expanded to include George McCartney and Robert Leathes (both ex Sovereigns), added the sailing ships *Golden Star* and *North Star* to their fleet.

By 1663, trade had increased to such a level that there were 29 ship owners in the town. Of these ships, which bore names like *Grizell, Salmon, Anne, Betty* and *Martha,* 15 of them were registered as having been constructed in Belfast, with the vast majority of their owners being or having been the Sovereign of the town. These vessels ranged in size from small barges of six tons up to sailing ships of 50 tons and would have been constructed from the local timber in the forests around the town. There are no records available of where, when or by whom these vessels were constructed by, as the shipbuilding was still carried out in a very adhoc nature. The Sovereigns and Belfast Corporation were aware that improvements were needed in the harbour area and one Sovereign, George McCartney, who had been responsible for organising a new water supply to the town by laying wooden piping from a local water source, had the quay at the river Lagan extended around the year 1675. This extension was made in land that was owned by the Sovereign, no doubt a case of early profiteering. Two years earlier McCartney had appointed a Mr John Dean as water bailiff for the town. Dean's duties included collecting fees for anchorage, ensuring that there were no obstacles to navigation and that "rubbish and filth were not deposited in the harbour".

The first mention of any notable ship being constructed was in 1699 when a 250 ton sailing ship, the *Loyal Charles*, was built and launched in the town, and again it was owned by local merchants.

Surprisingly there are no records of any organised shipbuilding or memorable launches in the town for the next 86 years, but in 1729, Parliament passed an Act which required the cleaning of the Port, Harbour and Rivers of certain towns including Belfast. This Act also gave authority to establish a Ballast Office in the town. The main purpose of the Act was to ensure that the ports would be in good condition and that revenues collected would be returned to Parliament. The Act was doomed to failure as the only things permitted to the Corporation were the supply of ballast at a charge to incoming vessels and keeping the river clear. Another and possibly the main reason for the failure was that two merchants, Rainey Maxwell and William McCartney, wanted to raise the fees for port dues by around 300 %, from two pence per ton to six pence. This was seen by the Belfast public as being blatant profiteering and was to lead to the Act failing.

In 1785 the Belfast Harbour Act was promulgated. This new Act took authority away from the Corporation and established a new body for "preserving and improving the Port and Harbour of Belfast". This new body from the beginning was referred to as the Belfast Ballast Board and had 15 members including the Right Honourable Arthur, Earl of Donegall, Waddell Cunningham and Sovereign George Black. The Principal Officer of the Ballast Board was to be called the Ballast Master and Samuel McTeir was the first to hold the position with a yearly fee of 50 guineas.

The construction and repair of ships in the town was still very disorganised with only a few men periodically engaged in this work, but this was all about to change. In March 1791, following a request from some local merchants, William Ritchie from Saltcoats in Scotland came to visit Belfast with a view to setting up a shipyard on the banks of the Lagan. Ritchie who had been born in Scotland in 1755 had two other brothers, John born in 1751 and Hugh born in 1767. In 1775 William Ritchie had established his own shipbuilding yard in Ayrshire. Whatever thoughts or images of the area around the Lagan that Ritchie saw when he visited will never be known, but he indeed saw the possibility of establishing for himself a brand new shipbuilding yard free from any competition. He arrived back in Belfast, just four months later on 3 July with ten workmen, equipment and materials, and his younger brother Hugh, who had been serving his apprenticeship in the Scottish yard. William Ritchie was to be the catalyst for this new organised venture. It would be here in Belfast that he and his brothers would set up their homes and shipyard, and plant that seed that would grow and put the city at the forefront of the world's shipbuilders.

Quite quickly Ritchie set up his yard on the banks of the Lagan at the Old Lime Kiln, roughly in the area where Corporation Street is today. The Ballast Board had agreed to build a graving platform for the new yard. This was an early

William Ritchie and John Ritchie, brother of William.

(From paintings held in the collection of the Belfast Harbour Commissioners.)

form of Graving Dock, in which the ship could be hauled out of the water to allow work to be carried out on the hull. William Ritchie's first ship, the 300-ton, wooden sailing ship *Hibernian*, was launched into the river Lagan on the 7 July 1792. The ship sailed to New York on its maiden voyage six weeks later. So keen were her owners for trade that they were to use a detail of the ship's construction as a means of having American custom duties reduced. They announced that on this maiden voyage any persons shipping goods would save 5% of the American custom duties due to the ship having an "American bottom".

The graving platform constructed earlier was to be of limited use to Ritchie. What was really needed was a conventional dry dock into which a ship could be floated, the gate closed behind it and the water then pumped out. The Ballast Board agreed that a dry dock should be constructed and in 1796, only five years after Ritchie came to Belfast, the Board agreed to have a dock built. Ritchie completed this work himself, which was finished by 1

William Ritchie's shipyard c. 1791–1792

(From paintings held in the collection of the Belfast Harbour Commissioners.)

January 1800. The cost of the dock was around £7,000 and it was large enough to allow three ships each of 200 tons to docked at the same time. The dock, which was called 'No.1 Clarendon Graving Dock', is still in existence today at the rear of the Belfast Harbour Commissioners Offices, although it should be added that it is no longer in use.

In 1798, the year that Henry Joy McCracken was publicly hanged in High Street in Belfast, Hugh Ritchie, who had started as an apprentice with his brother William, left and set up his own shipbuilding yard just north of the main Ritchie yard. Hugh died on the 1 January 1808 aged just 41 and was succeeded by his brother John, who was now aged 57. The name of new the shipyard was changed to John Ritchie and Sons.

In those early days, the new shipbuilding industry that was growing on the banks of the Lagan drew attention from many local people, none stranger than that of a young boy called Thomas Romney Robinson, who was born in 1792. His father Thomas was an accomplished painter and he was later to present a painting of William Ritchie to the Belfast Harbour Commissioners. In 1802, the young Robinson, who no doubt had travelled with his father to witness the burgeoning new industry, was obviously so impressed by what he saw that it encouraged him to compose a poem entitled *The Triumph of Commerce* in honour of Ritchie.

The Triumph of Commerce

Ingenious Ritchie! Commerce may now smile
And shed her blessing o'er Hibernia's Isle
Go, teach her sons to raise the ship on high
The pointed mast, high towering to the sky.

With every effort of the useful art,
With every passion of the feeling heart
Go, claim the crown excelling virtue brings
A prize more precious than the wealth of kings.

Thy numerous works are trophies of thy fame,
Which Envy's poisonous breath can ne'er defame.[2]

Romney Robinson, 'child bard of Belfast'.

Romney Robinson, who at one stage was referred to as the 'child bard of Belfast', was to have a collection of his poems entitled *Juvenile Poems* published in 1802. He would eventually go on to become Director of the Armagh Observatory and pursue science as a career. In later life he invented the cup anemometer, a device that would accurately measure wind speed, an invention that is still in use today. He also contributed much to the world of science, and died in 1882 at the ripe old age of 90.

In July 1811, William Ritchie wrote of his early experiences of shipbuilding in Belfast when he stated:

"Since the commencement I have built 32 vessels, and my brother eight, besides several lighters and small ones. The vessels I have built were from 50 to 450 tons burthen the greatest part about 220 tons.

When I came to Belfast there were only about six jobbing ship-carpenters being without any person to direct them, they were not (by that means) constantly employed, as the vessels belonging to the town were purchased and repaired in England and Scotland.

Since I came here, I have brought from Scotland several ship joiners, block-makers and blacksmiths. In my blacksmith's shop all kinds of ship work are done in the best manner, also anchors of all sizes to 14 cwt. There are now employed in the two shipyards, 44 journeymen carpenters; 55 apprentices; seven pair of sawyers; 12 blacksmiths, and several joiners; the weekly wages about £120. The increase of this business is partly owing to the accommodation of a good graving dock, capable of containing at one time three vessels of 200 tons each. These shipyards and graving dock stand on ground that I reclaimed from the sea by embankments and quays fronted with stone.

In 1796, I engaged with the Ballast Office Corporation to build the dock mentioned, which I completed 1st of January 1800. When I came to Belfast in 1791, the Liverpool traders consisted of four sloops, each about 80 tons burthen, and the London traders of four brigs of 160 tons. There are now in the London trade 10 brigs averaging 270 tons, and in the Liverpool trade eight brigs of 160 tons each; there are also two brigs that trade to Bristol of 150 tons one brig and two sloops in the Dublin trade averaging 90 tons. The above 26 vessels trade constantly to their respective ports; the 10 London traders are armed and fitted out in the completest manner. All the other vessels are kept in the best state of repair and equipment. In addition to the above, there are 12 ships and brigs trading to the West Indies and other parts that will average 350 tons each, all armed and fitted out in the best manner also a number of other vessels of various sizes that trade to different parts. The greatest part of the traders and West India vessels have been built in Belfast several of them with Irish Oak and it is but justice to say that for elegance mould fastness of sailing and utility in every respect they are unrivalled in any of the ports they trade to."[3]

One of the ships launched by Ritchie's yard, was called the *New System*. The ship was launched in front of many spectators and when launched, she was under ballast. The vessel was a schooner of around 60 tons and was constructed to a new method where there were no frame timbers, beams or any metal below the water line, except for a few bolts. The advantage of this method of construction was to reduce the cost to the shipyard of materials, and increase the strength and durability of the vessel. So new and radical was the design of the *New System* that a Mr William Annesley produced a pamphlet with drawings, designs and calculations that the shipyard used when they planned and constructed this new sailing ship.

In the same year John Ritchie left his brother and formed a new partnership with Alexander McLaine, who came from the Isle of Skye in Scotland. This new partnership was to found another new yard, which was called Ritchie and McLaine. In 1826 this shipyard was credited with building *The Chieftain*, the first steamboat to be constructed in Ireland.

The Ritchie's not only set up their yards and helped early Belfast prosper but they became involved in the affairs of the town. When proposals were laid to form the new Academical Institution, William and Hugh contributed over £33 to the fund. William, a Presbyterian, was a great supporter of the Reverend William Bristow and assisted with his successful campaign to be elected Sovereign of the town. In 1796 he donated two guineas to the 100 guinea reward for information relating to the arrest of the person responsible for the murder of local man William McBride.

By 1820, then aged 65, William Ritchie retired from shipbuilding and allowed his manager Charles Connell to continue to run the yard for him. In 1824 Connell, who had been born in Irvine in Scotland, was in a position to purchase the yard from Ritchie and he then renamed it Charles Connell and Sons. Ritchie was elected onto the committees of the General Hospital, the Pipe Water and the Police Committee, and was Chairman of the management committee of the Charitable Society in the Town. He died on the 18 January 1834 and was buried at the new Burying Ground at Clifton Street. A few days after his death the *Bible Christian* published the following eulogy about him:

> "There was no institution in Belfast of a public nature, whether literary, scientific or charitable, which was not largely indebted to him for support. No project could be started in which the welfare of his fellow townsmen was concerned without receiving his prompt and zealous aid.
>
> In the Second Congregation of Presbyterians, of which he was a member, those who witnessed his exertions to promote its prosperity and aid the furtherance of Gospel truth will long cherish his memory.
>
> Amiable, charitable and actively benevolent, he retained through life the esteem of all parties and of all sects, and left the world without having incurred the hostility of anyone.
>
> The estimation in which his character was held might have been inferred from the numerous assemblage who attended his remains to the meeting house in which he had been a worshipper to hear a funeral address from his minister and friend, the Rev. J. Porter, and from thence to the place of interment."[4]

John Ritchie, who had earlier gone into partnership with Alexander McLaine, died on 4 April 1828 at the age of 77 and was buried in the same graveyard as his brother. His yard was taken over by his Partner who took his own sons into partnership to form the shipyard of Alexander McLaine and Sons. Hugh, the youngest Ritchie, had died in 1808 and was also interred at Clifton Street.

The deaths of the Ritchie brothers was to bring about the closure of the first family involved in placing Belfast at the forefront of the shipbuilding world. Sadly, the only memorial to this family and all that they achieved are the weathered and worn gravestones in the little known graveyard at Clifton Street in Belfast.

CHAPTER 2

The Next Steps Forward

The legacy left by the Ritchies was a firmly established shipbuilding operation in Belfast. While it may not have been massive by today's standards it was nonetheless quite an achievement for this period of time.

Yards operating on the County Antrim shores of the Lagan over the ensuing years were those of Charles Connell and Sons, Alexander McLaine and Sons, Kirwan and McClune, which would later become Thompson and McClune, Coates and Young of the Lagan Foundry, and McIlwaine and Lewis. McIlwaine and Lewis would later become McIlwaine and McColl, be bought over by Workman Clark, and subsequently be bought over by Harland and Wolff.

In those early days there were some notable vessels built and launched. In the year 1820 Coates and Young built the first wooden hulled steamship in Ireland that was propelled by paddle wheels, which were set on each side of the hull and powered by a 70 horsepower engine. Some years later, in 1838, this firm also built an iron hulled ship, *Countess of Caledon,* which is thought to have been the first such steamship built in Ireland. In 1844 they constructed the *Seagull,* another iron ship. In 1833 the *Hindoo,* the largest sailing ship so far constructed anywhere in Ireland, at 440 tons, was commissioned and built by a yard in Belfast for the trade routes to India.

Major problems with navigating the river Lagan were coming to a head around this period of time. As previously mentioned, not only did the river Lagan meander quite badly from the quay at High Street to the lough, but also the depth of water at high tide was just sufficient to allow vessels to come into the port. At low tide the depth of water was so shallow that, after discharging and loading up, the ships would have to wait for the next high tide on which to depart. This delay would not only frustrate the ship owners but would also affect their profits. Incoming vessels faced a similar situation, if they misjudged the state of the tide.

The problems regarding the depth of water and the meandering of the river into the harbour area were well known to the Ballast Board. In 1830 the Board had consulted a firm of engineers, Messer's Walker and Burgess, to find a solution to both of these issues. Mr James Walker of the company visited Belfast and eventually presented the Board with a very full and exhaustive report, in which he proposed two solutions, with costs ranging from £180,000 to £200,000. He suggested making two straight cuts at the bends of the river, in effect making one straight channel and also deepening the river by dredging to at least 12 ft.

Walker and Burgess' report was accepted with enthusiasm by the majority of the Board and the town's merchants, including Lord Belfast and Sir Arthur Chichester. However, an Act had to be passed in Parliament to allow the Board to carry out the report's recommendations and a sub-committee, comprising of William Tennant, William Boyd and Robert Grimshaw, was established to go to London to lobby Parliament.

As is Belfast's way of doing things, there was some opposition to the proposed works by those who felt that their personal interests were not being represented. Several locals lobbied Lord Donegall and managed to get him to agree with their views. His Lordship was influenced to write to his son, Lord Belfast, and get him to change his mind and to offer the most strenuous opposition to the proposed Bill unless the Members of Parliament for Counties of Down and Antrim, the towns of Belfast and Carrickfergus and the Sovereign of Belfast, Sir Stephen May, would be installed as members of the Ballast Board. The local paper, the *Northern Whig* ran a campaign against this interference and in a leader column stated:

> "Reformers of Belfast, Lord Belfast has refused to present your petition for reform; merchants and freeholders of Belfast, his papa has ordered him to oppose the very first Bill you apply for, to mend your quays and improve your harbour."

The article continued with an attack on the whole system of representation by concluding:

> "However, the whole procedure admirably illustrates the base and villainous corruption on which our representative system is founded; and ought to urge us all the more strenuously to procure such a Reform as will extricate the people out of the hands of the Aristocracy." [1]

The members of Belfast Corporation did not look on Donegall's proposals favourably. Their fears were further exasperated when Lord Belfast, in an attempt to dispel any opposition, made a further proposal which suggested that, in order to protect the rights of all concerned, the Ballast Board should consist of six members from the Belfast Corporation, in addition to members from County Antrim, Belfast and Carrickfergus. This proposal was thrown out by the Belfast Corporation but finally a compromise was agreed and a Bill received the Royal Assent in August 1831 with the title of 'An Act for the further improvement of the Port and Harbour of Belfast in Ireland and for other purposes.'

This new Act, while still drawing the Board's members from the members of Parliament, the Counties of Antrim and Down, and the Boroughs of Belfast, Carrickfergus and Downpatrick, allowed another 16 members to be elected on a rotational basis. These members would serve for no more than four years and, more importantly, local owners of registered shipping using the Port would now be granted voting rights to elect these extra members. The Ballast Board were given the right to purchase land and private docks to divert, deepen and direct the river Lagan, to make any such improvements as it felt necessary and to raise revenue by way of port dues.

The newly constituted Ballast Board applied to the Board of Public Works for a loan in the region of £60,000 to enable them to bring into operation Walker and Burgess' report. There was to be 'toing and froing' for several years, which would see the Board purchase around 900 acres including the portion of the river Lagan from High Street and the Long Bridge that led across the river to the east of the town, to where the river discharged at Garmoyle into Belfast Lough. Eventually, in 1837, seven years after the initial report, an Act was passed which allowed the Board to make alterations to the river so improvements could be made to the Port of Belfast. This new Act repealed the previous one and dissolved the Ballast Board. A new board was brought in, still with the same title but with 18 members. The Board then set about appointing a contractor for the project of finally straightening and deepening the river and chose to engage the services of William Dargan.

William Dargan, the son of a tenant farmer, was born on 28 February 1799, in County Carlow. Sadly, little is known of the early life of this vastly underrated civil engineer, whose contribution to numerous constructions in Ireland has never been fully examined. He was educated in England and his first job was in the surveyor's office in the firm of civil engineer Thomas Telford. In this employment he was involved in the construction of the road to Holyhead in 1820. Following the completion of that project he returned to Ireland and set himself up in his own business, which in these early days included constructing the road from Dublin to Howth. Within a few years he became involved with laying railway lines and was responsible for the construction of the first railway track in Ireland from Dublin to Kingstown. By 1853 he had been responsible for the laying of more than 600 miles of railway track in Ireland.

He was also responsible for the opening of the Ulster Canal, which ran from Lough Erne to Belfast, as well as constructing the Newry Canal. He was also heavily involved in the construction of the docks at Liverpool. So large did his business become, that at one stage he commented that in a 14 year period he paid over £800,000 in wages to his work force, which numbered over 50,000 men. This made him the then largest employer in Ireland, controlling industries as diverse as agriculture, linen production, civil engineering and ownership of a steamboat. This enterprise put him at the height of his career in the 'millionaire class'.

Dargan was contracted by the Ballast Board and made two cuts to straighten and also deepen the river Lagan. In 1840 his first cut was started and took a year to complete at a cost of around £42,000. The mud that was dredged up was initially to be dumped around the mouth of Belfast Lough near Whitehead, but a decision was made to deposit

William Dargan

any further mud on the County Down side of the river just adjacent to the area where the Queen's Bridge now is. The spoil that was dredged up over the next eight years was to form an area of around 59 acres in size. Dargan then made a straight cut across the front of where he had dumped the spoil (*see map on page 28*). In doing so he created an island, as the natural flow of the river Lagan was allowed to continue to flow behind this area on the County Down side.

When he had completed this first cut of the river, the City Fathers decided that, in his honour, this newly formed island was to be called Dargan's Island. Once the ground had settled it was to be laid out as a public park for the residents of Belfast. To gain access to the island rowing boats plied from the County Antrim side of the river carrying passengers there and back for a payment of one penny. One Belfast resident, Charles C. Russell, in an article in the *Northern Whig* newspaper, remembered that most of the ferrymen would be found sitting on the quayside smoking. It was only when the boat had filled up with sufficient passengers that the ferryman would collect the penny fare and start rowing them across the river. There were several occasions when those who had travelled over to the island forgot to get back to the ferryboat on time and were left stranded on the island overnight.

A bird's eye view of the completed cut which created Dargan's Island in the middle of the river lagan.

(Detail from 'A Bird's Eye View of Belfast' by Jacob Henry Connop (1863). Painting produced courtesy of Linen Hall Library.)

This new attraction for the Belfast citizens, contained in an area of 17 acres, consisted of a winter garden, a wooded area with walks laid out and various amusements, including a small zoo, with a golden eagle, monkeys, raccoons and a pelican on display, and a mechanically operated piano which played tunes when a penny was placed in a slot. There was also a large glasshouse, or 'Crystal Palace' as it was known locally, 112 ft in length and constructed of glass, iron and wood. Its centrepiece was a beautifully sculptured Italian fountain. On top of the fountain there was the figure of Neptune, with crown and trident, sitting on a large shell drawn by two fish horses, with water flowing from their mouths. It was later thought that this glasshouse was subsequently transported to the Botanic Gardens, but this is not the case. The existing glasshouse in the South Belfast Gardens was built prior to the one on Dargan's Island being demolished.

One side of the island was laid out with bathing boxes for the intrepid swimmer to change in. At the north end of the Island, was a battery of cannons, which were used on ceremonial occasions for firing salutes. It was also possible to take a balloon ride from the Island and in the winter months wild fowl shooting was organised as well as badger baiting competitions. A fete was held on the Island in September 1851, which drew around 10,000 visitors.

It was recorded in the local newspaper, that a visit across the river gave an experience of a sea journey after which the citizens of Belfast could compose themselves on one of the many seats placed for their convenience. Eventually a causeway was constructed and the Island would be firmly attached to the County Down side of the town, but the area would still be lovingly called 'an island.' In 1864 the Crystal Palace was destroyed by fire and the building was allowed to fall into disrepair. In 1992, local historian and descendent of William Dargan, Vincent Dargan, discovered the lower part of the fountain still intact and being used to house goldfish. Thankfully, Mr Dargan photographed that section of the fountain (*pictured above*) because only a few years later it was totally destroyed in an act of vandalism.[2]

The bottom section of the Fountain that was the centre piece at Dargan's Island.
(Courtesy of the Vincent Dargan collection.)

At this time the Island, or 'The People's Park' as it was often referred to, proved to be very popular with the local people of Belfast. However, the Belfast Harbour Commissioners, who succeeded the Belfast Ballast Board in an Act in 1843, had, with their new powers, been buying up all the private land on both sides of the river. These purchases nearly brought shipbuilding in the town to an end, as they were then controlling how much land could or could not be used for industrial purposes, ending the unregulated expansion that was taking place. The longer term view taken by the Commissioners was to try and establish, under their control as allowed in the Act, a viable and new harbour and port for the town. The Commissioners were reported as stating that shipbuilding had started in a spirit that augured well for its future success and importance. They could see that

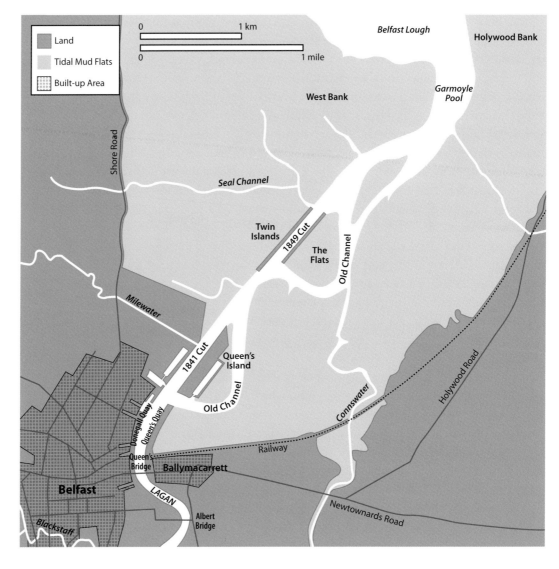

Plan showing the result of straightening the River Lagan by William Dargan.

(Based on Walter and Burges' 1846–7 Plan of Belfast Harbour.)

the smaller yards were starting to construct larger and larger vessels, and that to assist them and the port of Belfast it would be a wise move to allow for expansion. The newly formed Dargan's Island held the potential to allow shipbuilding to progress.

By 1849, William Dargan had completed the final cut to the river and the Lagan was now both straighter and deeper thus allowing ships of greater draught to enter the new harbour and quays that were being laid out. The new channel was inaugurated on the 10 July 1849. From mid-morning on that day, crowds of people had started to arrive at the quayside on the river to witness the official opening ceremony. According to newspaper reports, the day was warm and sunny with a gentle breeze. Moored along the quay adjacent to High Street were the vessels that would take part in the ceremony, the Royal Mail Steamer *Prince*

Engraving of the opening of the Victoria Channel.
(© National Museums Northern Ireland, Collection Ulster Museum Belfast.)

of Wales, a steam schooner *Erin's Queen*, a tug *Superb* and two locally owned yachts *Fawn* and *Gannet*. Further down the river were stationed the steamboat *Whitehaven* and the tugboat *Ranger*. All these vessels were decorated with flags and there were several other small craft in the river, which were there to spectate but not officially taking part in the proceedings.

At 1.30 pm the Belfast Harbour Commissioners and their guests including William Dargan, boarded the *Prince of Wales* along with the band of the thirteenth Irish Regiment. The *Prince of Wales* ship bell was sounded and the flotilla started towards the new cut in the river, with the tug *Superb* leading. As the procession passed Dargan's Island, (although by this date it had been agreed that the name of the Island would change to Queen's Island), a battery of four cannon fired a salute from the Island. The flotilla came to a stop and on board the *Prince of Wales*, Captain William Pirrie, a member of the Belfast Harbour Commissioners, made a short speech, poured a bottle of champagne into the river and officially named the channel The Victoria Channel. At the same time, from the mizzenmast of the ship, a red flag bearing the words 'The New Channel Opened' was unfurled. The battery of cannons again fired a salute and the band struck up 'Rule Britannia'.

The flotilla then split into two groups, both sailing towards the mouth of the lough, with one half sailing along the Antrim shore while the other group sailed down the Down coastline. During the voyage there were several toasts proposed including one to the health of the constructor William Dargan, to which he replied "that his acquaintance with the people of Belfast had made a strong impression on him and that to be a Belfast man would ever give any person a claim upon him". The vessels eventually returned to the High Street quay, with *Erin's Queen* being the last to arrive at around 8.00 pm, while rockets and fireworks were being let off from Dargan's Island.

The same year saw the completion of the infilling of the areas behind the new Donegall, Princess and Albert Quays, providing both much needed space for the handling of cargo and a continuous roadway behind the quays. During the dredging and laying out of Dargan's Island, the Harbour Commissioners had a pond constructed on the island for holding timber that would be used in ship building. The pond at the County Down side of the island was around 1,500 ft long and 270 ft wide. They also had a 650 ft long patent slipway built adjacent to the pond. This slipway, a cheaper version of a dry dock, would allow shipbuilders to haul their vessels, of weights up to 1,000 tons, out of the water by making use of a 20 horse power steam engine, and enable workmen to access the hull, rudder and propeller. In the first year of its use, 14 vessels were hauled out of the water for repairs.

Access in the town was further improved when, around 1850, several of the narrow lanes which provided the only access between the lower ends of Ann Street, High Street and Waring Street were removed, and Victoria Street was laid out as a broad continuation of Corporation Street, across the top of Queen's Square and Albert Square which were formerly occupied by the old docks.

The Harbour Commissioners were now getting ready for the next phase of their plan, which would eventually lead to them granting permission for large-scale shipbuilding on Dargan's Island. However, with all this excitement and building work that was going on there was one man who must have been slightly disappointed. That man was William Dargan, the contractor and after whom the newly formed Island was named.

On the 13 August 1845 Queen Victoria visited Belfast. To mark the occasion the town fathers had decided to rename Dargan's Island as 'Queen's Island' in honour of Her Majesty's visit. Several years later, on 29 August 1853, William Dargan and his wife were visited by Queen Victoria and Prince Albert, at Dargan's home (Dargan Villa) in Mount Annville. During the visit Her Majesty offered Dargan a Baronetcy, which he refused. What Her Majesty thought when this offer was refused is not recorded, but perhaps this refusal of the Baronetcy, was Dargan's way of showing Queen Victoria that *he* was not amused.

Several years later in 1866, Dargan was seriously injured following a fall from his horse and died on the 7 February 1867 at his Dublin home at Fitzwilliam Square East. Today, the only reminder of a man who was one of Ireland's greatest civil engineers is a statue of him which is situated in the grounds of Leinster House in Dublin. Simply inscribed on it is one word, 'Dargan'.

Statue of William Dargan in the grounds of Leinster House, Dublin.

CHAPTER 3

The Emergence of Iron Men

In my Introduction, I said that Belfast was a strange place to see the creation of shipbuilding yards that would come to dominate the shipping world. For those men engaged in the early days there was nothing really going in their favour. There were no deposits of iron ore or coal to be found in large enough quantities to make the production of iron a financial success. However, there had been several unsuccessful attempts to do just that.

Around 1798, Messer's McClenaghan and Stainton established an iron foundry in Ballymacarrett in East Belfast. Within a few years they took the name of the Lagan Foundry, so as not to be confused with another foundry in the east of the town run by Benjamin Edwards. By 1802 both McClenaghan and Stainton had died and a younger Partner Victor Coates took ownership of the Foundry. Later on in 1820, he would supply two engines producing 70 horsepower, for the shipyard of Ritchie and McLaine to be fitted into their new wooden steamship the *Belfast*. The 115 ft ship was a steamer of approximately 200 tons, which was under the control of Captain Pashley, and was to be engaged on the cross channel run from London to Calais. In the same year Coates took a Mr J. Young into partnership and changed the name of the company to Victor Coates, Son and Young. They advertised the company as 'brass and iron founders, millwrights and engineers' with an address at the Old Lagan Village. The company was also to build a steam powered iron towboat that was engaged on Lough Neagh.

Other foundries were to spring up around the town. The Falls Foundry of Combe, Barbour and Combe, that was established around 1845 would occupy a site of around five acres. At this point it is interesting to note that the Barbour in the firm was James, who was a relative of the Barbour family that owned the Barbour Thread Company of Lisburn. A daughter of that family, Helen, would later marry Thomas Andrews, one of the designers of the *Titanic*. Ritchie and Hart established another foundry under the name of the Mountpottinger Foundry in 1863.

Other foundries in the province of Ulster were opened including A. Brown and Sons in Foyle Street, Londonderry; John Taylor in Strabane; John Kane in Harryville, Ballymena; and in Belfast, an Iron Works at Eliza Street was opened by Thomas N. Gladstone and Robert Pace.

Gladstone and Pace had begun construction of their foundry in 1849, with the hope that they would be able to draw on reserves of iron ore and coal, which they mistakenly assumed were in abundance in the extensive estates of the Marquis of Downshire. The works, with the name of the Belfast Iron Works and complete with tall, 'graceful' chimneys, were to take almost two years to complete. The first boilerplates in Ireland were rolled out in December 1851, amid much excitement, when the managers asked the Marquis of Downshire to assist them in the operation. The press reported that during the official opening, the Marquis came forward, took off his topcoat and rolled up his sleeves to assist in the operation of transferring the first heated iron ingot from the furnace by placing it in the rolling machine, only for Gladstone and Pace to suffer the embarrassment of having their machinery breakdown in front of the invited guests. By the time the offending machine was repaired the initial ingot had cooled down, so another ingot was hastily heated up in the furnace and successfully transferred with the aid of tongs into the rollers. Under power from a 64 horsepower steam engine, a sheet of iron around 20 ft by 6 ft was then rolled out. The Marquis then retired to the Managers office where a 'great repast' was served exclusively for him and his party. The workforce of around 50 men, who most probably had done all the hard and dirty work, had to wait until the Marquis and invited guests had finished their meal and at around 8.00 pm they were invited into the Manager's Office where they were allowed to eat what had been left.

Sadly for Gladstone and Pace, the hope that they would be able to draw on deposits of local iron ore or coal was not to be. All their raw material had to be shipped into Belfast, which made the finished iron much more expensive and proved their venture to be impractical on a large-scale. Within a short period of time Robert Pace was complaining that everything that he had was tied up in the Works and that his backers, the banks, were putting pressure on him.

Gladstone decided to approach the Harbour Commissioners to see if they would consider allowing the two of them to open an Iron shipyard on Queen's Island. This would at least be a way of using up the iron that they were producing and may even allow them to at last profit from their venture. The Commissioners were interested in this proposal and established a sub committee under the chairmanship of Captain William Pirrie to fully examine the suggestion of them granting permission for an iron shipyard on the Island. Within a few months Pirrie came back with a favourable report and advertisements were placed on behalf of the Commissioners granting land for shipyards to establish on the island.

Following this, Gladstone and Pace were approached by a gentleman called Robert Hickson, who expressed an interest in taking over the running of the Iron Works. With all the pressure that the two Partners were under from the bank it is not surprising that they happily accepted this offer, which would see them, resolve their financial problems, and get out of the predicament that they were in.

Robert Hickson, who was born in Tralee, County Kerry, in 1815, was one of seven children, five sons and two daughters, to Edward and Rose Hickson. The five sons opened a timber yard in Tralee. When Robert was aged 15 his three eldest brothers left Ireland and emigrated to Canada, leaving the timber yard to be run by Robert and his older brother William. Eventually Robert decided to broaden his horizons and also left the timber business. He ended up in Liverpool where two things, both connected with the one family, would shape his future.

Firstly, he married Jane Elizabeth Spence who had been born in Liverpool in 1819. Between them they were to have six surviving children. The first child was born in Tralee, while three of their other children were born in Belfast. Secondly, Hickson established a partnership with a local Liverpool businessman, James Spence and they traded the newly formed business under the name of Robert Hickson and Company. It cannot be proved if this James was the father, brother or another relative of Hickson's wife, Jane, but it would not be beyond the bounds of possibility that his new Partner was in fact related to him through marriage, as this practice of mixing business and marriage was quite a common occurrence. This new company was not only to eventually take over the running of the Gladstone and Pace Iron Works in Eliza Street but also to lease land on Queen's Island from the Harbour Commissioners and establish the first iron shipyard there. Once Gladstone and Pace had sold the Iron Works to Hickson, there was no sense in them keeping the option on the lease for the Iron Shipyard, so they transferred their holding as part of the sale of the foundry.

Hickson was a ship owner, with his vessel registered in his hometown of Tralee, and could see the possibilities of using this iron in the construction of ships. He took the bold step and wrote to the Belfast Harbour Commissioners on the 5 September 1853 proposing to lease a plot of land, 100 ft by 550 ft and adjacent to the patent slipway, for his new ship building venture. In his letter he proposed taking on, with effect from the 1 November 1853, a 21 year lease on the area, with rent starting at £50 a year in the first year and rising to £200 per year by the 15th year. He also requested that within a period of six months, the Harbour Commissioners would spend at least £1,500 on laying out a launching slipway and sheds for him. In fact the Commissioners got away with spending just over £1,100. Hickson further requested the Commissioners to ensure that the water in the river Lagan was kept to a minimum depth of 15 ft to allow him to launch his ships. He agreed that his yard would not encroach on the pleasure gardens and that he would maintain the steam engine at the patent slip at his own expense. In a further letter on the same day, he also requested use of a strip of waste ground to the north west of the proposed shipyard for a timber yard. Permission for this was granted, with the lease being signed by Edmund Getty, the secretary of the Harbour Commissioners. A few months later, on 14 January 1854, Hickson leased another plot of land between his existing yard and the Victoria Channel. In his letter he requested that the Harbour Commissioners spend a further sum of 393 pounds 2 shillings and 9 pence, the amount making up the short fall that the Commissioners had not spent in the previous September when he took out his original lease.

On the opening of Hickson's shipyard on the County Down side of the river, the Belfast Harbour Commissioners stated:

> "that the business has been commenced in a spirit that augers well for its future success and importance, the vessels contracted for being of a very large tonnage and the proprietor already finding it necessary to ask for additional space. It is also proper to observe that the other yards* for timber built ships are extending their business and laying down vessels of a much larger burthen than formerly." [1]

> *The 'other yards' mentioned in the statement refers to those on the County Antrim side of the river.*

With both the iron works and a newly laid out shipyard in place, Hickson went looking for orders for ships for his new venture and it is not surprising that, with his connections in Liverpool, the first order would come from that seafaring city. An order came from Edward Bates, a Liverpool ship owner, for a 1,289 ton, wooden sailing ship. The *Silistria*, Hickson's first ship, was successfully launched in September 1854 and, as he had no facilities in Belfast, the vessel was towed across the Irish Sea to Liverpool and was fitted out there. While construction of his first ship was ongoing, Hickson obtained an order for a second vessel, the 1,273 ton *Khersonese*, an iron ship that would be commanded by Captain Thompson, and was built for two local Belfast businessmen, Frederick Lewis and Edward

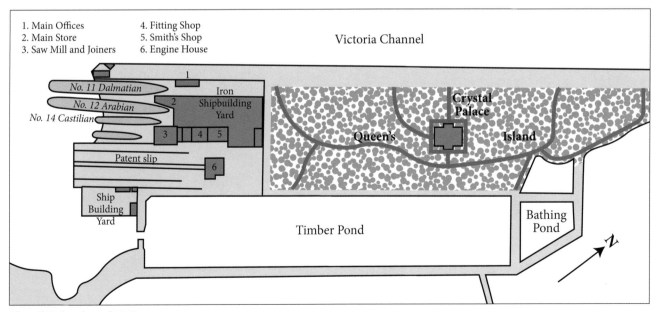

Plan of Hickson's yard 1862.

Geoghergan. Lewis, who lived at 'Nettlefield' in Ballymacarrett, in East Belfast, was a timber merchant owning the local firm of Thomas Corbett and Company. Geoghergan, who lived at 'Royal Terrace', Lisburn Road, was the local Agent in the Belfast area for the Bank of Ireland. He was a very wealthy man in his own right and made an ideal sleeping Partner to finance Lewis. The *Khersonese*, which the Partners registered in Liverpool, was to be engaged carrying cargo from that port to America. During the launch of the *Khersonese*, the ship started down the slipway, and then, to the embarrassment of those gathered, it stopped and refused to move. Hickson's manager, who was on hand, saw what had happened. He managed to overcome the problem and the ship continued down the slipway before the stationary weight of the vessel caused it to collapse the slipway and sink into the ground underneath.

A few months earlier the press in Belfast had taken notice of the progress that Hickson was making when the *Belfast Newsletter* commented on the potential that lay in his enterprise:

> "There are, we think, tolerably good grounds for anticipating the speedy pre-eminence of Belfast over all other Irish ports as regards the shipbuilding trade. The recent improvements in our harbour, the large accommodation about to be afforded by the reclamation of the slob between the Queen's Quay and the line of the Holywood Railway, the vastly increasing commerce of the port, and the almost unparalleled activity of our merchants, have given an impulse to the earlier efforts in this branch of trade which will not be weakened until the Lagan becomes the Clyde of Ireland."[2]

The signs for the continued good fortune of shipbuilding, according to the newspaper article, boded well for the future. Events just a few months after the article was printed were to rock the fledgling shipyard to its very core and would see a transformation that would propel Belfast shipbuilding into the premier league of world shipyards.

Hickson knew his limitations with regard to shipbuilding and during the construction of the *Silistria* he had taken on a Mr John Jordan of 4 Garmoyle Street as a manager to assist him with the growing amount of work. Within a few months of Jordan being engaged Hickson was to dismiss him, just prior to the launch of *Silistria*. The main reason for the dismissal appears to be that he was not strict enough with the workforce and that the work was not progressing at a satisfactory rate. Left in the position of having no manager, Hickson advertised in the national press for a new manager. Eventually in December of 1854, while the *Khersonese* was still at the beginning of construction on the slipway, a 21 year old gentleman from Scarborough in England was to take up the post. His name was Edward James Harland.

CHAPTER 4

Edward J. Harland

Edward James Harland was born in Scarborough, England, in May 1831. He was the sixth out of eight children born to William Harland, a medical Doctor and part-time scientist who practised in the town. His mother, Anne, was also gifted with a practical nature and would be seen helping her husband in the preparation of his plans for his inventions. She was also an accomplished model and toy maker, and would help her boys to make toy carts, horses and boats, while her daughters would make dresses for their dolls and sails for their brothers' boats. Edward Harland recalled, "the nursery soon became a little workshop under her directions."

In 1827 his father had invented and obtained a patent for a road going steam carriage that incorporated a multi-tubular boiler. He also experimented with the new electricity and, well ahead of today's standards, he got involved with organic fertilizers. Harland senior even considered that it might be possible to have laid an electric cable across the Atlantic to light up America. He went as far as costing the whole operation.

Harland attended Grammar school and, like most young boys, he was not that interested in his early schooling, apart from drawing and geometry. He stated that he was happiest when visiting the local workshops, where he would watch or even assist the skilled workmen in their various trades. This 'hands on', practical knowledge that he gained at a young and impressionable stage of his life was to stay with him throughout his working life. The local industry that he most enjoyed visiting as a youngster was the shipyard of William and Robert Tindall. William Tindall was one of the founding members of Lloyds of London. By all accounts Harland must have spent all of his free moments wandering around the yard, observing the various techniques of that trade. The Tindall brothers were building wooden ships of up to 1,000 tons and Harland commented that, "scarcely a timber was moulded, a plank bent, a spar lined off, or launching, without my being present to witness them." He was to take this interest further by building himself model-racing yachts.

Harland was then sent to Edinburgh Academy where he studied for two years and relied on his brother for academic assistance. This same brother was to help him build and plan models of buildings and machinery. He was so much involved in things mechanical that on one occasion, while travelling by rail to Edinburgh, a gentleman in his company enquired what a screw propeller that would be fitted to a ship would be like. As they were passing a windmill young Harland pointed to the tail blade and replied "it is just like that."

His mother died in 1844, when he was aged only 13. He continued his education until he was 15, when his father suggested that he pursued a career in law with a view to becoming a Barrister. Harland, with his mechanical instinct, had a different career path in mind, as he wanted to be an Engineer. Eventually he talked his father around into letting him pursue engineering and, to assist his son, Harland senior called on an old acquaintance George Stephenson. Between them they felt that it would be a good idea to let Edward carry on and arrangements were made to place him in the engineering works of Robert Stephenson in Newcastle upon Tyne, as a gentleman or premium apprentice. His five year apprenticeship began in 1846 and he was placed in the drawing office of the company by the time he entered its final year.

Those early working days were to be long and hard. Work started in the morning at 6.00 am and would continue until at least 8.15 pm. Saturdays saw the workforce finish at 4.00 pm and have all day Sunday off, making a working week of 80 plus hours. It was around this period of time, in the summer of 1850, just before his apprenticeship was finished, that Harland became aware of a competition organised by the Duke of Northumberland, who was offering a prize of 100 guineas (£105 or around £4,500 at today's exchange rates) for someone to design a new lifeboat. Harland came up with an idea of a cylindrico-conical design that would have space inside the sealed craft for passengers

Edward Harland as a young man.

(Courtesy of the V. Morrison collection.)

and would be fitted with two propellers, one at each end, the idea being that at least one of the propeller screws would be submerged at any one time and give propulsion for the craft. He spent many evenings drawing up his plans and then making a scale wooden model. This model was constructed using copper plates and was around 32 inches long. Eventually, after many full nights of work, he took the model for its sea trials, which it passed with flying colours, always self-righting and he said he was pleased that it was also watertight. Once the model had satisfactorily passed all his tests, he took the unusual step of drawing up full plans and specifications and submitting these to the Patent Office in London. Finally he submitted his plans and model for the competition. There appears to have been quite some interest in Northumberland's competition, no doubt spurred on by the large prize fund. Over 280 designs were entered, with the award eventually being given to Mr James Beeching, whose winning design was adopted and put into commercial service. Harland heard no more about his design, although he did keep the model and many years later, when he moved to Belfast, he would delight guests by demonstrating his lifeboat on the lake at his Belfast home at Ormiston House.

The firm of Stephenson's had received an order from the Government for large caisson gates for a dock, the construction of which at that time was similar to that of a ship. With Harland's interest in ships, he was given the position of assisting with the work. He was also to spend his free time looking at other engineering feats in the area and stated, "that unless a young fellow takes a real interest in his work, and has a genuine love for it, the greatest advantages will prove of no avail whatever." It appears that during this period Harland built up a great deal of respect for Mr William Hutchinson, a Partner of George Stephenson, and would seem to have learnt from him the man management skills that he would put to good use later in life. He also looked up to the head draughtsman of the firm, William Weallans, and said of both these men that he "had the benefit of the example and the training of these very clever men." His five years of training ended in May 1851 when he was aged 20. Throughout this period of training he had slept in only twice, and now was listed as a journeyman, on the 'big wage' of 20 shillings (£1) per week.

He decided to take some time off work and headed to London to see the Great Exhibition that was being held at the newly constructed Crystal Palace at Hyde Park. The building, which was designed by Joseph Paxton, was over 1,800 ft long and consisted of iron arch girders holding miles of glass in place. Here at the exhibition he marvelled at all the mechanical and technical advances of the age and spend two months walking around and inspecting the exhibits. He then briefly returned back to Scarborough, before travelling to Glasgow to the marine engine building firm of J&G Thomson where he was employed, still with the pay of 20 shillings (£1) a week. In later years and following many mergers, Thomson's shipyard would become more commonly known as John Brown.

It was here, on the banks of the Clyde, that he was able to satisfy his curiosity and interest in ships. With so many shipyards on the Clyde he was to spend all his free time walking up and down the river, taking in all he could see. He was especially keen to visit the yard of Robert Napier, where ships for the Cunard Line were being built. Tod and McGregor was another yard that he spent time at. This shipyard was at the forefront of constructing ships with propellers and they were building vessels for the Peninsular and Oriental Company, more commonly know, as P&O. Here he would observe the various methods of ship construction, boiler design and passenger accommodation.

His employers, Thomson's, decided to go into the business of shipbuilding and hired an experienced naval draughtsman, with Harland being placed as his assistant. Gradually Harland was being given more and more work to do, so that when the chief draughtsman was offered a promotion with a new yard on the Tyne, the job of head draughtsman was given without question to Edward

Harland. Initially his wages stayed at the 20 shillings but after a period of time these were increased. One funny and interesting thing happened while he was in this position. He was required to design a new furnace and was not quite sure the best way to proceed. However, there was one man on the Clyde who had all the answers that Harland needed, but the problem was that the man in question was rarely sober. Harland approached him and after some cajoling and the promise of some liquid refreshment, a liberal supply of Glenlivat whisky, the man gave Harland all the details that were required. It turned out to be the best that had been designed and built.

In late 1853, word of the capabilities of Harland had spread around the shipbuilding and engineering industries. Thomas Toward who operated a shipyard at St. Peters, about three miles from Newcastle upon Tyne, was on the look out for Manager. His father's old friend and his own first employer, George Stephenson, recommended Harland for the position. Harland accepted. On his arrival at the yard he found the quality of work to be 'rough and ready'. Drawing on his previous experiences of working on the construction of around 12 ships and the guidance already given to him by his previous managers, he was able to raise the standard of work without any additional expense and to have the orders ready on time. The owner of the yard, Mr Toward, was in poor health and was preparing to spend more time abroad. This placed Harland in a difficult position. Here was a young man with energy, drive and determination who, with Toward away, was not being given full responsibility and was only able to run the yard on a day to day basis. What frustrated Harland was that Toward would not devolve down full responsibility for the running of the yard. This lack of authority given to Harland was to see him questioning his position, or lack of it, at Toward's yard and Harland began looking for a new position, somewhere that he could push himself forward.

As I mentioned at the end of the last chapter, Robert Hickson was, in his shipyard in Belfast, having serious problems. His manager Mr Jordan had been sacked for being too slack with the workforce. It seems that he wanted to be favoured by them and was not the disciplinarian that was required by Hickson. Following his dismissal Hickson placed an advertisement in the national papers looking for a new Manager. Back on the Tyne, Harland became aware of this vacancy and made several inquiries about both Hickson and his yard. He applied for the vacant post and took up the position as Manager in December 1854. On arrival in Belfast he was impressed with the facilities and later stated:

> "The yard was a much larger one than that on the Tyne, and was capable of great expansion. It was situated on what was then well known as the Queen's Island; but now, like the Isle of Dogs, it has been attached by reclamation. The yard, about four acres in extent, was held by lease from the Belfast Harbour Commissioners. It was well placed, alongside a fine patent slip, with clear frontage, allowing of the largest ships being freely launched."[1]

His arrival in Belfast did nothing for the workforce. After Jordan's departure, there now appeared this young Yorkshire man, who from the moment he arrived was to be a lot stricter with the workforce than before. Harland quickly made his mark. Noticing that the wages paid were higher than in England and that the quality of the finished work was of a much lower standard, he immediately reduced the wages of the workers to the standard rate, banned smoking in the yard and went about increasing both the quality and quantity of work. He continually roamed around the shipyard inspecting the standard of work. With him he always carried a piece of chalk and an ivory rule. Any defective work discovered by him was 'ringed' in chalk and the workman responsible for the poor work was made to repair it at his own expense. It was said that he could see everything that was going on, and most probably he could 'hear the grass grow'. On one occasion, while 'doing his rounds' in the shipyard, he stopped in his tracks, looked down at a saw pit, flipped open the lid and discovered a 'wee man' sitting puffing on his pipe. No doubt the crafty smoker was shown the door.

All of this really didn't go down well with the Belfast workers, who had been used to a more relaxed regime with Jordan in charge. Even though they had built and launched the first ship, and had started construction of the second one, the workforce did what they felt they could do best. They took the view that nobody was going to treat them like that and promptly downed tools and went on strike. To add insult to injury, Jordan had taken over the lease of the old small shipbuilding concern of Thompson and Kirwan on the County Antrim side of the river and appeared to have got an order for a ship. He was offering work to any of Hickson's men who were dissatisfied with the new working regime being imposed by Harland. Undaunted by Jordan's actions Harland brought workmen from the Clyde to augment those who had left. At the same time Hickson and his Partner James Spence were having cash problems with their bank, which were threatening to foreclose on their loans. Hickson and Spence had by now closed the Iron Works, which never really lived up to the expectations that they initially had, and put the Works up for sale by way of public auction.

In order to satisfy the demands made by the bank Hickson and his Partner announced that, on 24 July 1855, the Iron Works were being put up for auction. The auction was scheduled to take place on Wednesday 5 September at 12.00 o'clock noon. In their description of the Works, Hickson and Spence painted a very rosy and confident picture of what the Foundry could do. The site was, they said, laid out to produce up to 120 tons of finished iron per

Extract from the Belfast Newsletter.

SALE BY AUCTION

OF THE

BELFAST IRON WORKS.

TO BE SOLD BY AUCTION,

At the Premises, on WEDNESDAY, the 5th of September, at the hour of TWELVE o'clock, THE ABOVE WORKS, CONSISTING of Plate and Angle Iron, Merchant and Puddle Bar Mills, with a Tilt Hammer for Forgings—the entire worked by four Engines; together with Roll Lathe, Cupola, Smith's Shop, Store Houses, and all other necessary appliances for carrying on the Works.

Ship Plates of the largest size have been made at these Works, within the last six months. The Mills are laid out to produce from 100 to 120 tons per week of Finished Iron, and are now in good working order. The Buildings are all new; and the whole of the extensive Concern is enclosed by a high wall. There is a local demand for Iron Ship Building and Engineering, equal to the entire make of the Works, which are within a few hours' sail of Ayrshire, the cheapest existing source of supply of Pig Iron and Coal, the freightage on which ranges from three to four shillings per ton.

The Premises are held under a Lease for lives renewable for ever, at a low rent.

This is a good opening for a practical working man with a moderate capital, the consumption of Iron of all sorts being far greater in Belfast than any other town in Ireland, and the rates of labour low.

Should this Property be not Sold together as it now stands, it will then be put up in Lots, consisting in part of the following Materials, &c.:—Four powerful Steam Engines and Boilers, Gearing, Nine Pair Large Rolls (some never used), Flooring and Levelling Plates, Two Pair of Shears, Four Pair of Small Rolls, Fifty-nine Spare Rolls for Merchant Mill, Water Troughs, Three Large Cranes, Weighing Beams, Weighbridge, Grindstones, Drilling and Screwing Machine, Pumps and Gearings, Screw Jack, Over One Hundred Spare Rolls, Sixteen Plate Mill and Puddle Furnaces, Contents of Cupola, Carpenter and Smith's Shop, Castings, Plates, Malleable Iron and Shafting, Office Fixtures, with sundry other Articles, of which a Catalogue will be issued previous to day of Sale.

Should it be a convenience to any purchaser of the entire concern, a considerable part of the purchase-money may remain on mortgage.

For further particulars, apply to JAMES SPENCE, Esq., 5, York Buildings, Liverpool; or to the IRON COMPANY, Eliza Street, Belfast.   1974 week. In order to attract interest they stated:

> "There is a local demand for Iron Shipbuilding and Engineering, equal to the entire make of the Works, which are within a few hours' sail of Ayrshire, the cheapest existing source of supply of Pig Iron and Coal, the freightage on which ranges from three to four shillings per ton."

Hoping to generate interest from potential bidders, they added:

> "This is a good opening for a practical man with a moderate capital, the consumption of Iron of all sorts being far greater in Belfast than any other town in Ireland, and the rates of labour low."[2]

Unfortunately for the Partners, on the day of the Auction there was no interest from anyone. They advertised another date for the sale in November but again no acceptable offer was received. The problem with an unworkable plant and the resultant cash flow difficulties placed a terrible burden on them. In the interim period Edward Harland had to pay the wages of the 250 or so workmen employed in the shipyard, while Hickson and Spence entered into discussions with their bank to discuss the future of not only the Iron Works but also their shipyard. Due to the fact that Hickson had orders for ships, the bank relented somewhat and allowed him to continue shipbuilding as they could see the possibility of a profit being made. This would then clear Hickson's debts, however, there was no way in which they could save the Iron Works and Hickson and Spence were forced to close the foundry.

In the middle of all this financial dealing, some friends of Edward Harland naturally suggested that maybe he would be better away from all these on going problems. Harland must have seen something in this shipyard which made him want to stay because he told his friends "that having mounted a restive horse, I would ride him into the stable."

As I have already mentioned, Harland had been repeatedly travelling to the Clyde to entice men to come to Belfast to work at the shipyard. However, Jordan was doing his best to stifle his efforts by trying to stop these men working. One such example of this ended up in the local courts in September of 1855. Carson Clawson and several other men from Hickson's yard had finished work on Friday 31 August, and were travelling home using the ferry to cross the Lagan. When they reached the County Antrim side of the river at Pilot Street, they were set upon by Peter McCann and Edward Hill who were leading a group of men from Jordan's new, up-and-coming yard. The local constable arrested McCann and Hill, both were charged with assault and they appeared in Court the following day before Judge John F. Ferguson. On hearing the evidence of how Clawson was beaten around the head, the Judge found both accused guilty. McCann was sentenced to one month in jail and Hill was bound over to keep the peace and had to find a surety of £40. The Judge was concerned that there was a conspiracy against Hickson's workers and told the accused and their supporters that they should abandon this idea because, the Judge added, if there were a conspiracy, and if that fact could be proved, then the prisoners would receive a far higher punishment.

At this stage in his career in Belfast, Harland had a couple of lucky breaks. Firstly, following the Court case against Jordan's men it would seem that an uneasy calm broke out. This was helped by the fact that Jordan's experience of shipbuilding and man management was non-existent. The unnamed ship he was constructing was now abandoned and nothing more was heard from him or his ship. The second piece of news that Harland received was that his previous employer, Mr Thomas Toward, who had been suffering from ill health had passed away. Never one to rest on his laurels, Harland quickly seized the opportunity of engaging the services of Toward's head foreman, Mr William Hanson, who also brought to Belfast some of the more experienced leading hands from the English shipyard. With these men 'on board', Harland was able to complete the ships that were on the order book to the satisfaction of both Robert Hickson and also the ships' owners.

Work continued at Hickson's shipyard and by now the yard was branching out, not just building ships, but also engaging in repair work to ships. In 1857 two young brothers, Walter Henry and Alexander Basil Wilson, were taken on by Hickson as the first gentlemen or premium apprentices. Walter Wilson, who will be discussed later in the book, was to rise from this lowly position to become an outstanding marine engineer and a Partner with Harland and Wolff.

Orders were placed for further ships with Hickson, which included, in 1857, the *Circassion*, for the North Atlantic Steam Navigation Company. The vessel was 1387 tons with a 350 horsepower engine, and was engaged on the Liverpool to Portland route. The ship was placed in the charge of Captain Powell. That same year also saw two other ships being constructed; the *Dewa Gunghadu*, an iron ship ordered by Edward Bates and the *Mayola*, a 400 ton iron ship for Liverpool ship owner William Porter.

The year 1858 was to see another new face coming into Hickson's yard, that of Gustav Wilhelm Wolff, who was to take up a position as a draughtsman. Through marriage, he was a distant relative of Edward Harland. Gustav Wolff was born in Hamburg, Germany on the 10 November 1834. His father was Moritz Wolff, a local merchant who had married Fanny Schwabe, who was the sister of Gustav Schwabe, the financier who in a few short years time would play such an important role in the formation of the partnership of Harland and Wolff. Schwabe would later introduce them both to Thomas Ismay and his family, the owners of the White Star Line. Following direction from his father, it was decided that, at the early age of just 14, Wolff should take up engineering as a career and he moved to

Liverpool where he attended Liverpool College. It was here that he lodged with his uncle Gustav Schwabe. He left school at 16 and was apprenticed to the Manchester engineering firm of Joseph Whitworth and Company. In 1855 the firm selected him to represent the company at Great Exhibition in Paris. Following this, Wolff moved to Goodfellow and Company, where he was employed as a draughtsman. He then moved to Robert Hickson's yard in Belfast and took on the same role as draughtsman. On his arrival in Belfast he was looked after by another distant relative, Daniel J Jaffe. Sir Otto, a relative of this Jaffe, would on two occasions, 1899 and 1904, be elected as Lord Mayor of Belfast.

At this early stage in Belfast, while managing Hickson's yard, Harland took Wolff on as a personal assistant. The shipyard was continuing to progress, one ship had been built in 1854, one in the following year and by 1857 there were orders for three more vessels. Wolff then decided to go to sea and was taken on as an Engineer, sailing on the Mediterranean, most likely on one of the Bibby Line ships. He made this decision in order to study the engines of ships while at sea. By this time, Edward Harland was encouraged by the success of not only the shipyard, but more importantly his competence and capability in running the building work. He decided that now was the time for him to establish his own shipbuilding business. His initial thought was to establish himself in Liverpool, and encouraged by Schwabe, he approached the Council in that City with a request to lay down a yard at Garstang, and also at Birkenhead. The Council, who were concerned at his young age and inexperience in running his own business, refused his application.

The Belfast shipyard in 1858 had just launched two ships, the *Norah Graeme* an iron sailing ship at just over 1,000 tons (as a third order from Edward Bates of Liverpool) and the *Adjutant*, a tugboat designed to serve ships sailing from the Mersey. There was one further ship being constructed, the *Oceola*, but due to financial conditions, the owner pulled out of the contract. In order to keep his yard 'afloat', Hickson decided to transfer the ship to his name and complete the construction himself. This venture, while keeping his good name as a shipbuilder, stretched the finances of the yard, and, if further orders were not obtained, it would most probably have the effect of forcing Hickson to close the concern. Happily for Hickson, word of Harland's intention to move from Belfast eventually came to his notice. With this in mind, Robert Hickson decided to offer to sell the shipyard to Edward Harland. He offered the yard to Harland for the sum of £5,000, which at today's value would be in the region of 3 million pounds. Harland, as a young 27 year old, obviously didn't have that sort of capital to draw on, on his own account. But financial help was at hand.

Gustav Schwabe had been born on 10 October 1813 in Hamburg in Germany and was christened Gustav Christian by his father Philip. From 1820 members of the Schwabe family had moved to England where they would establish new businesses. An uncle of Schwabe opened a fabric printing company in Manchester

43

Gustav Wolff
(© National Museums Northern Ireland, Collection Harland and Wolff, Ulster Folk and Transport Museum)

Gustav Schwabe
(Courtesy of the David Man Collection)

Helen Dugdale
(Courtesy of the David Man Collection)

and cousins opened new business premises in Glasgow. Gustav moved to Liverpool and by 1838 he was in a partnership with Edward Little, running a commission agency. It appears that, when Little died, all his estate including property passed to Schwabe. He continued in the shipping business with various Partners and in June 1842 he married Helen Dugdale, the daughter of one of his Partners, John Dugdale. When Schwabe died in 1897 he bequeathed his entire fortune to Gustav Wolff, who was his nephew. Edward Harland was also distantly related to Schwabe, which meant that Harland and Wolff were distant cousins. Schwabe was also a Partner in the Liverpool based Bibby Line. No doubt Schwabe's mind was working overtime when he considered the possibility of making a loan to Harland with which he could purchase the shipyard. This is indeed what he did, with the suggestion to Harland that he should consider bringing Wolff back from sea and engaging him in the yard. Edward Harland took up the offer of financial assistance from Schwabe and on 21 September 1858 he received a letter from Hickson offering the shipyard to him. In the letter Hickson makes one provision when he requests:

> "It is understood that I am to be allowed to finish the present ship (*The Oceola*) now building and use whatever materials that may be required, as also to make use of the labour of the present workmen until the ship be launched – say in January 1859."

The takeover letter also stressed that Harland's offer was subject to the Belfast Harbour Commissioners agreeing to transfer and assign the existing lease to him, and that Hickson would do all he could to ensure that this transfer of the lease was concluded. The date for the transfer of the concern was set as 1 November 1858 and that an agreed joint stocktaking should be undertaken by 1 January 1859. Finally in the letter Hickson referred to the matter of payment for the shipyard and stated:

> "Terms of payments, Cash or equal thereto, but that £100, (£60,000 by today's values) shall be allowed in the shape of discount for prompt cash in the case of the purchase of the concern."[3]

Harland accepted this discount and paid the discounted price of £4,900 for the shipyard. Following this, Hickson, his family and four servants, who lived at University Road, Belfast where the present Student's Union building stands opposite Queens University, moved to Devonshire Place in Woodchurch on the Wirral. Here he and his wife lived with their two daughters and four sons. They also had three servants and a Governess to look after them. He carried on as a shipowner until his untimely death aged 54 when he died in December 1869. Following his death, his wife Jane then moved to live in Hastings in Sussex with one daughter and two sons.

Harland arranged for Gustav Wolff to return to Belfast and, as suggested by Schwabe, had him take up again the position of personal assistant, along with his role as Head of the Drawing Office. To ensure that the new venture on Queen's Island succeeded and also to try and guarantee that the loan would be repaid, Schwabe set about lining up potential customers for Harland. As Schwabe was involved heavily with the Bibby Line, it really is not surprising that he persuaded the board of the shipping line to place an order with this young man in Belfast. Not only did the Bibby Line place an order, but also they took a massive risk, and placed an order for three ships. These ships, numbers 1, 2 and 3 on Harland's order book, were called he *Venetian*, the *Sicilian* and the *Syrian*, and were placed in service for the shipping company on their Mediterranean routes.

When the order for these three new ships was announced there must have been some raised eyebrows in the shipbuilding world. Bibby's, the well-established shipping line, was placing an enormous order with such a new and untried shipbuilder. The Bibby Line, which was founded in 1805, had for many years dealt exclusively with the Clyde shipbuilders J&G Thomson. Harland had in the early stages of his career worked for Thomson's and no doubt in the course of his time there he had met with the Directors and staff from Bibby Line. On the face of it, the announcement that Edward Harland was to receive this order for three ships was to say the least strange. Thomson's must have been extremely surprised when it was announced where this large order was being placed. What they most likely didn't know was the extent that Schwabe was involved, by giving financial assistance to Harland and using his position on the board of the Bibby Line to have this large order placed with a new and totally untried shipbuilder.

The existing shipyard at Queen's Island would not be large enough to accommodate this new order and so to allow for expansion of the existing facilities, Harland leased an area of land on the Island, adjacent to his shipyard. This land had once been used for a much smaller shipbuilding and repair works for Thompson and Kirwan, which at one stage constructed wooden ships for local Belfast businessmen. Also at this time, Harland's new shipyard did not have the capability to construct the marine engines that would be needed for the Bibby ships, so he approached the marine engineering firm of McCabe and Company of the Clyde and subcontracted them to supply the motive power for the new ships. He also went to his old employers J&G Thomson and had them supply the cranes for the order. The *Venetian* bears a very special place in history as the first vessel that Harland constructed in his new shipyard. It is interesting to note that from this first ship built in 1859 until the *Anvil Point* (a roll on roll off ferry for the Ministry of Defence) was floated out in 2003, Harland and Wolff constructed around 1,651 vessels over a period of 144 years, giving an average of 11 ships launched per year over that period. (Note: This figure of 1,651 takes into account vessels allocated a ship number in the order book which were then subsequently cancelled.)

The *Venetian* was a four masted barque, 290 ft in length, with a breadth of 33.7 ft. The gross tonnage was 1,508 and the iron-hulled ship had a cargo capacity of 2,500 tons. The vessel was equipped with a two cylinder simple steam engine, which produced 450 horsepower and could propel the ship at an average speed of 6–7 knots. Under sail power the vessel could accomplish an increased speed of 10–12 knots. At the design stage the owners had requested a system be introduced whereby the single 15½ ft diameter propeller could be raised out of the water when the vessel was under wind power, thus reducing the drag caused by a stationary screw. First class accommodation was situated aft in the poop area, with eleven two-berth cabins, while there was also a six-berth ladies cabin, which had a private bathroom and toilet. For the second class passengers accommodation was by way of a ten-berth cabin amidships. The *Venetian* was later re-engined in 1872 and 1880. The ship was launched on Saturday 30 July 1859 at 11.00 am. Robert Hickson's wife Jane was given the privilege of christening the ship. Immediately following the launch, the slipway was cleared and preparations were made to lay the keel of the third ship, the *Syrian*.

The Venetian, *the first ship built by Edward Harland in Belfast*

(Courtesy of the Bibby Line Group picture library)

The *Belfast Newsletter* in reporting the event stated:

> "The steamer was built under special survey for the highest class at Lloyds, and certainly she does great credit to the constructors, as she is one of the finest models we have had the pleasure of examining."

Referring to the mechanism for the lifting propeller, the newspaper continued:

> "… the screw can be unshipped … above the waterline so that when the vessel may be sailing under canvas, with a fair wind, the use of the screw can be dispensed with."[4]

One reporter in his article for a local paper may not have been listening as intently as he should have been, as he later quoted that the owner of this new shipyard was "Mr Harlan". After the launch the VIP's partook of a splendid déjeuner in a special marquee that was erected at the shipyard. That evening, Edward Harland, treated all the foremen and heads of the various departments of his yard to a special supper at the Clarendon Dining Rooms in Belfast.

Around this time two events were to change in Harland's life. Firstly, in his own words:

> "Everything went on prosperously; and, in the midst of all my engagements, I found time to woo and win the hand of Miss Rosa Wann, of Vermont, Belfast, to whom I was married on the 26 of January, 1860, and by her great energy, soundness of judgement, and cleverness in organisation, I was soon relieved from all sources of care and anxiety, excepting those connected with business."[5]

The Wann's lived at Pakenham Place off the Donegall Pass in Belfast. Rosa's father, Thomas, who had married Mary Hyndham, was connected to the Gallaher tobacco family and he was the Secretary to a local Bank.

The second thing to influence Harland, was the continual pressure of the business. He had to travel away from the Belfast yard on quite a few occasions and in doing so he was not in the position to keep watch over the progress of the yard, which by now was employing around 1,000 men. He needed to have someone upon whom he could fully trust and depend on. The answer to this problem was to make Gustav Wolff, who had also been acting as his Personal Assistant, a full Partner in the enterprise.

The historic Agreement was drawn up and dated 11 April 1861, and contains 21 clauses. In the document the two principals seemed to have thought of most things. Their initial agreement was to run until 1 January 1869, at which time they could by further agreement extend it or dissolve the partnership. The business was to "be in the name and style of Edward James Harland". This could

Rosa Wann as a young woman (V. Morrison Collection)

be changed at Wolff's request, when the name of the firm would change to that of Harland and Wolff.[6]

The initial capital of the firm was to be £2,416. Harland would contribute £1,916 and receive ⅔ of the profits. Wolff would contribute £500 and receive ⅓ of the profits. From the annual profits the Partners could withdraw funds for their own personal use, Harland was permitted £700 and Wolff £500. They could also raise personal loans from the company and would be charged 5 % interest.

One clause, number 11, laid out the procedure in case one of the Partners invented any process or made an important discovery. This clause added that a Patent should be taken out and that the invention or process would be used solely to benefit the partnership. On the dissolution of the partnership the rights of the Patent would revert to whichever Partner made the application.

Clause 13 stated that both Partners should devote all their time to the partnership and should not pledge credit or cash belonging to the partnership to anyone else. This clause also stated that neither Partner should bet, gamble or play any game of chance whereby either may loose more than £5 in a period of 24 hours. In the event that the partnership would be dissolved, any profits should be divided on a basis of ⅔ to Harland and ⅓ to Wolff.

Finally, in clause 21 they stated that, in the event of a disagreement, then the sole Arbitrator of any dispute should be Mr James Bibby of the Bibby Shipping Line. In the event that Bibby either died or was reluctant to take on this role, the Partners agreed that Mr James Dugdale of Manchester was to be called upon. (Dugdale was the brother in law of Gustav Schwabe). The witnesses to this historic agreement were Mr John Bailey and Mr Priestly.

The Bibby Line were well pleased with the first three ships that Harland constructed for them, so much so that within a few months they placed an order for three more ships, that would be called *Grecian, Italian* and *Egyptian*. Edward Harland was aware that previously, in 1851, J. Reid and Company on the Clyde had built a steamer called the *Tiber* for the Bibby Line, which incorporated a new hull design. Harland, who at that earlier time had been employed by J&G Thomson when they supplied the engines for the ship, would have had first hand knowledge of the vessel. The striking feature of this ship was that she had been constructed with a longer and narrower hull in comparison to most ships of that time. The ship's length was 231½ ft long and only 28¼ ft in beam (or width). This was further enhanced in 1861 when the length was increased to 274 ft and the beam was only increased 1 ft to 29¼ ft. The shipping world at the time felt that ships of this type of dimension were dangerous, but the *Tiber* sailed on until she was wrecked in 1894. Harland approached the Bibby's and suggested to them that it may be an opportune time to consider building the three new ships in a similar manner. He was convinced that adopting this radical design to the ship's hull would result in an increase in both speed and power, and also offer more accommodation space for passengers. The Bibby Line agreed to this proposal

48

along with other modifications including constructing the four masts for the ships in one continuous length and only having yards on the two forward masts (the cross members on the mast), which would result in fewer crew members being needed to man the ships, thereby reducing operating costs. Yards were not fitted to the *Grecian* and her two sisters.

Since the introduction of steam engines into ships, there had always been a problem of getting the steam to condense back into water on its return from the engines. A Mr Spencer in England had previously invented a system using India rubber to seal the boilers and stop salt water contaminating the steam, which was recycled as pure water back into the system. Spencer's idea had only ever been tried out on land and Harland suggested to Bibby's that one of their existing vessels the 657 ton *Frankfurt* should be used to test this new method of sealing the boilers. This proved to be a great success and resulted in a fuel saving of around 20%. Harland purchased the patent for the discovery and these innovations were included in the three new ships.

There was a lot riding on these new innovations of Harland's. He had successfully on his own account built three ships for the Bibby Line, breaking a long established link that they had with the Clyde Shipbuilders. However, now he and Wolff would have to surpass themselves with this new order and 'pull out all the stops' to give the ship owners vessels that would be at the forefront of new technology and ships that both builders and owners could be proud of.

The first of these was the *Grecian*. Harland put into practice his ideas of lengthening the ship and for this vessel he had the length extended to 310 ft (40 ft more than the *Venetian*), but kept the breadth the same as the previous ship (28¼ ft). In his memoirs many years later, Harland recalled that when these new ships, the *Grecian* and her two sisters *Italian* and *Egyptian*, were seen by the 'old salts' on the Mersey at Liverpool, their thoughts were:

> "They were too long! They were too sharp! They would break their backs! They might, indeed, get out of the Mersey, but they would never get back!"[7]

The ships, however, sailed and they made rapid and prosperous voyages to and from the Mediterranean. They fulfilled all the promises which had been made. They proved the advantages of our new build of ships; and the owners were perfectly satisfied with their superior strength, speed, and accommodation.

The old sea salts of Liverpool gave these new ships the nicknames, of the 'Bibby Coffins' because they were so long and narrow.

Satisfied with the ships that they had purchased, the Bibby Line ordered a further five ships. In the Order Book of the Harland and Wolff shipyard, the Bibby Line were to purchase 11 out of the first 16 ships that were built. Further advances were made in the next Bibby ships that were constructed. In fact Harland and Wolff managed to extend the length of the ships up to 360 ft on the *Persian*, and still maintain the same breadth as the *Grecian*. They made the bottom of their new ships flatter and squared up the bilges, which again earned a nickname from the 'old hands' in Liverpool, the 'Belfast Bottoms'. Also adopted was the idea of straightening the bow and stern of their designs.

There was a problem in joining the various materials used in the construction of the ships at that time, particularly the joining of iron and timber. Harland and Wolff came up with another radical idea of using Portland cement. Harland recalled:

> "Having found it impossible to combine satisfactorily wood with iron, each being so differently affected by temperature and moisture, I secured some of these novelties of construction in a patent, by which filling in the spaces between frames, &c., with Portland cement, instead of chocks of wood, and covering the iron plates with cement and tiles, became general practice, and this has since come into very general use."[8]

The rise in the fortunes of the shipyard of Harland and Wolff was to continue. Within five years of Edward Harland buying out Robert Hickson, the company built 26 ships and created many new jobs at their Queen's Island yard. Expansion of the shipyard was the next thing that Harland wanted to consider and also the provision of a dry dock facility. Edward Harland's gamble in 1858 had paid off. He and Gustav Wolff had taken on the established shipyards on the Clyde and Newcastle upon Tyne, and had, with their new ideas, built ships that now would be copied by other yards. Their initial designs would become the 'norm' for constructing ships.

However, there were events happening in the wider world which would have a major impact on the shipyard, and perhaps none more importantly than when a young Canadian born boy, aged just 16 years of age, started in the shipyard as a gentleman apprentice. With time he was to grow into a position of power and he would then take the Harland and Wolff shipyard and place it in the premier league of shipbuilders. The boy's name was William James Pirrie. In that same year Edward Harland was to make Gustav Wolff a full Partner and then establish the shipyard with the name of Harland and Wolff.

One other significant event happened in England when a small shipping line went bankrupt and collapsed. The line was called the White Star Line and it was bought over for a nominal sum by a gentleman called Thomas Ismay. In forthcoming years Ismay came to the Belfast shipyard of Harland and Wolff to have all his new ships built.

50

CHAPTER 5

Partners

In 1845 Henry Threlfall Wilson and John Pilkington founded a shipping company called the White Star Line, which was based in Liverpool. Their company was established with the name Pilkington and Wilson, and they acted as shipbrokers and agents, initially engaging a number of American owned clipper sailing ships. In 1849 they commissioned their first newly built ship, the 879 ton *Iowa*. By 1851 the company's fortunes took an upturn when gold was discovered in Australia. It was estimated at the time that around half a million people left the United Kingdom to seek their fortune and Pilkington and Wilson were to prosper from this increase in travel. Other ships owned by the Line included the *Red Jacket*, *Star of Shalimar* and the ill-fated *Royal Standard*. On 4 April 1864, while on a return journey from Australia to the United Kingdom, the ship, a 2,033 ton clipper, collided with an iceberg and nearly sank. Quickly the vessel had to put into Rio de Janeiro for repairs.

The ill-fated Royal Standard (Illustrated London News, 18 June 1864)

It was reported at the time that all of Pilkington and Wilson's ships had a Red Indian Chieftain as the figurehead of their vessels. Carved on the figure's chest was a five-pointed white star, which went on to give the company the name of White Star Line.

The Line's flag was a red swallow-tail flag with that white star in the middle of it.

There had, however, been a previous company called the White Star Line. In 1825 George Thompson of Aberdeen set up a shipping company to trade between Scotland and Canada, carrying passengers on the outward journey and returning home with a cargo of timber. He named his line the Aberdeen Line and his house flag was half red and half blue with a six-pointed white star in the middle. Thompson's company became known as the Aberdeen White Star Line, and continued in business totally separate from the Liverpool White Star Line of Pilkington and Wilson. By 1837 Thompson's Line was operating with a fleet of 12 sailing ships and eventually in 1905 the concern was sold to the Shaw Savill Line.

In Liverpool, in 1863, John Pilkington left the White Star Line. Henry Wilson replaced him with his own brother in law, James Chambers and the name of the firm was changed from Pilkington and Wilson to H.T. Wilson and Chambers. This new partnership only lasted two years and in 1865 Chambers left. Chambers was replaced by John Cunningham and the company name changed once again, this time to Wilson and Cunningham. The Line was still involved in the Liverpool to Australia route and advertised that its ships could take passengers there in just 68 days. This new, reformed White Star Line was starting to suffer from financial problems due to the Henry Wilson's over-spending and wastefulness with money and purchases. The company merged with the Black Ball Line and The Eagle Line, but following attempts to expand the whole company, debts of around £527,000 were amassed. To the dismay of Wilson and Cunningham, their bankers, the Royal Bank of Liverpool, collapsed in October 1867. This in turn brought down the White Star Line of Wilson and Cunningham.

In his home in Liverpool, Gustav Schwabe was keeping up to date with the financial downfall of the Bank and the subsequent failure of the local White Star Line. In his mind he was starting to hatch yet another financial plan. As I have already said, just a few years previously he had given Edward Harland a loan to buy the shipyard in Belfast. In order to assist both Harland and himself he had introduced the Bibby Line to Harland, and this had proved a very happy and prosperous business arrangement for all concerned. Now the White Star Line had gone bankrupt. If Schwabe was able to get someone interested in buying the Line, then there was a possibility that the new purchaser would be in the market for acquiring new ships, which would benefit his investment in Harland and Wolff.

Schwabe didn't really have to wait too long. Not long after White Star's downfall, Thomas Henry Ismay had put in a successful bid of £1,000 for the flag and goodwill of the bankrupt company, and set himself up trading between Liverpool and Australia. Ismay had been born on 7 January 1837 in Maryport, Cumberland, England. At the age of 16 he was apprenticed to the Liverpool ship broking firm of Imrie and Tomlison. Following his period there he went to sea travelling to South America. On his return he established a small shipbrokers in Maryport, along with Philip Nelson, an old sea Captain, which traded under the name of Nelson, Ismay and Company. This partnership didn't last too long as Nelson was very set in his ways and was possibly not as forward thinking as the younger Ismay. Nelson was replaced with William Imrie, a relative of the Imrie in the Imrie and Tomlison firm that Ismay had originally worked for. They set themselves in business trading under the name of Ismay, Imrie and Company with offices at 30 James Street in Liverpool. Thomas Ismay, as well as running his own business, also became a Director of the National Line, another shipping company, and by the time he was 32 years of age he had amassed a personal fortune of £500,000.

In Belfast, Harland and Wolff had just been left with an almost constructed ship that the owners had cancelled. The Partners were endeavouring to complete this vessel, which was ship number 44, when Schwabe suggested to them that he might be able to get a buyer for it. He approached Thomas Ismay with the suggestion that he should buy the ship and also offered to put up a quarter of the cost of the ship through the books of Harland and Wolff. Ismay happily accepted and the ship was named *Broughton* after the Schwabe family home in Liverpool.

Thomas Henry Ismay

53

Now that Schwabe had seen the deal struck with Ismay and Harland and Wolff, he turned his attentions fully to Ismay. Schwabe was by now living at Broughton Hall in West Derby, within the greater Liverpool area and it is reputed that he invited Ismay to dinner at his home. Following the meal and during a game of billiards, Schwabe suggested to Ismay, that he would offer financial assistance and backing to the new company if Ismay would consider starting up a new shipping line to trade on the North Atlantic route out of Liverpool. Schwabe further suggested that Ismay should consider going to the Belfast shipyard of Harland and Wolff to have his ships built there. Schwabe also promised to bring in other local businessmen to further back this new venture.

Ismay, the astute business man, didn't take to long to think about this offer and on the 6 September 1869 he established his new shipping company, which was to trade under the name of the Oceanic Steam Navigation Company. The new Line was formed with a capital of £400,000 in £1,000 shares. Ismay took 50 shares while G.H. Fletcher (who would become a Partner of Ismay's in this new venture) took another 50 and Schwabe purchased 12 shares. Edward Harland and Gustav Wolff also took shares in the new company. The White Star Line was now established, as was the link with the Harland and Wolff shipyard, which would continue for the next sixty years.

The next major event to shape the future of shipbuilding was to happen in Belfast, when William James Pirrie was apprenticed to Harland and Wolff on 23 June 1862 as a gentleman apprentice. Pirrie was born in Canada on 31 May 1847. His parents James and Eliza had travelled and married there in 1844. In 1845 another child was also born in Canada, a girl called Eliza. Their father James was the son of Captain William Pirrie, mentioned earlier in this book. James died of cholera on 20 August 1849. Eliza took the major decision to travel back to Ireland with her two young children and took up residence with her father in law, Captain Pirrie, at his home at Conlig in County Down. William and his sister Eliza were to be educated at the grandfather's home in their early years.

William James Pirrie
(Jefferson, Herbert, *Viscount Pirrie of Belfast*, W.M. Mullan & Son Ltd, Belfast: 1948)

James Pirrie father of William James Pirrie

(Jefferson, Herbert, *Viscount Pirrie of Belfast*, W.M. Mullan & Son Ltd, Belfast: 1948)

Through this education, both of them were taught to respect their mother's wisdom and good advice. For William, she taught him that he had to make his own way in life and instilled in him the need to be industrious, persevering and patient.

It would appear that the grandfather, Captain William, took quite an interest in the young Pirrie and by all accounts this bond was mutually shared. On many occasions the pair could be seen side by side walking the lengths of the harbour in Belfast, with the older Pirrie no doubt recounting adventures of the sea to the younger. It was during these walks that the sea was to get into the veins of the young William Pirrie.

When William was aged 11 he was enrolled in the Royal Belfast Academical Institution, in the charge of the Headmaster, John Carlisle M.A. Carlisle, who was known as 'Jack Carlisle of the Inst', was born in 1823 and died in 1884. He was married to Catherine Montgomery, the sister of Eliza Swan Montgomery, who was James Pirrie's widow. This then made 'Jack of the Inst' and the 11 year old Pirrie uncle and nephew. There were to be closer family ties created within these two families when Jack Carlisle's two children became very closely involved with Pirrie. A son of Carlisle's, named Alexander, would become a Managing Director on the board of the shipyard of Harland and Wolff and Carlisle's daughter Margaret would marry her cousin William Pirrie.

Young Pirrie's education at Inst came to an end on his 15th birthday in 1862. At school he had taken a normal interest in games but showed more aptitude towards mathematics. For sometime he had been pressuring his mother into allowing him to enter the business world when he left school. Some of his uncles and aunts were involved in the shipping world, perhaps the most noticeable of those ventures being the Heyn Shipping Line, which was based in Belfast. His grandfather, Captain William, who had been a life member of the Ballast Board also had had close contacts with those in the local shipping circle, so it was really no great surprise that his mother made an appointment with Edward Harland with a view to taking him on as a premium apprentice with the shipyard. This was agreed and William James Pirrie, aged 15 and 23 days, signed an indenture to be trained in the noble art of shipbuilding. He entered the shipyard and over a five year period passed through various departments, becoming a 'jack of all trades' rather than a master of just one. Finally after this period of training he would become a draughtsman, Assistant Manager, Sub Manager and then progress to Works Manager.

Royal Belfast Academical Institution

Those first few days of his time in the shipyard must surely have brought back vivid and happy memories of his grandfather Captain William Pirrie, the walks and tales that they swapped as they walked around Belfast Lough and the port of the town, and the very strong connection that the elder Pirrie had with the sea and ships. Pirrie senior, who had been born in Port William in Scotland on 24 January 1780, had died in 1858, the year the young Pirrie was enrolled in Inst.

At an early age, Captain William went to sea and became an American citizen and ship's Captain. In the early 1800s, during the Spanish and French Peninsular war, Captain Pirrie was operating from the Spanish port of Malaga. On one occasion, while transporting contraband to Spain, the French intercepted his ship and the hapless Captain was captured and held as a prisoner for 12 months. He managed to escape from his captors and in an open boat made his way across the English Channel to the safety of England. He then made his way to Belfast where he settled as a merchant and ship owner. He was approached by the newly constituted Belfast Ballast Board and asked to join, and was subsequently made a life member of the Board. One of the main changes he made in Belfast was to ensure that ships could reach the centre of the docks in Belfast and he was responsible for the creation of the Victoria Channel. During this work he ensured that the newly formed Belfast Harbour Commissioners could possess any new land formed by the excavations of the river Lagan. The Belfast Harbour Commissioners later leased this land to Edward Harland on which he built his shipyard.

Captain William Pirrie had become a leading figure in Belfast, but he sought to put himself in that position. Herbert Jefferson in his book, *Viscount Pirrie of Belfast,* stated "that he was a man who meant to keep company with a class that

Grave of James Pirrie
(Courtesy of the McKenna Collection)

56

could assist him in business pursuits", he always aimed high. In 1810, he had married Elizabeth Morrison and between them they had a family of eight children, four girls and four boys. Captain Pirrie was also involved heavily with the Belfast Fever Hospital and assisted with fund raising for it. He, along his son in law John Sinclair, also founded the Presbyterian Church at Conlig in County Down, which was close to his home in that village.

On the 9 June 1858 he was laid to rest at the New Burying Ground at Clifton Street in Belfast.

CHAPTER 6

Pupils, Apprentices and Working Conditions

Prior to the decline of shipbuilding in the late twentieth century, it was generally felt that if a young boy could secure employment in the shipyard it would provide job security. Provided that over the ensuing years the worker kept their 'nose clean' the job would be a job for life. In the early days there were several ways of gaining employment. The first would be for the sons of the well to do. Very early in the life of the Harland and Wolff shipyard they introduced the Premium Apprentices system for 16 year old boys. This method of recruitment had been first pioneered by Robert Hickson. The basic idea was to encourage young men to join the shipyard with the possibility, through careful training, of becoming the future mid and senior management for the yard. These young boys would also be referred to as shipyard pupils. Parents of a 'pupil' would make a payment to Harland and Wolff, generally of around 100 guineas (£105) and then the young boy would be indentured to the yard for a period of five years. During this period of apprenticeship, the youngster would have to work in many departments and then undergo a period of study, which would ultimately lead to a technical qualification. While entry into the pupilage system could mean advancement through the yard, that advancement would rest solely on the pupil's ability and determination. If the pupil were able to show that he had what it took, by way of hard work, study and devotion to the firm, he could look forward to promotion when he would come to the end of his apprenticeship.

The purpose of this system was to ensure that pupils had a good knowledge of shipbuilding and by the end of the five years they would become a 'jack of all trades' rather than a master of any one specific trade. Normally the pupils were placed in the various departments around the shipyard for a period of time, beginning with the Joinery Department for six months, followed by two months in the Main Store. For the next five months they would work alongside the shipwrights, and then spend two months in the Moulding Loft. There were two months with the painters and then eight months with the Iron Shipwrights. The next placement was for six months with the Fitters, followed by three months with the Patternmakers. The Blacksmiths took a further eight months and, finally, they were placed in the Drawing Office for the last 18 months of the five year period. When they moved into the Office building, gone would be the greasy

■ 58

3859

DUPLICATE INDENTURE OF APPRENTICESHIP (to be retained by the Apprentice).

This Indenture

MADE THE

Fourth day of *September 1922.*

BETWEEN HARLAND & WOLFF, LIMITED, of Queen's Island, Belfast, Shipbuilders and Engineers, (hereinafter called " The Employers ") of the one part, AND

Francis J. Parkinson,
35 Distillery St,
Belfast

of

(hereinafter called " The Apprentice ") of the other part, WITNESSETH as follows :

1. In consideration of the Covenants by the Apprentice hereinafter contained, the Employers hereby Covenant with the Apprentice as follows :

(a) To receive the Apprentice into their employment as their Apprentice for a period of Five years from the date hereof, which period shall be reckoned in the manner hereinafter specified as the term of his Apprenticeship under this Indenture.

(b) Each year of said Apprenticeship shall be reckoned as consisting of the recognised standard of ordinary working hours for tradesmen employed in the Employers' Works, prescribed from time to time, but shall in no case be less than one calendar year.

(c) In case the actual time (including overtime) worked by the Apprentice up to the end of each year of his Apprenticeship falls short of the full number of working hours constituting the working time for one year, the Apprentice shall make up by work whatever hours he is short; and until the full number of working hours for each year is completed, he shall not be deemed to have completed that year of his apprenticeship, nor shall he be entitled to receive any increase of pay for the succeeding year, but overtime shall not reduce the period of apprenticeship.

(d) During the term of said Apprenticeship to provide said Apprentice with work, and, so far as may be necessary and practicable, instructions relative thereto as a *Joaier*

(e) To pay the Apprentice

Six shillings per week of full working time during the first year.
Eight do. do. second year.
Ten do. do. third year.
Twelve do. do. fourth year.
Fifteen do. do. fifth year.

(f) Overtime shall count as stated on Works Rules from time to time.

(g) To allow the Apprentice the following holidays in each year, but without pay therefor namely— Christmas Day, Easter Monday, and three whole holidays or six half holidays between 1st March and 1st October, and any other general holidays given in the Employers' Works, either alternatively for or in addition to the above.

2. In consideration of the premises, the Apprentice hereby binds and places himself as an Apprentice to and with the Employers during the aforesaid term of his Apprenticeship, during which time he shall diligently and faithfully serve the Employers, keep their secrets, and willingly and diligently obey their lawful commands; and shall not do any damage to the Employers or their goods, see any damage done by others without informing the Employers, or the Works manager, or the foreman of the department in which the Apprentice is working, concerning same; and shall not waste, or without permission, lend, give, sell, take away, or otherwise dispose of the Employers' goods, nor absent himself without permission from the Employers' service; but shall in all things behave as a faithful Apprentice ought to do, and duly account for any of the Employers' money or goods entrusted to him.

3. The Apprentice hereby accepts and undertakes that he will duly conform to the general rules of the Employers' Works, as they are now or may hereafter be posted up therein.

4. AND IT IS HEREBY AGREED as follows :—

If the Apprentice shall be guilty of disobedience, misconduct, or disrespect towards the Employers, their manager, or any foreman to whom the Apprentice is reponsible for his work; or of vicious or immoral conduct; or of repeated absence without leave; or of disobedience of reasonable orders; or of any offence which, in the opinion of the Employers, is deserving of either of the penalties hereinafter set forth; or if he commit any breach of the general rules of the Employers' Works, the Employers may dismiss the Apprentice or may suspend him for any period, and such period of suspension shall be excluded from the calculation of the term of Apprenticeship to be served by the Apprentice under this agreement.

IN WITNESS whereof the parties above-named have hereunto respectively set their Hands and Seals, the day and year aforesaid.

Signed, Sealed, and Delivered on behalf of the said Harland & Wolff, Limited, by

Chas Payne

(duly authorised for that purpose), in the presence of

HC Hayes

Chas Payne

Managing Director.

Signed, Sealed, and Delivered by the said Apprentice in presence of

Samuel Wilson

Francis John Parkinson

Indenture of F. John Parkinson issued in 1922

(Courtesy of Belfast Titanic Society)

overalls that had been wearing for the last three and a half years. This new formal setting required them to arrive for work properly dressed in collar and tie.

Following a successful apprenticeship the young men, who would then be aged 21, would be given their first role in authority, normally as a Junior Manager in one of the outside works. They would also be expected to wear the badge of office, a bowler hat, and be called Mister by the workforce. Some very prominent people passed through this system. Frank Workman and George Clark were both pupils of Edward Harland and they left once their pupilage was completed to set up their own shipyard in Belfast with the name of Workman Clark. It was forever in the shadow of Harland and Wolff. Others included Walter Wilson and his brother Alexander, Alexander (or Alick) Carlisle, Thomas Andrews and of course William James Pirrie. They would all undergo training in the pupil system and would eventually make their mark on the progress of the yard, as they were promoted to the Board of Directors.

The other simpler way of gaining employment with the shipyard was to be taken on as an apprentice and undergo five years training 'on the job'. As the success of the shipyard grew so did the number of apprentices taken on. On average around 200 such apprenticeships would be offered each year.

A young 16 year old boy would nervously be brought down to the shipyard, generally by his father or maybe an uncle who already worked in the Yard. There the anxious and bewildered youngster would be interviewed by a Manager before being presented with his 'Indenture of Apprenticeship'. For most this would be the first time in their young lives that they were presented with a formal legal document. It firstly outlined what the shipyard would agree to do for them and secondly clearly stated what was expected of the new apprentice. In the agreement Harland and Wolff promised that, over a five year period, they would train the young apprentice and would assist him to become a tradesman in his chosen discipline. Probably for the young boy and his family, the most important part of the Agreement outlined what wages he would receive each year throughout the period of the Indenture. The apprentice in signing the agreement stated that he would obey all company orders and "diligently and faithfully serve his Employers."

Whilst the new apprentice may have been 'over the moon' at securing his position, he was in for a rather rude awakening, when he actually started work. The young boy who had just finished school had been used to a reasonably relaxed regime, compared to what was waiting for him once inside the gates of the shipyard. There would be no more lie-ins or gentle starts to the day, he would have to report for work along with the rest of the workforce and clock on no later than 6.30 am in the morning daily. Managers were expected to be at their post by 6.00 am to keep a watchful eye on the workforce as they clocked on. The 'knock off whistle' would not sound until 5.30 pm in the evening, and on Saturday the working day was from 6.30 am until 1.30 pm. Meal breaks were permitted on weekdays between 8.20 am and 9.00 am and again between 1.00 pm and 2.00 pm. Only a breakfast break was permitted on a Saturday, which gave a working week in excess of 54 hours. Unpaid holidays were allowed, and the apprentice would be off on Christmas Day, Easter Monday and a further three days or six half days between March and October. Wages would have been in the region of only a few shillings a week, but would have risen for each of the five years of the apprenticeship.

Another way of gaining employment in the shipyard was the casual labour scheme. This in hindsight was really a very cruel and hard way of trying to gain employment. Every morning between 6.00 and 6.30 am many unskilled and unemployed labourers would be gathered at the main gates looking for a day's work. The foreman, resplendent with bowler hat, would walk up to the crowd and announce that for the day he needed perhaps 50 or so men. He would then select those he wanted from the gathered mass. If a man had been taken on before and worked well, and impressed the foreman there was a good chance that he might be employed for the day. On the other hand if the foreman didn't like the look of a certain individual, there would be no possibility that he would be enlisted for the day, no matter whether he was a good worker or not. For those gaining employment there was the payment at the end of the day to look forward to and this would be taken home to the wife and family. No work meant no pay for the day and, with no assistance forthcoming from the Government, the man's family would have to make do with less money coming into the house.

For the workforce in the shipyard there was the dreaded 'wet horn'. If the weather was so bad that it was impossible to continue working, the horn would be sounded and the work for that day would stop, the workforce would then go home and would only receive pay up until the horn had sounded.

There were financial penalties for any workman who did not obey the company rules. The gates of the shipyard would be closed on the stroke of 6.30 am and any man who did not get in on time would have to wait until 7.30 am when the gates would be opened again, he could then 'clock in' but his wages would be docked by the one hour, that he had been 'locked out'. Any workman who was discovered clocking on and then 'beaking off' work would lose all his wages for that day. Another trick that was frowned upon was 'clocking on' your mate who was taking an 'unofficial' day's leave. If either man were caught, both would face the harsh discipline of the yard, which generally resulted in both men being dismissed. No reference of good character would be given to the dismissed man and without this it was impossible to gain further employment.

The list of misdemeanours that would result in a fine was a considerable one. Some of those that could incur a fine included:

- Leaving a candle, lamp or fire burning after use.
- Stopping work or preparing to stop work before the appointed time.
- Any wastage of oil, pitch, tar, oakum, paint, candles or nails.

RULES

To be observed in these Works and subject to which all persons employed are engaged.

1. Ordinary working hours from 6.20 till 8.20 o'clock; from 9 till 1 o'clock; and from 2 till 5.30 o'clock. On Saturdays work will cease at 1.30 o'clock, but without interval for dinner. Wages will be paid by the hour; and only the number of hours actually worked will be paid for. Any workman commencing work and absenting himself without leave until the termination of the ordinary working day, will not be entitled to payment for any time he may have worked on the day in question.

2. The first two hours of Overtime, Saturdays included, to be paid for as time and a quarter, and further Overtime to count as time and a half; but no time will be counted as Overtime until the ordinary number of hours for the day has been completed. Sunday work, when absolutely necessary, will be paid for as double ordinary time.

3. Workmen on the night shift to start work at 5.30 p.m., and continue until 6.20 o'clock the next morning; intervals for meals from 9 till 9.25 p m., and 1.35 till 2 o'clock a.m. For the hours worked on the night shift, time and a quarter will be paid.

4. Wages will be paid fortnightly on each alternate Saturday, at 1.30 o'clock—to be counted up to the previous Thursday night, and from it the amount of any fines, debts, or damages will be deducted. Men off work on the pay day will not be paid until after those working have received their wages.

5. All hands will enter the Works through the Time Offices at starting time, and also on resuming work after breakfast and dinner. Each workman to draw his Time Board on commencing work; and on resuming work after breakfast and dinner, must, as he enters the Works, take his Token off the Board and put it into the receiving slot. On leaving work each workman to pass out through the Time Offices and hand in his Time Board, with the amount of time worked and for what purpose written thereon, and on each Thursday evening the total amount of the previous week's time to be written thereon. Any breach of this Rule will subject him to a fine, and any workman not delivering his Token or Time Board personally at the times mentioned will forfeit all claim to wages for that day. All workmen passing through the gates during working hours must show their Time Boards to the Gatekeeper and give any explanation that may be demanded as to their business; non-compliance with this will forfeit wages for the day and subject the offender to fine or dismissal.

6. Those provided with Tool Boxes or Lockers to leave the keys thereof at the Office or Store before quitting work, if so ordered.

7. Any one causing disturbance in the Works, neglecting the orders of his Foreman, avoidably absent for more than one day without the leave of his Foreman, bringing spirituous liquors into the Works, or appearing here in a state of intoxication, will be subject to fine or dismissal.

8. Any one carelessly or maliciously breaking, injuring, or defacing any Machine or Tool, altering any Template, removing Shores without leave, or committing any other mischief, to pay the cost of repairing the same, or, in the option of the Employers, to be fined.

9. Those provided with Tools must satisfactorily account for the same before leaving the employment, or the value of any that may be missing will be deducted from the wages due.

10. Any one entering or leaving the Works except by the appointed gates, or carrying out material to ships without having it charged by the Storekeeper and also giving account of same to the Gateman, will be subject to fine or dismissal.

11. No person is allowed to take strangers into any portion of the Works without first having obtained an authorized pass.

12. Any one stopping work, or preparing to stop work before the appointed time, will be fined or dismissed.

13. Any one wasting, injuring, or destroying Oil, Pitch, Tar, Oakum, Paint, Candles, Nails, or any other material, to pay the cost thereof.

14. Any one smoking, or preparing food during working hours, or smoking at any other time near combustile material, will be fined or dismissed.

15. Any one leaving a candle, lamp, or fire burning after use, will be fined.

16. In the event of work being spoiled by the carelessness of workmen, the labour expended thereon will not be paid for, and those in fault will be held responsible for the loss of the material.

We reserve to ourselves the right of fining for any irregularity or offence not specially mentioned in the foregoing Rules.

HARLAND & WOLFF.

Shipbuilding and Engineering Works,
Belfast, 30th May, 1888.

Harland and Wolff company rules.

(Courtesy of the The Deputy Keeper of the Records, Public Record Office of Northern Ireland)

- Anyone smoking or preparing food during working hours.
- Spoiling work or carelessness.
- Causing a disturbance.
- Neglecting orders from a foreman.
- Being absent for more than one day without permission from a foreman.
- Bringing spirituous liquors into the yard or appearing drunk.

Any of these would result in the person concerned having their wages docked or reduced, and in times when money was hard to come by any reduction in the weekly wage packet could lead to harsh times at home.

Then there was the strange clocking on and off system employed by the yard. On entering the shipyard of Harland and Wolff the new employee was given his works number and his board. This small piece of hardwood known as 'the bourd' was the preferred method of timekeeping. The bourd was 3 inches in length, 1½ inches wide and 5/16 of an inch thick (76 mm × 39 mm × 7 mm). Cut out on top of the bourd was an indent, just over an inch wide, and in that space, on the top edge, the employee's works number was stamped.

The Harland and Wolff bourd.

The bourd was probably the most important item belonging to the workman and it had to be well looked after, because its issue was the way in which the shipyard would calculate the wages to be paid to the workman at the end of the week.

In the simplest way of working, when the worker 'clocked on' at the Time Office in the morning, he would call out his works number to the Timekeepers in the Office, and be issued with his bourd which he would keep with him all day. At the end of the day when he 'clocked off', the workman would then give the bourd back to the Timekeeper. With this information the Timekeeper could then calculate the hours worked and on payday the workman would collect his wages.

The bourd was also used for many other things in the shipyard. If, for example the workman finished early or worked overtime, he would have to go to his foreman who would rub the board with chalk, then write these extra details on the back of the wooden bourd prior to it being left with the Timekeepers.

The Timekeepers, the clerks in the Time Office, could also have a hard time of it. When it came time to 'clock off' the shipyard workers would want to get away as quickly as possible. With many hundreds of them going through the Time Offices at the same time, to speed up their exit, generally one man in the squad of workers would gather up all the bourds and take great delight in throwing them through the small window of the Time Office, trying his best to hit the poor Timekeeper. There were variations on this theme. The bourds that were gathered from the squad would be loosely tied with string and when this 'missile' was hurled through the window, depending on the aim of the 'launcher', the incoming projectile on contact with a hard surface would 'explode', showering the Office with bourds. This was much to the annoyance of the poor Timekeepers, who then had the job of trying to collect each individual bourd and record its owner's details in a large book. This book would later be used to calculate the wages to be paid. The bourd was then placed in a slot in a large open wooden cabinet in the Office.

On payday, clerks from the Accounts Department would help the Timekeepers prepare the wages for the workforce. When the hours and wages for the individual had been calculated they would then assemble the payment in readiness for handing out the wages at the end of the day. In those early days the workforce were not issued with a wages slip or a wages envelope. The wages were instead wrapped up in the paper money, for example if the wages came to three pounds, ten shillings and six pence, the Timekeepers would lay out the three pound notes on the desk and in the middle of the notes they would place coins to the value of ten shillings and six pence. The paper money would then be neatly folded over the coins and the 'package' subsequently placed in the bourd slot of the appropriate workman. At the end of the shift on pay day (this would be the only day that there would be no 'flying bourds') each man would patiently queue up to collect his own wages in person, this was done by him handing in his bourd and then receiving his neatly prepared wages, which could be taken home.

When the young apprentice joined the shipyard he would, at his own expense, have to provide his own set of tools. In most cases the youngster would be helped with these purchases by his own family and would also receive some assistance from the journeyman, under whose care he had been entrusted for the period of his apprenticeship. The very first thing that the apprentice would do on gaining a new tool would be to stamp his name on it, denoting that it was his. Woe betide anyone who was ever caught with a hammer or other tool with someone else's name on it. The wronged apprentice would certainly have something to say about his missing tool. The 'discussion' would probably be non-verbal, take place out of sight of anyone else and would end up with someone suffering at the least a black eye. The hammer in question would be returned to its rightful place.

However there would always be occasions when a workman, even with a full toolbox, would require a specialised tool for a certain job that he was to undertake, perhaps a large hammer or crowbar. He would then go to the Main Store and from there could borrow whatever it was that was needed. When the job was completed and the tool finished with it would have to be returned to the Store. Bearing in mind human nature, unless there was some form of incentive, the tool would probably be abandoned and left lying where it had last been used. It may even have been stolen by another quick-eyed workman and possibly never returned to the Main Store. A very simple system was put in place to stop this happening. To borrow the tool the workman had to leave his bourd as a deposit, quite simply if he couldn't be bothered to return the tool by quitting time his bourd would be confiscated and handed in to the Timekeeper by the Storeman, this would result in the man receiving no wages for the day and probably fined as well, so the threat of a reduction in his wages was the lever that would see the tool returned.

There was another use for the bourd, and it would be used when the workman went to the toilets. In an environment like a shipyard, you would be forgiven for thinking that the toilets, that were scattered throughout the yard, would be given a name suitable to a maritime setting, like the Royal Navy's use of the term of 'heads'. However, the shipyard of Harland and Wolff referred to the toilets as 'the minutes' and in charge of them was 'the minute man'. This term came about because the workforce were only allowed seven minutes in the toilets, not per go but per day.

On entry into the minutes, the workman would deposit his bourd with the minuteman. He would then collect four sheets of toilet paper, which the minuteman had already 'packaged'. The workman would then proceed to one of the stalls or cubicles, which were only provided with half doors. There he would do what was needed, and on leaving, collect his bourd. The minuteman would keep a record in his ledger of the time of entry and exit of the worker which would give a running total of the time spent in the minutes. This was the preferred method of management in order to discourage lingering in the toilets and certainly there would have been no time available to the workman to smoke too many cigarettes or read too much of the paper, until his 'number was up'.

In later years the requirement to deposit the bourd was dropped, but the time limit stayed in place. On entering the minutes the workman would call out his number and proceed to an empty stall. Like before, the bourd number would be recorded by the minuteman in his ledger. Some of the braver or foolhardy apprentices would, on finishing in the toilets, crawl out unseen under the area where the minuteman sat. After a period of time the poor minuteman would realise that several of his 'customers' had not vacated after their seven minutes and he would spend time looking for the missing person, much to his annoyance and the fun of the apprentice. The minutemen, like the elephant, had a long memory and on his next visit the wayward apprentice would more than likely get a clip around the ear and have his seven minutes 'unofficially' reduced.

There would always be an occasion when the workman needed an extra visit to the minutes, perhaps after having been out the night before and consumed the proverbial bad pint. With his stomach heaving he would have to go cap in hand to his foreman and plead for some extra minutes. The foreman depending on his mood would then chalk the back of the bourd and on it marks a number, which represented some extra time in the minutes.

There were occasions when a squad of workmen would be working far away from the minutes, and in these cases a latrine would be dug, and a large plank of wood with suitable openings strategically cut, and held up on blocks that would be placed over the latrine. The men could squat down on the plank in view of their neighbour and do what was required. The young apprentices, like all young men, were full of devilment. Playing and thinking up new pranks, and getting away with them was one way of breaking the boredom of the day. The young apprentices not wanting to miss a chance would get a rag, soak it in petrol and when lit, would from a concealed hiding place, throw the flaming rag into the latrine. You could imagine the shock that would result from having the nether regions warmed and the quick exodus that would be made from the latrine, with a lot of verbal abuse being hurled towards the 'arsonist'.

Those who worked in the East Belfast shipyards look back at their time there with great fondness, but the reality was that it was also a very hard place to labour. The work was extremely hard, death and severe injury were never too far away, the hours were long, and the workplace was dirty and noisy. It was always thought that there was some form of unofficial death figure, stating that for every 10,000 tons weight of ship that was constructed, the shipyard could expect one man to be accidentally killed. Certainly the yard was a dangerous place to work. For example during the construction of the *Olympic*, nine men were killed and 220 injured, while on the *Titanic* things weren't much better, as eight men were killed and over 240 hurt or injured.

In common with all large workplaces there were characters that would always stand out from the workforce, as would the nicknames that were given, sometimes cruelly,

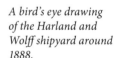

A bird's eye drawing of the Harland and Wolff shipyard around 1888.

(The Pictorial World, Linen Hall Library)

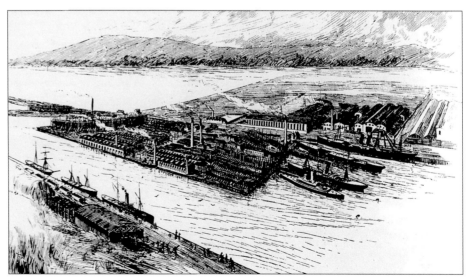

to other workmates. When a young 16 year old boy was taken on at the shipyard there would be many ingenious attempts to embarrass and humiliate him. At some period in his first few weeks of employment he could be sure that his tradesman would send him to the Stores for a pot of striped paint or a bucketful of blue steam, or perhaps he would be told to go to the Storeman and ask for a long weight. What the unsuspecting youth didn't realise was that he was asking for a long *wait*! After the allotted wait the embarrassed youngster would be given a clip around the ear and told that his long wait was over and red faced he would return to his work colleagues. He would never fall for that same trick again. You could also be sure that at some stage in those first few weeks the young apprentice would be grabbed by his workmates, have his pants unceremoniously lowered and liberal amounts of grease slapped onto the nether regions. Only after these initiation ceremonies were complete could the new recruit feel at home.

The joiners used to play a joke with new apprentices. They would be given an adze (a specialised type of axe used in shipbuilding) and a chalk mark put on a wooden board in front of him. The apprentice would then be told to hit the mark with the blade of the axe. After a few attempts the apprentice would be able to continually hit the mark. The men would then ask him to try it blindfolded and they would take off his flat cap or 'duncher', as it was known, while a blindfold was tied around his eyes. The apprentice's duncher was then placed on the ground over the mark and he was then told to try and hit the mark again. Whether he hit it or not he was told to keep trying. Each swing of the blade would see another slice cut out of the brand new duncher. After a few moments the blindfold was removed and a shocked apprentice would see the damage he caused to his own cap.

Then there were the nicknames that were given. It was always said that you weren't part of the group until you had been given your own special name. 'Weebit' was a stager who had been climbing up a ladder. He fell off from a height of about 10 ft and landed badly on the ground. Fortunately he didn't break any bones but he did suffer from aches and pains in his back following the fall. His nickname came about by the way he would always reply when his workmates would ask how he was, "Ah you know still a weebit sore."

Tommy McBride who started in the yard in the 1910s was known not only there but in practically all of East Belfast as 'The Duke'. Now Tommy would have had you believe that this nickname was given to him following a meeting with the Duke of Windsor, but there were others who felt that his name came about when it was his turn to buy a round of drinks in the pub, and, Tommy, it was said, would do anything to 'duke' or get out of paying for the round.[1]

There was also the story of Sammy. He was being elevated to foreman, which would entail him wearing a bowler hat and from that moment on become 'one of them' – management. Some of his very close mates on his first day of promotion bid him good day and called him Sammy, to which the new hat replied "men from now on it will be Sammy no more" and 'Sammy no more' stuck with him to the end of his service in the yard.

Other names circulating were 'Woodbine Willie', who chain-smoked Woodbine cigarettes, 'Bungalow Brains' because he didn't have too much upstairs, 'the Slobber' because he generally talked a lot of nonsense. Then there was 'Forty Watts', who was deemed to be a bit dim.

Theft was another major problem in the shipyard. It has always been said that there was enough material stolen or in the local dialect, 'prucked', to rebuild *Titanic* several times over. The shipyards were very hard on anyone caught stealing. In 1902, a workman by the name of James Stewart was given a sentence of 14 days imprisonment with hard labour by the Judge, for the theft of two tins of paint. Others who tried to hide scraps of brass, lead or copper down their trousers, risked, if caught, being taken to court and facing the inevitable jail sentence. They could also expect never to gain any type of employment at the shipyard again.

It was said that the workforce in the shipyards loved it when it was announced that an order had been received from a new Shipping Line. This would mean that new paint would have to be mixed and soon after the front doors of houses in nearby East Belfast would take on the same hue as the new ship. Now on most days at lunchtime a local 'hell fire and brimstone' preacher would arrive at the yard and start preaching in order to save the souls of those who would listen. The story is told that one such preacher, when moralising about honesty scared 'the willies' out of the men so much, that they 'borrowed' blowtorches from the stores and when they arrived home, they used the torches to burn the paint off the front door of their houses that had previously been prucked from the yard. One version of the story states that one man even tried to return the burnt paint.

There was also a story told about quite a brazen theft. A certain man was in the last few days of his employment before he retired from the shipyard. For many years he had used a ladder in his work and he had become very attached to it, so he decided to take it into retirement with him. If he tried to smuggle it out the chances are that he would be caught and what meagre pension he was to receive would no doubt be forfeited. The best way he felt to get the ladder out of the shipyard was to be quite open about it. On his last day he got the ladder, put it over his shoulder, collected a bucket of water and a chamois leather and marched out into Queen's Road outside the Harland and Wolff shipyard and headed for the nearest lamp post. The ladder was pitched and he climbed up, took out the chamois leather and cleaned the lamp. He then came down and went to the next lamp post, moving in the direction of the security hut and the way out. This lamp post was also cleaned, as was every other one up to the gates at the way out, when he reached there, he nodded to the Security Man and muttered something about that was all he could do today and that he would finish the job off the following day. Needless to say neither he nor the ladder were ever seen again, as they both headed out of the shipyard and into a 'joint' retirement.

CHAPTER 7

Building the Ship

To build and then successfully launch a ship was such a massive task that it required the skills of many people. The work was both complex and dangerous and everyone who was involved needed to know and perfect their own particular skills in the construction process. In this chapter I will attempt to explain to the reader, in very simple terms, how, in the period at the beginning of the twentieth century, the shipyards at Queen's Island actually went about planning and building a ship, followed by the very difficult task of, in full view of the public, actually getting the hull of the new vessel into the water without any mishaps.

Most shipyards would be split into two distinct sections, the Shipyard and the Engine Works. The former being the area where the ship would be constructed and the latter being where the propelling machinery and boilers were built. It should be added that there was also a third element to the shipyard and that was the Office and the staff associated with it.

In both the Shipyard and Engine Works there were many different trades, some with very peculiar names. In 'Shipyard Trades' on page 202 I have listed the main trades that operated in both areas.

The Harland and Wolff Drawing Office.

(© National Museums Northern Ireland, Collection Harland and Wolff, Ulster Folk and Transport Museum)

The most important area in any shipyard has to be the Drawing Office. In Harland and Wolff there were many such offices, but the main Drawing Office was situated on the ground floor of the Main Office Building on Queen's Road. The Drawing Office had been designed with a large barrel ceiling, containing windows which would allow as much natural light as possible to stream in for the draughtsmen as they laboured on their plans. The outside wall at the back of the Drawing Office was covered in white tiles, again to reflect as much natural light as possible into the room below.

Laid out on large drawing benches, the draughtsmen, following instructions and design briefs from management, would draw out the many thousands of individual plans that would be needed for the construction of a ship. The first plans would be drawn on paper, and then finally the draughtsmen would transfer these pencil drawings onto rolls of linen, with ink pens. These linen plans were the reference set that could be safely stored in the office and copies would then be made by Tracers for the workforce to use in the shipyard. Today a few copies of these plans, especially those of the Olympic class ships are on permanent display at the Ulster Folk and Transport Museum at Cultra, County Down.

Once the plans were completed they were then given over to staff at the Moulding Loft. This building was situated at the Queen's yard adjacent to Queen's Road. The Moulding Loft took up the entire area of the first floor of the building which was 254 ft long and 74 ft wide (78 × 22 m). Internally it had no columns to support the ceiling. The roof of the loft was constructed in a slightly curved fashion and was made from scrap pieces of wood, which surprisingly made a very strong and rigid structure. This type of roof construction was called a 'Belfast roof' and importantly it allowed the floor area to be free from columns. This was essential as it was there that workmen traced out the plans of the new ship, which had been completed by the draughtsmen in the Drawing Office, in chalk on the black painted floorboards. Normally the plans were drawn out at a ¼ scale for the length and full size for the beam or width of the vessel. This system, obviously well before today's computers, could do the same thing and in 3D, which allowed

The Harland and Wolff Moulding Loft, where plans of new ships were drawn on the floor to create templates.

(© National Museums Northern Ireland, Collection Harland and Wolff, Ulster Folk and Transport Museum)

the builders to check that the plans and the planned run of the hull and ribs were correct.

Once the plans had been drawn and proved to everyone's satisfaction, the joiners took over. They then drew out on the floor, full size and one by one, all the frames or ribs that would attach to the keel of the ship. These frames radiated outwards from the central keel to where the hull would start to rise upwards and it would be onto these frames that the hull plates would later be riveted. Once the frame was drawn on the floor, a wooden template, which followed the outline of the frame would be made and numbered. When all these frames had been copied, the templates were then brought to the platers shop for the next stage in the process.

The floor in the platers shop where bending the frames took place was 5 ft by 5 ft and 4 inches thick (1.52 m × 10 cm). There were numerous holes about 1 inch in diameter and about 4 inches apart that had been precast into the metal floor. The platers would take the template that had been drawn in the Moulding Loft and then draw out the profile of the frame on the floor. Into the holes were then inserted small metal rods or 'dogs' that were slightly bent and these would trace the complete outline of each individual frame. Close by this was a furnace that could be anything up to 90 ft long, into which had been placed the straight iron frames. These were a bit like today's 'H beam'. The frame, once heated to white hot, was drawn from the furnace and with sledge hammers the platers would strike the frame to bend it into the required shape, which had already been marked on out the floor. This work had to be carried out quickly as the metal frame was cooling down. The platers would also use a small hydraulic press that could be anchored into one of the holes in the ground. Then, under hydraulic pressure, a ram would place more pressure on the frame to bend it.

Once the foreman was satisfied that the frame had been bent into the correct shape, it would be numbered and set aside to cool. While a lot of the frames would be the same shape, many of them, especially those near the bow or stern of the hull, would have peculiar shapes. For these the 'dogs' would be lifted, the next template placed on the floor and the whole process started over again. When riveted in place the frames would be about 3 ft apart and when you consider that the Olympic class ships were almost 900 ft long, there would be in excess of 600 frames to bend to shape.

Other platers would have been busy receiving and checking the massive 30 ft long iron plates that were continuously being delivered to the shipyard by ship from the iron foundries in

Frame bending

(Courtesy of the National Records of Scotland and University of Glasgow Archive Services, Lithgows Ltd collection, GB0248 GD323/13/10/3/4)

England and Scotland. These plates would have to be sorted and then, depending on where they were to be used on the hull or decks of the vessel, would need to be bent to shape, following the directions in the plans. Most of the plates that needed to be shaped were fashioned by a process called 'cold bending'. This involved bending the plates in a massive hydraulic machine fitted with rollers, a bit like your granny's old mangle but much larger! The plates would also need 1 inch holes punched into them to take the rivets that would later attach the plate to the frame.

Meanwhile, in the Engine Works, preparations were being laid for the start of the construction of the boilers, engines and all the other ancillary equipment that would be needed to propel the vessel.

In other parts of the shipyard craftsmen would be beginning to construct the many parts that would be needed for the comfort of the passengers. Shipwrights would be building doors, frames and wall panels, and would have used a frightful looking weapon called the adze. The adze had a curved blade like a hatchet but set at 90° to the shaft. The shipwright used it to pare away small pieces of wood from the main block, by using a chopping movement. So good were these tradesmen that the finished work would require no further finishing or sanding down. Cabinetmakers looked on themselves as the elite of the carpentry trade, they would make all the decorative carved mouldings and finished panelling that was seen on board by the passengers on the ship. They also made some of the furniture that was placed on the ship. Between both the joiners and cabinetmakers they would create full size mock ups of the cabins and other public rooms, that would then be shown to the owners who, if satisfied, would give the order to proceed with the work.

Joiners using the adze, a handtool used to pare away small pieces of wood from the main block.
(Gwynedd Archives Service)

Meanwhile, out on the slipway, the debris from any previous ship construction was cleared away. The slipways in the shipyard were laid out at an incline of around 3/8 of an inch to a foot, which means that for every foot of the length of the keel, it dropped by 3/8 of an inch. For a ship such as the *Olympic* that would mean that from the bow, to the stern, the slipway dropped around 28 ft (8.53 m).

On this incline the workmen very carefully laid out the large keel blocks, which were very heavy blocks of wood and they were precisely stacked on top of each other to a height of around 5 to 6 ft. These blocks had to be laid out in a perfectly straight line, and the shipwrights who laid them out used a process called sighting to ensure the blocks were laid precisely.

The most important moment of the ship's construction was about to take place,

72

Hydraulic riveting on the keel of Olympic.

(© National Museums Northern Ireland, Collection Harland and Wolff, Ulster Folk and Transport Museum)

when the keel was laid. The keel is really the backbone of the vessel and it is from this that the ship takes shape. There would be a simple ceremony carried out when the first plates were laid and riveted together. These first plates were placed exactly at the mid point on the length of the vessel, and there the riveters would join the plates together. Originally this was done by hand riveters, followed later by the hydraulic riveting machine.

Once the keel laying ceremony was over, the workforce then proceeded with the task ahead. Riveted to the keel plate was a vertical plate called the keelson. Coming outwards from the centre line of the keel, the workmen would attach the bottom plating of the hull, on top of which vertical side girders were riveted. On top of this, the tank top or top of the double bottom was laid out. The entire double bottom radiated outwards to the bilge and this is where the hull turned into the vertical plane. The hull plates were then attached to the vertical frames or ribs. These plates would be overlapped and normally the platers would work from the stern of the vessel to the front or bow. The reason for this was that the overlap would then be facing aft and as the ship sailed through the water there would be little resistance set up against the water. In some ways it is like the way tiles are laid on a roof, with the overlap facing downwards to allow the water to flow freely down the roof.

While all this was going on the shipwrights were setting up the standing way and sliding ways underneath the hull. These ways would run the entire length of the ship and would later be used to launch the hull.

There were many and varied trades that were required in order to produce a ship.

Considered by most to be the 'Kings of the workforce' were the riveters. Each gang consisted of five people. In charge of the squad was the right-handed riveter, who along with a left-handed riveter would between them hammer the head onto the hot rivet. They would work as a pair and once a successful pairing was established it would normally last for many years. Obviously there were thousands and thousands of rivets that would need to be put in place in the construction of a ship. Ensuring that a steady supply of red-hot rivets was continually provided for the two riveters was the role of the three other members of the gang, a heater boy, a catch boy and a holder up. For the whole system to work smoothly teamwork was needed.

The heater boy was generally just that, a very young and unskilled boy. He was in charge of the brazier that heated the rivets. The most important part of his job was to maintain a steady supply of correctly heated rivets. His initial training amounted to him being shown how to keep the brazier well stoked, how to ensure a steady supply of rivets being placed in the brazier and then, finally, watching the rivets heat to the correct temperature as determined by the colour of the rivet. The squad's pay was based on the number of rivets that they drove home; the more rivets in place the larger the pay out at the end of the week. Around the time of the construction of the Olympic class ships, in the early 1900s, the riveters

73

Hand riveting the plates making up the hull.

(© National Museums Northern Ireland, Collection Harland and Wolff, Ulster Folk and Transport Museum)

were being paid one old half penny per rivet that was hammered home. This meant that they had to put in 480 rivets to earn one pound. This then was divided between them. With this in mind it was of the utmost importance that the squad could start working as soon as possible from the beginning of each shift. This meant that the heater boy had to 'break into' the yard before starting time in the morning and get the brazier lit, and have it up to working temperature as early as possible, thereby ensuring that the squad could be at work as soon as possible. Meal beaks were also the time for him to tend to the brazier and ensure he had sufficient coke to fuel the fire.

A young heater boy.
(Tyne and Wear Archives and Museums, JL Thompson Archive, reference 1811/252/17)

Once the rivet was heated to the correct colour, the heater boy would take it out of the brazier with a large pair of tongs and give it to the catch boy. Again like the heater boy, the catch boy would also be quite young. Depending on how or where in the ship they were working, the heater boy would either slide the red hot rivet along a metal plate to the catch boy or throw it to him. The catch boy could catch it in a large asbestos mitt and then quickly throw it to the holder up, who would catch it in a large tin and with a pair of tongs swiftly transfer it to the hole in the plates that were being joined together. The catch boy would only ever receive one issue of the non-Health and Safety mitt. Once it wore out he would either have to try and make a leather patch and tie it to his hand, or else do without. This method would result in his hand becoming burnt very quickly and would callus over as he caught and then threw on the red hot rivet. Once inserted in place the holder up, again only a young boy, would use a wooden cradle against his shoulder and the rivet. On the other side of the metal work the two riveters would start hammering at the rivet and put the head on in less than a minute. They would then quickly progress on to the next rivet that the holder up would push through from the underside. From the minute the rivet was taken out of the brazier it was starting to cool down so it was vitally important that the rivet was quickly delivered to the riveters before it cooled to such a temperature that it would not be malleable enough to have the head hammered onto it.

Following after the squad were the unpopular rivet counters. Their job was to twofold, firstly to check that an acceptable standard of riveting was being met and also to count the number of rivets being put in. It was on this number that the wages of the entire squad would be based. If the riveting was below standard, the counter would draw a chalk circle around the faulty rivet and the squad, at their own expense, would have to have this rivet drilled out and then re-riveted.

Hand riveting was later replaced with hydraulic riveting, which took away the need for the right and left handed riveters. A large machine, similar in some ways to a horseshoe, would be suspended by a crane over the area where the rivets were to be placed. At each end of the arms of the machine were two rams that on the operation of a lever would close tightly under hydraulic pressure. The red-hot rivet would be put into the required hole, the riveter would line up the rams, which had metal cups at their ends. These cups would hold the rivet in place while the rams were pushed together compressing the rivet. Once that was done the riveter would increase the pressure in the machine to full power and the cups, under enormous hydraulic pressure, would close tightly and in doing so would then form the head on the hot rivet. This method was quicker than hand riveting and when it was finished the rivet would still be red-hot and contracting, which would make it pull the plates together and make a tighter joint in the plates. This hydraulic system while faster could not be carried out in confined spaces, so there was always the need for the hand riveters.

The squad had to work very closely with each other. In fact if one of the hand riveters didn't turn in for work it would have been very difficult for the other riveter to work with anyone else, as they both worked in tandem. Communication between the squad was difficult due to the incessant noise that was created by all the riveting squads throughout the yard. Normally they used a 'morse code' tapping on the hull to tell those on the other side what they wanted. Deafness would also have been a major problem for these men as they were subjected to continuous loud noise without any form of ear protection. By today's Health and Safety standards this would most certainly not be allowed and the riveters would be queuing up to claim compensation, but in those days if, because of your work, you became deaf then people would just have to shout at you.

In a day's shift these squads would hammer home many rivets. In June 1918 the smaller yard of Workman Clark held a competition amongst their rivet

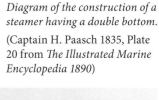

Diagram of the construction of a steamer having a double bottom.
(Captain H. Paasch 1835, Plate 20 from *The Illustrated Marine Encyclopedia 1890*)

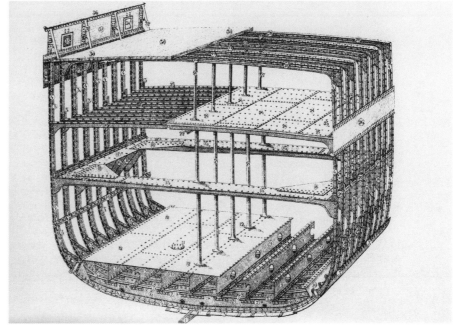

75

squads to see how many rivets one man could place in a nine-hour shift. The eventual winner was a Mr John Moir, who drove home a total of 11,209 rivets. This was verified by Lloyds of London and the British Corporation Surveyors, which ensured that all the rivets were up to standard. Moir, aged 44, was also known as 'Dundee Jock', as he was born in Scotland. He lived at Alexandra Park Avenue in Belfast with his wife, three daughters and two sons. During the competition he was attended by four boys and given lime juice to drink through a tube. One can only imagine the effect that this had on his arm muscles by the end of the day, but he set a record that to the current date has never be bettered or broken. He was presented with a rose bowl by his employers and two years later awarded the M.B.E. Today with these skills now long gone it would be nearly impossible to find anyone who would know how to drive home a rivet. Mr Moir can truly rest in peace with the knowledge that the record he set all those years ago will stand forever. He is the true rivet king of Belfast.

As the riveting was taking place on the outside of the hull, inside construction was already progressing on the decks. Iron beams ran from the inside of the hull across the ship. These beams were supported by stanchions. On top of these were then riveted the plates that would make up the various decks. Bulkheads were also constructed along the length of the vessel. These bulkheads would generally be watertight and were designed to both strengthen the ship and also to make compartments in the hull along its length.

At the forward end the stem post would be attached while aft the sternpost, which would also hold the propeller shaft or shafts, would be fixed into place. These massive shafts would be fitted into the hull while it was still on the slipway. Work would also start on the structure of the accommodation although no fitting out of the ship would be started at this construction stage.

By now the whole hull was fully plated and preparations were being made for the complicated procedure of launching the hull. There were basically three ways for a shipyard to launch a hull. Stern first, bow first or sideways. The second two were really difficult to perform and could cause major embarrassment, as they were fraught with the potential for danger. The shipyards in Belfast had always chosen the classic stern first launch system, and when you consider that in 1912, Harland and Wolff launched 12 ships, the whole process was carried out with a procedure 'like a well oiled machine'.

However, as an aside, there was one ship at Harland and Wolff that 'launched itself'. The ship in question was *HMS Formidable*, ship number 1007. At just over 28,000 tons the ship was launched on 17 August 1939. The launch party had got themselves in position and just before the lady sponsor could name the ship and break the bottle of champagne over the bows there was a massive noise from under the hull, which then over rode the launch trigger and started down the slipway. The wooden props under the ship were being ejected at an alarming rate. A lady called Mrs Kirk was struck by one and killed and several others were hurt. Happily this 'going it alone' only happened once in the whole history of the Harland and Wolff yard.[1]

The standing way and sliding ways would have been put in place, under the hull, many months earlier. At this stage large wooden launch cradles were built at the bow and stern of the hull to support these areas during the launch. Underneath the hull a large hydraulic ram had also been installed. The purpose of this ram was not to push the hull, but to stop it moving until the required time for the launch. Chains were attached to the hull and from there they ran to drag chains which were set out at both sides of the hull. Drag chains were also dropped into the water at the end of the slipway, lowered in by a floating crane. These chains would then slow the progress of the ship down the slipway and bring it to a halt in the water. There would be nothing more embarrassing than to launch the hull into the water and for the momentum created to cause it to float further away down the river.

On the morning of the launch, men would be under the hull performing the very dangerous task of knocking all the wooden props away, the pressure in the hydraulic ram had been built up, and for just a few seconds before the order was given to launch, the hull would be held back by the ram. Once the ship had been named and the bottle of champagne broken, the ram was released and the vessel would start down the ways into the water. It should be noted that the White Star Line did not believe in a christening ceremony. No one would ever break a bottle of champagne over the bows of their vessels. At the appropriate time they were instead 'shoved in'.

Following the successful launch, the hull, once the check wires and launch cradle were removed would be towed to the out fitting wharf where work would start on completing the ship. Here the engines, boilers and ancillary machinery would be installed, cabins would be completed and the whole interior of the ship would be finished.

CHAPTER 8

Yards, Yards and Yards

When William Ritchie started his small shipbuilding yard in 1791, he could not have foreseen that what he started then would eventually grow and expand to place the shipyards in Belfast as major players in the shipbuilding industry in not just the United Kingdom, but the entire world, with Harland and Wolff being the predominant shipyard. By way of mergers the Ritchie brothers' shipyard eventually became two separate yards, that of Charles Connell who bought William's yard and also the shipyard of Alexander McLaine who married John Ritchie's daughter Martha and took the yard over at John's death.

In 1824 Charles Connell, who had been the manager of the shipyard set up and run by William Ritchie, bought it over from Ritchie, and established his yard under the name of Charles Connell and Sons. In those early days all of the ships were constructed from local timber. The first ship built by Connell was a schooner named *Jane* and launched in June 1825.

Connell had already made a name for himself in the port prior to this, when in June of 1820 he undertook a most dangerous and difficult salvage operation. A sloop, the *John and Mary*, that was carrying coal had become stuck at the entry to the harbour and was blocking access to Belfast for other ships. In his attempt to salvage the sloop, Connell decided not to use other vessels or pumping equipment but rather chose brute force. He approached Captain Cockburn, who was the Officer in Charge of the local garrison and asked if he could borrow some soldiers. He set about having hawsers attached to the sloop and then at high tide he got the raw power of the soldiers to pull on the hawsers. The hawsers broke on two occasions, but with the continued effort from the soldiers they finally were able to haul the sloop to an area above the high tide mark. Connell was then able to get access to the vessel and set about discharging the cargo. This allowed the sloop to float and be towed away, which freed up the entrance to the harbour.

His next ship to be constructed was a brig called *Brian Boru*, of about 300 tons. This vessel was launched in December 1826 and traded around the world. Other vessels constructed by Connell were, *Joseph P. Dobree* in 1829; *Fanny*, 300 tons in 1832; *Pennington*, 500 tons in 1833; *Tickler*; *Hindoo*; *Brigand* and *Splendid*.

Between 1837 and 1838 Connell built two steamboats and a schooner. One of the steamboats, the *SS Victoria* of 1837, was only the third steamer built in

Ireland with Coates and Young of Belfast manufacturing her engines. The *SS Aurora* of 1838 was used on the Belfast to Glasgow route. This vessel was to set the quickest crossing from Scotland to Ireland on several occasions. By 1842 this busy shipyard had constructed 32 ships of varying sizes.

Another vessel from Connell's yard was the *Oceanica*, a sailing ship for local man James Lemon. The vessel was used for many years to transport tea. The hull was painted green and she flew a green burgee with an Irish harp on it. When launched the ship was even christened with a bottle of Irish whiskey. Charles Connell died in 1875 and is buried in the Old Churchyard at Carnmoney.

In 1838, two gentlemen called Kirwan and McCune established a shipbuilding yard on Queen's Island and quite quickly launched their first ship, the 114 ton schooner *William and Mary*. Little is known or recorded of their business, but after 13 years McCune dissolved the partnership and was replaced by a Mr Thompson. At the same time the Belfast Harbour Commissioners laid out a slipway for this new partnership on Queen's Island. Again little is known of this company but by 1858 they had gone out of business and their yard, which for many years lay semi-derelict, was finally bought over in an expansion bid by Edward Harland, who added it to his own shipyard.

John H. McIlwaine was another early shipbuilder. His yard concentrated mainly on the construction of iron barges for use on the then Lagan canal. They also built small steamers, with four being purchased by the Cork Railway Company. Over the years McIlwaine was to have several Partners including, in 1867, Welshman Richard Lewis, who lived at Ty-Isa in Strandtown, East Belfast. In years to come, Lewis's grandson, Clive Staples Lewis would write many books, including the very popular children's book, *The Chronicles of Narnia*.

The partnership between McIlwaine and Lewis was dissolved when the business relationship between the two men became so bad that it was impossible to keep the partnership alive. McIlwaine was to take on a new Partner called Mr Hector McColl. This new partnership in 1888 took its first order from H&J Scott of Belfast for a 1,608 ton schooner. The vessel had a length of 280 ft, was powered by a triple expansion engine and was named *Titanic*. This first Belfast built *Titanic* was launched on the 4 May 1888 and changed owners and names several times throughout its service, including the *Luis Alberto* and eventually the *Don Alberto*.

Over the years, John McIlwaine and his

A family group circa 1900. Richard Lewis, Partner in McIlwaine and Lewis shipyard and grandfather of C.S. Lewis, is in the back row, second from right.

(Bresland, R.W., 'A Backward Glance: C.S. Lewis and Ireland', Belfast: Institute of Irish Studies, 1999)

Don Alberto, *previously known as the first Belfast built* Titanic *(1888).*

(Courtesy the Joseph A. Carvalho Collection, *Titanic* International Society, www. titanicinternationalsociety.org)

Paul Rodgers and his workforce in Carrickfergus. Rodgers is on the extreme left.

(© National Museums Northern Ireland, Collection Ulster Folk and Transport Museum)

various Partners not only built over 58 vessels of all sizes up to the largest of 5,000 tons, but also constructed their own engines. Eventually McIlwaine decided to sell his interest in his shipyard to Workman Clark and he then worked as a ship repairer.

Belfast should not be seen as the only area where shipbuilding was taking place. At Carrickfergus, on the northern shores of Belfast Lough, ships were also being built. It was recorded that, in 1845, a brig called *David Legg* of 147 tons was launched. The vessel was named after the Town Clerk of the seaside town and was owned by a local businessman, Paul Logan. Just six years later a shipyard was established by Bowman, Logan and Company. It is possible that the Logan in this yard may have been the same person who owned the *David Legg*. Bowman and Logan launched their first ship, the *Carrickfergus*, a brig of 196 tons, in 1851.

In 1852 Bowman and Logan took on Paul Rodgers, an 18 year old, as an apprentice shipwright. Logan went bankrupt in 1856 and his share in the business was taken over by a Robert Johnston, whose daughter Janet later married the young apprentice Paul Rodgers. They could keep it in the family in Carrickfergus, just as well as they did in Belfast. By 1858 Rodgers had completed his apprenticeship and was made Yard Foreman, and by 1868 he was Shipyard Manager.

Johnston's first ship, the 200 ton brigantine *Dorothea Wright*, was constructed from Irish oak and launched in July 1861 with Paul Rodgers being responsible for the design of the vessel. Within nine years Rodgers became the owner of the yard, launching his first ship, a 160 ton brig called the *Accrington*, in 1874. The honour of christening the ship was given to Rodgers' daughter. Over the next 18 years he and his work force of around 100 men constructed and launched 30 ships, including *Thomas Fisher* and *Richard Fisher*. In 1885 he both constructed his last timber-hulled schooner, the *Edith Crossfield*, and his first metal hulled tug ship *Emulator*. By 1888 he was in financial difficulties and entered into partnership with a local linen merchant Elias H. Bell, the company being renamed Paul Rodgers and Company. His partnership with Bell collapsed in 1892 and the yard was sold to Robert Kent of Ayr in Scotland. His main customer, Fishers, had by this time taken their business to McIlwaine and McColl in Belfast. In 1893, Kent launched a ship previously started by Rodgers, which was perhaps the most famous vessel of all to come out of Carrickfergus, the *Result*. This vessel, which now is in the safe keeping of the Ulster Folk and Transport Museum at Cultra, just outside Holywood, was a 122 ton, three masted schooner. It was originally owned by Thomas Ashburner and Company of Barrow. The vessel saw service in the First World War, when the Admiralty commandeered it and fitted it out as a Q-ship, installing a quick firing gun on the stern of the vessel. In February 1915 the *Result* engaged with and caused damage to a German submarine U-45. In 1950 the vessel, with some modification, was used in the filming of *An Outcast of the Islands*.

Back in Belfast, successful opposition to Harland and Wolff came from Frank Workman and George Clark, two premium apprentices of Edward Harland. In 1879 they set up in partnership their own shipbuilding yard, Workman Clark and Company Limited, that would come to be known as the 'wee yard' compared to Harland and Wolff's 'big yard'. This affectionate term for Workman Clark's really does them down when you consider that within six years of their founding they employed 3,500 men and were the fourth biggest shipyard for output in the United Kingdom.

Both Workman and Clark were distantly related through the Smith family of Glasgow who owned the City Shipping Line. Within a year of establishing their partnership they had their first order for two cargo ships, *Ethel* and *William*

Paul Rodgers' shipyard in Carrickfergus.

(© National Museums Northern Ireland, Collection Ulster Folk and Transport Museum)

81

Hinde. Quite quickly the family connections helped when the City Line placed an order for a passenger and cargo ship, the 2,576 ton *City of Cambridge*. In 1891 the firm decided to construct its own engines for their ships, which had up until then been made by an outside contractor. Charles Allen, the son of a senior Partner in the Allen Line, joined Workman Clark and by 1894 they were producing almost half as much as their rivals Harland and Wolff. As if to add insult to injury, they were starting to take orders away from Harland and Wolff, by accepting orders for ships for the Head Line and then Corrys Line, whose Directors were also related to Frank Workman.

A major acquisition occurred in 1894 when Workman Clark bought over the derelict yard of McIlwaine and McColl on Queen's Island. This then gave the firm yards on both sides of the river Lagan, something Harland and Wolff never did. Their output of ships was staggering and in 1901 they overtook the output of Harland and Wolff. By 1902 they were employing around 5,000 men. Their expansion continued and in 1909, Workman Clark claimed to employ over 9,000 men and that their output of tonnage exceeded that of any other shipbuilding company in the United Kingdom. 1904 saw their largest ship, the *Victorian*, a passenger ship for the Allan Line of 10,630 tons, completed and launched. Customers on their order books included Cunard, P&O, and the Shaw Savill Line. During the First World War they produced ships for the Admiralty. Whilst Edward Harland and Gustav Wolff must have been worried at the loss of some clients to the smaller yard it did not seem to hinder working relations between them. In fact during industrial disputes they would even cooperate with each other. Workman Clark were not really in competition with Harland and Wolff, as the smaller yard directed their attention towards specialised shipping, when they started to construct cargo ships for the transportation of frozen products. This resulted in them becoming one of the main builders of refrigerated ships in the United Kingdom.

In early 1920 the 'wee yard' was sold to the Northumberland Shipping Company and within a year Frank Workman and George Clark had left and severed all their connections with their former company. This was quite closely followed by a slump in ship orders and by 1926 the yard had made losses of around £3 million. This debt and the sale of the yard was really the beginning of the end for the 'wee yard' and by 1935 the yard finally closed. It had constructed around 530 ships in its 55 year history.

CHAPTER 9

Expansion at Queen's Island

The firm of Harland and Wolff was well established by 1865. After six years in business they had constructed 43 vessels with many ship owners placing multiple orders. The Wilson brothers were being singled out for promotion, whilst William Pirrie was nearing the end of his apprenticeship.

In those early years, the Harland and Wolff shipyard on Queen's Island was quite restricted in its size. It was bounded by the People's Park and the large timber pond, and the only way of getting a ship out of water was to drag it up the patent slip or tow it over to the County Antrim side of the river and dock it in Ritchie's small dry dock. The Belfast Harbour Commissioners, as I mentioned earlier, had been buying up land along the river with a view to laying out docks and quays as well as promoting shipbuilding. But their plan nearly came unstuck when it was announced that the Commissioners were going to build a new dry dock that could accommodate ships up to 137 m or 450 ft in length. The news that the Commissioners were planning to construct the dock on the County Antrim side of the river Lagan concerned Harland and Wolff. This decision really would not have suited Edward Harland who would much have preferred the dock to be closer to his yard. This would allow him to control the dock and also make it a lot easier for his yard to use the docks facilities. The ideal location for Harland would be to have the dock constructed on Queen's Island.

The Commissioners' proposal was to start a debate over the location of the new dock that would last many months. At a meeting of the Commissioners in November 1862 a letter signed by, amongst others, Valentine Whitla, George McTear and Gustavus Heyn called for the dock to be located on the County Down side of the Lagan. The meeting became so hot and heavy that the press were removed from the proceedings. Finally after many weeks of wrangling, including a veiled threat that Edward Harland would move his shipyard away from Belfast, (a threat that the company was to use on several occasions in later years) and the submission of a letter with 4,000 signatures of local tradesmen that was handed in to the Commissioners, they finally agreed that the dock be constructed on the County Down side of the river. The vote at ten members to six was not unanimous but it was still carried through, and the cost to the Commissioners would be less as it was reckoned at that time that land on the Antrim side of the river would cost around £1,500 per acre while it would be considerably cheaper on the County Down side at £300 per acre.

Even though the vote had been taken, agreed and passed, the row still rumbled on as to the location of the dock. Several months later, at another meeting of the Commissioners, the matter was raised again by Commissioner John Thompson, supported by the Belfast Mayor and noted architect, Sir Charles Lanyon. Thompson argued that the Belfast Harbour Commissioners did not have the legal right to put the dock on the County Down side. He stated that there would be an increase in the time workmen would take to travel by rowing boat to Queen's Island. Finally after another very heated meeting, another 'final vote' was taken by the Commissioners with the result being seven to five votes in favour of the County Down location. On hearing this news John Thompson promptly resigned from the Commissioners Board. The Belfast Shipwrights were also concerned about their members crossing the Lagan in overcrowded boats, especially in the dark mornings or evenings of wintertime.

However, it was obvious to all that there was the potential for expansion of the shipyard of Harland and Wolff, and this led to all finally agreeing to construct the new dry dock on Queen's Island.

Work started in 1863 at the area of the old channel basin that fronted the slipways of Harland and Wolff and McIlwaine and Lewis's yards. Here the new dry dock was constructed at 450½ ft long, 82½ ft wide and at high tide 15½ ft deep. The old channel basin was reformed into a massive open basin of about 12 acres in size. The total cost of the work was around £250,000 and was overseen by Mr Lizars, the Engineer from the Belfast Harbour Commissioners.

The new basin and dry dock was officially opened on Wednesday 2 October 1867, when James Hamilton, Marquis of Abercorn, Lord Lieutenant-General and Governor General of Ireland undertook the naming of the Abercorn Basin and Hamilton Dry Dock. The Marquis arrived at the Harbour Commissioners' Office at 11.30 am. The similarly named Chairman, Mr James Hamilton, accompanied by William Thompson, the Secretary of the Harbour Commissioners, greeted him on his arrival and read and then presented an address outlining the construction of both the dock and basin. The *Belfast Newsletter* in reporting the event stated that the Harbour Office "was as gay externally and internally as flowers and foliage and banners could make it". The party then walked to the steamer *Wonder* that was moored at the Clarendon Dock and proceeded to cross the river towards the Abercorn Basin. When they arrived at the middle of it the Marquis stated, "I name this the Abercorn Basin and now declare it open."

There was a Royal Salute from cannons and a large banner with the words 'The Abercorn Basin' inscribed on it was unfurled. They then proceeded on to the quayside at the Basin where the dignitaries landed and walked around and inspected the new dry dock. During the inspection, Mr Lizars pointed out the workings of the dock and gate to the Marquis. The Marquis then said, "I name this the Hamilton Dry Dock and declare it open." Another banner was unfurled on the caisson gate with the name of the dock written on it. The party then returned to the steamer and sailed to the *Wolff*, a paddle steamer that was waiting at the mouth of the Basin, which then took the guests on a short voyage down towards Belfast Lough.

That evening, in the Long Room in the Harbour Commissioners' Office, invited guests held a celebration dinner at which the caterer Mrs Linden, served them oysters, followed by turtle soup, with a fish course of turbot sole, haddock and whiting.

Exactly who is the Hamilton Dry Docked named after? It is quite clear that the newly formed basin of water was named after James Hamilton, Marquis of Abercorn. What is not so clear is whether the Hamilton Dry Dock is also named after him or in honour of the Chairman of the Belfast Harbour Commissioners, of the same name. When it came to naming the new massive Thompson Dry Dock in 1910, it was named in honour of Robert Thompson M.P. D.L., the then Chairman of the Commissioners. Looking through the records of the Commissioners and reports in the local newspapers, it was simply stated that this new dry dock would be called the Hamilton Dry Dock. Perhaps the only solution is that the descendants of both James Hamiltons can rightly claim that it was named after their predecessor.

In the same year when the new basin and dry dock were opened a minor disaster occurred in Belfast Lough when the *Wolff*, a cross channel mail paddle steamer, owned and operated by G and J Burns, sank following a collision with the steamer the *Prince Arthur*. The *Wolff* lay in around seven fathoms of water off Whiteabbey and was beginning to become a danger to other ships using the port of Belfast.

The shipyard of Harland and Wolff impressed the shipping world when they succeeded in raising the paddle steamer from the waters of the lough. The initial idea had been to send down divers, attach dynamite to the hull of the vessel and then subsequently blow the *Wolff* up. There had been much discussion between the interested parties as to what to do with the ship, but finally the Insurance Company agreed that permission be given to try the idea suggested by Edward Harland that his yard be allowed to undertake a salvage attempt to raise the vessel. This was even by today's standards quite an audacious plan. The *Wolff* weighed in excess of 800 tons and, apart from being at a depth of around seven fathoms (42 ft or 12.8 m), the paddle steamer was further embedded into the mud on the seabed by eight feet (2.43 m).

Edward Harland came up with an ingeniously simple plan – he would winch the *Wolff* up from the seabed. The idea may have seemed simple but in reality it was to take a lot of planning and hard work from those undertaking the task of winching the vessel up. Firstly in the shipyard he had constructed four massive metal floating tanks that were to be placed two over the bow and two over the stern of the ship. On each tank he had constructed an enormous winching system, at the centre of which was a massive six foot long metal screw to be turned by a gang of five men. The four tanks would need twenty men at a time to operate the system of winches. From these screws on the floating barges he had attached massive chains that had their respective hooks fixed by divers into the sidelights or portholes of the *Wolff*.

By July 1868, the tanks were in place and all was ready for the attempt to lift the *Wolff*. A total of 250 men were engaged in the project and support vessels were standing by with extra men, tools and provisions. As work commenced a massive gale gathered in Belfast Lough and the attempt had to be abandoned. When the weather became more settled the salvage was restarted. It took over six long hours of slowly turning the winches to raise the *Wolff* out of the mud. The work continued for eight days and by the end of that time Harland and his workmen had managed to fully raise and refloat the *Wolff*, which was then towed into the shipyard for repairs and successfully placed into the newly opened Hamilton Dry Dock. Harland later recalled "that hardly anyone would recognise us as we had not shaved or undressed during that anxious time."[1]

Satisfied with the recently opened dry dock and the additional water frontage in which he could move and fit out his new ships, Edward Harland set out to gain

The SS Wolff *being lifted by the use of four floating winching platforms.*

(Millin, S., *Sidelights on Belfast History*, W&G Baird, Belfast: 1938)

more orders for his shipyard. By this stage, Gustav Schwabe, who many years previously had backed Harland's bid to buy the shipyard, had suggested to Thomas Ismay that he should consider having his ships for the new shipping line he had just purchased built by the Belfast shipyard. Ismay placed an order for four ships for his newly acquired Oceanic Steam Navigation Company. These new vessels, which were for the North American route, were around 3,800 tons and capable of sailing at 14 knots. The four were called *Oceanic, Atlantic, Baltic* and *Republic*. Before the *Oceanic* had been handed over the order was increased to six with the *Adriatic* and *Celtic* being added. This was the beginning of the partnership that would see around 60 ships being built for Ismay's White Star Line.

The first ship in the order from Ismay, the *Oceanic,* was launched on Saturday 24 August 1870. The ship was 128 m long and 12.4 m breadth (420 ft × 40.9 ft). Twelve boilers provided the steam at 65 psi to turn the 4 cylinder 1,990 hp engine that propelled the ship with one propeller to a top speed of 14 knots.

The *Oceanic* was described as having graceful lines that gave her the appearance of a millionaire's yacht rather than a passenger ship. Thomas Ismay had collaborated with Harland and Wolff on the design of these new vessels and for the first time the accommodation in the ship was extended to take in the full width of the hull of the ship. First class accommodation was moved from the stern to the middle of the ship where there would be less vibration and movement from the propeller that would be felt by the passengers. Accommodation was proved for 160 First class and 1,000 steerage. At the beginning of her service a single fare from Liverpool to New York via Queenstown was 18 guineas (£18.90) or return 25 guineas (£26.25).

Prior to the launch day, the Belfast Harbour Master, Captain Tate, had all vessels removed from the Abercorn Basin. He also arranged for the cross channel ferries from England to be moved from their berths and tied up at buoys in the river in case there were any problems during the launching of the hull of the *Oceanic*. At 10.30 am, the locking pins under the hull were released and the ship slid down the slipway into the water. As soon as the bow of the hull entered the water, a lady called Miss Hoeley officially named the ship, which resulted in loud cheers from the assembled crowds. The hull took longer to stop than was anticipated, but when it did it was towed to the quayside at the Abercorn Basin. It was here that her engines, which were supplied by Maudslay, Sons and Field of London were later fitted. The rigging and sails for the ship were supplied by S. Wilson and Company of Belfast.

The same month in which *Oceanic* was launched, saw a young 16 year old boy by the name of Alexander Montgomery Carlisle enter the shipyard as a gentleman apprentice. He was to rise through the ranks of the yard and end up as Chief Naval Architect and designer of the Olympic class ships. His sister, Margaret, would later marry William Pirrie.

By now Edward Harland and Gustav Wolff had singled out Walter Wilson and

SS Oceanic.

(© National Museums Northern Ireland, Collection Ulster
Folk and Transport Museum)

William Pirrie as possible successors to themselves. Harland later recalled, "The works were now up to the mark in extent and equipment, Mr W.H. Wilson, the manager and Mr W.J. Pirrie, the head draughtsman."

In just over 12 years, the company had taken Edward Harland's original purchase of a fledgling shipbuilding yard situated on a few acres of mud and turned it into to a massive shipyard, at what was now named the Abercorn yard. In that period of time, Harland and his workforce had built 72 ships (whilst *Oceanic* was ship number 73, a previous vessel numbered 4 on the order book had been cancelled in 1860). This amounts to an average of six ships launched every year, with an overall tonnage of over 70,000 tons. Ship number 50, however, was not a ship but the caisson or gate for the newly created Hamilton Dry Dock.

Here at the Abercorn yard were laid out six slipways, a patent slipway for hauling smaller ships out of the water, and, of course, the newly completed Dry Dock. The yard had also built a platers shed, blacksmiths and fitters shop, as well as offices. While in 1870 this was large enough for the shipyard, a growing order book would see the shipyard expanding even further. Within a few years, the shipyard expanded and took over the entire area of the Island.

CHAPTER 10

A New Beginning

Edward Harland and Gustav Wolff were both shrewd businessmen, and by the mid 1870s, just eight years after they formed their original partnership, Edward Harland stated that his estimated wealth by then was £125,000. Allowing for inflation, by today's monetary standards, this would be worth around 75 million pounds. As I have already mentioned, when the Abercorn Basin had opened, a newly established marine engineering firm of McIlwaine and Lewis had taken the opportunity to secure a site at the opposite side of the Basin to that of Harland and Wolff. McIlwaine had been a pupil in Robert Hickson's early yard when Harland had first arrived in Belfast. Also, another one of Harland's early apprentices, Frank Workman, had gone into partnership with George Clark and opened a shipyard in competition to them on the County Antrim side of the river.

It must have been a major concern to both Harland and Wolff that their new star pupils, the Wilson brothers and Pirrie, might at some stage in the future want to break away and set up on their own shipbuilding yards, bringing more unwanted competition. With this in mind Harland and Wolff dissolved their 1862 partnership and, in 1874, offered the young men a position as Partners in the newly constituted company of Harland and Wolff. Between the five of them they invested over £76,000 into the new company. The largest shareholder was Edward Harland with 42%, Gustav Wolff held a 21% share, while William Pirrie held 17% with Walter and Alexander Wilson each investing a 10% share. Pirrie and the Wilson brothers were to invest around £29,000 in this new venture, and it would be incredible to think that they personally would have amassed this sort of wealth in such a short period of time, bearing in mind that Pirrie was only aged 27 and Walter Wilson was aged 35. In order to invest these large sums of money, they must have borrowed the capital from friends and family.

Between Pirrie and the Wilson brothers, it was Pirrie who had invested the most capital by way of £10,000. Whilst Walter Wilson had been the first apprentice started by Robert Hickson, he therefore was senior in service to Pirrie, but it was Pirrie who now set out to be the leading one amongst the junior Partners.

William Pirrie was sent to the Clyde, to see how the Scottish shipyards went about building and fitting out their newly completed vessels. He also travelled widely on the continent to study the interior designs that were incorporated into hotels. This information would later be incorporated when designing the passenger accommodation on new ships. Gustav Wolff also took Pirrie aside and shared his experiences in ship design and saw to it that the yard's business dealings were fully explained to him by John Bailey the firm's bookkeeper. The two Wilson brothers were, on the other hand, more interested in the technical matters of shipbuilding. Alexander was in charge of engine design and Walter would come to solve many problems that dogged shipbuilding, including finding a way to stop corrosion around the propeller when the ship was in motion.

Quite soon after the partnership was established Alexander Wilson left the shipyard. He moved to take up the role of Managing Director of John Rowan and Sons, a local Belfast general and marine engineering works. This move, while it suited Wilson, also benefited Harland and Wolff, as they were at that time purchasing engines from Rowan's for a new vessel called the *Thursby* that was being constructed in the Belfast yard. Walter Wilson took over his brother's shares when he left.

The year 1877 was a particularly bad one for shipbuilding on the island, with Harland and Wolff launching only three vessels. The following year saw an upturn in the order book, and it also saw Alexander Carlisle promoted to the position of shipyard manager. The company also bought over Alexander McLaine's engineering business for £7,000. This was quite a shrewd move as it now opened up the possibility of Harland and Wolff starting to build their own engines in this newly purchased engineering concern.

1878, the following year was also a poor one, with only three ships being launched. J.P. Corry and Company, a local timber importing company, had been a very good customer of Harland's from practically the creation of the shipyard when they had the *Jane Porter* built for them as ship number 3 in the order book. However, in 1878 they moved their business to the newly formed Workman Clark shipyard. In a book written by one of the Corry family, the explanation given for this move of business was that Edward Harland had, on a visit to the Corry home, as a joke, placed a piece of coal in a bedtime glass of milk that was destined for a family member, and that many years later the young Corry was eventually getting his own back on Harland. The family story may be correct, but what is nearer to the truth is a lot simpler, the Corry family were related to both Frank Workman and Ernest Clark and that was most probably the main reason why they switched allegiance.

While there may have been a slow down in the current orders, the shipyard had, over the previous seven years already built ten ships for Thomas Ismay's White Star Line. The shipyard was also building ships for local Belfast customers, one of whom was businessman Samuel Lawther, who had for many years been involved in the timber importing business and had a large fleet of wooden and iron ships. He was also prominent in local politics by becoming an Alderman on Belfast Council and on one occasion he was elected to the position of the High

Sheriff of Belfast. He worked tirelessly for improvements in the harbour and also served as a Harbour Commissioner.

Lawther had gone into partnership with another local businessman, Thomas Dixon, and in 1875 they jointly placed the first of five orders for iron ships. In a tribute to Edward Harland and his new Partners, Lawther and Dixon's ships would be named *E.J. Harland*, *G.W. Wolff*, *Walter H. Wilson*, *W.J. Pirrie* and *Queen's Island*.

The *E.J. Harland* was described as a beautiful full rigger of around 1,270 tons. Her maiden voyage from Ardrossan in Scotland to San Francisco took 130 days. The Master of the ship was Captain English who stated that the vessel was well received by the people of San Francisco. On the return journey from America the ship made the crossing to Queenstown in Ireland in 103 days. At the time a parody from an old sea song was penned about the ship:

> "It's of a bold packet, a packet of fame,
> The flash packet, *E.J. Harland*'s her name.
> She sails to the westward where the stormy winds blow
> Bound away in the Harland to the westward we go."[1]

The ship sadly ended her career, when she was in collision with the steamer *Lake Champion*.

The next ship of the five was the *G.W. Wolff*, which was larger than the *E.J. Harland*. Captain English was transferred to captain the vessel before the loss of the *Harland*. Her best crossing of the Atlantic was from Philadelphia to Belfast in 13 days while under the command of Captain Duckworth. In 1902 the ship was sold to a new owner who resided in Swansea, Wales, and there she continued to sail for another 10 years.

Walter H. Wilson *a four masted iron barque of the Lawther Shipping Line.*
(Nautical Photo Agency)

The *Walter H. Wilson* was the only one of the ships that was given the full first name of a Partner, rather than just the initials. The ship, at 2,518 tons, was a large four masted barque and remained with Samuel Lawther for over 20 years. It was then resold to Edgar and Company and renamed *California*. On 15 January 1913, after giving 31 years service, the vessel, while undertow in ballast near the Tyne, was caught up in a heavy gale and pushed onto rocks on St. Mary's Island in Whitley Bay. She broke her keel and the mate and eight

of the crew were lost.

Fourth in the fleet was the *W.J. Pirrie*. She was in reality a sister ship to the *Walter H. Wilson*, launched in May 1883, just under a year later. Her maiden voyage was under the command of Captain Duckworth and was from Dundee in Scotland to San Francisco. In 1889 the ship set a record time on the journey from Calcutta to Great Britain in 97 days. In 1898 the ship was sold to J.M. Campbell and Son of Glasgow and in 1904, while near Tocopilla, her cargo of nitrate caught fire resulting in the ship being completely burnt out. By 1919 she had been salvaged and was in use as a five masted schooner, but in 1920, while under tow in the north Atlantic off Washington, she sank with a loss of 16 lives and only two crew members surviving.

The last of the five ships was the *Queen's Island*, which was launched in 1885 and rigged as a three masted barque of 2,093 tons. At that time the ship was the largest in her class in the world. She stayed with the Lawther fleet for five years and then in 1890 was sold to the Aberdeen White Star line and renamed the *Strathdon*. She was again sold on five years later, in 1905, to a French company and was called *Gers*. Finally the ship was broken up in 1925 in Bruges.

W.J. Pirrie *a four masted iron ship for the Lawther shipping Line.*
(Nautical Photo Agency)

CHAPTER 11

Approaching the End of an Era

Edward Harland and Gustav Wolff had now set up a new partnership with the younger men Pirrie and the Wilson brothers. Even though both principals were still only in their early forties they decided that it was time to start becoming less involved in the day to day running of the yard and to leave it to the younger men.

Harland had been approached in 1870 by the Belfast Harbour Commissioners and was co-opted to serve as a Commissioner. While initially taking on the role, he found within a few short months that his commitments in the shipyard meant he could not fully participate in the responsibilities being asked of him. He therefore reluctantly stood down from the Board. However, two years later, with Pirrie and Wilson now taking a bigger role in the shipyard, Harland was in a position to seek re-election to the Commissioners. He was successfully elected to the Board in 1872, and within three years he was elected as their Chairman.

Meanwhile, around this period, Gustav Wolff was becoming involved with his role in establishing the Belfast Rope Works in East Belfast.

Both men also became interested in politics. Harland, in 1883, was elected to serve as a Councillor on the Belfast Town Council representing the St. Anne's Ward. He went on to serve as Mayor of Belfast for two years in 1885 and 1886, and in 1885 a Baronetcy was conferred upon him. He also represented North Belfast as its Member of Parliament from 1889 until his death in 1895. Wolff too served as a Member of Parliament, representing East Belfast from 1892 until 1910.

Since the initial order for the *Oceanic* had been completed in 1870, Harland and Wolff had, within two years, completed and handed over an additional seven ships to the White Star Line, with a combined tonnage of 24,161 tons. The new Partners in the shipyard now continued to push ship owners for orders and to build ever bigger and bigger ships.

In 1873, the White Star Line were to place an order for two new vessels that to that date, at just over 5,000 tons each, were the largest vessels ever constructed by Harland and Wolff. These vessels were named *Britannic* and *Germanic*, and were 455 ft long. To accommodate the extra weight of the vessels during construction, the shipyard had to enlarge the berths at which the ships were fitted out and new equipment also had to be purchased.

94

SS Britannic, *ship No. 83, launched February 1874.*

(© National Museums Northern Ireland, Collection Ulster Folk and Transport Museum)

Both ships were costed at around £200,000. *Britannic*, yard number 83, was originally to be called *Hellenic*. Considering the record size of the tonnage of the vessel, the *Britannic* was launched without a mention in the local Belfast press on 3 February 1874. For the next 17 weeks fitting out took place. The ship was 450 ft long, with a breadth of just over 45 ft. Her compound four cylinder engine, with a rated output of 760 hp was supplied by Maudslay, Son and Field of London. The ship was fitted with two funnels and four wooden masts. There were three decks, two of which were made of iron and were covered with wood, while the hull was divided into eight watertight compartments. The upper or weather deck had a very pronounced camber built into it to allow the seawater to quickly drain away through the scuppers on the side. This type of deck construction was referred to as 'a turtle deck'.

Internally the main saloon and first class staterooms were positioned amidships. This became very popular with passengers, as it reduced the amount of vibration from the ship, while at sea. The upper deck had accommodation for the Officers and Engineers, as well as the ship's galleys and smoking rooms and toilets. The Grand Saloon was unique in some ways, having a real open fireplace fitted, around which were arranged armchairs and a piano. Mr Mullan of Donegall Place, Belfast, installed a library with a collection of 265 books. He was to provide similar books, all bound in leather with the White Star logo for the majority of the ships in the line. The first class staterooms were plumbed with cold water and some of them had bunks fitted. Forward of the staterooms was a dormitory. This space was thought to be the first ever such dormitory that was fitted out in a ship. Bunks provided for 22 people and it was reported as being large and comfortable, the berths were arranged in such a manner that it was possible to rest on one and hold a conversation with a neighbouring passenger at the same time. The main idea behind the dormitory was that it might encourage large groups to travel. Another first in the fitting out of the ship was the inclusion of bridal berths. The local newspaper reported on this by stating, "They are luxuriously furnished and provided with every requisite that can possibly add to the pleasure of a 'honeymoon trip.'"

Originally the vessel was fitted with an adjustable propeller shaft that could be raised or lowered. The thinking behind this new idea of Harland's was that when the shaft was raised and the ship under sail, it would reduce drag and allow for an increase in the speed of the ship. However after a few voyages it was deemed not to be a success and *Britannic* was brought back to Belfast to be fitted with a standard propeller shaft. Captain Hamilton took the ship on its maiden voyage, leaving Liverpool bound for New York on 25 June 1874. *Britannic* covered the journey in 7 days and 2 hours. Following the alterations to the propeller shaft that time was bettered by several hours.

Unknown to the shipyard of Harland and Wolff, they would make history, when on 15 July 1874, again with little interest from the local press, they launched the *Germanic*, the sister ship to the *Britannic*. Hundreds of people had come to watch the launch, some even climbing onto a ship in an adjacent slipway at the Abercorn yard to watch the spectacle. The large wooden props holding the bow up were knocked away, the ship settled onto the slipway and slid quickly into the water. There was concern that the vessel if, not stopped in time, could hit the quay at the opposite side of the Abercorn Basin, but as the hull was going down the slipway, workmen high up on the hull dropped two anchors attached to chains into the water. The ship was pulled up well in time and then towed to the quayside near to the Hamilton Dry Dock.

What was historical about this launch was that when the *Germanic* was handed over to her owners she would continue to sail for around 75 years. The ship would in that period of time have several different owners and would sail until she was scrapped in 1950. The *Nomadic* (yard number 422) would be the only other Harland and Wolff ship to surpass that record, afloat for some 100 years after its construction at Queen's Island.

The year 1880 was a special one for Harland and Wolff. Firstly they purchased, for around £7,000, the small shipbuilding and repair yard of Alexander McLaine and Sons, which had facilities on the County Antrim side of the river. The owner, Alexander McLaine, had died and his son had no interest in continuing with the business, so he was quite happy to sell up to the large yard across the river. At the same time Harland and Wolff leased extra land from the Belfast Harbour Commissioners opposite their existing yard on Queen's Road. Here, for the first time, they established their own Engine Works. This finally allowed them to

The main office and administration block for Harland and Wolff.

provide the ships they built with their own engines, instead of having to buy them in from outside engineering firms. Over the next few years the shipyard expanded rapidly from the small beginnings at the Abercorn yard, where they had started with five slipways, to the new Queen's shipyard, where an additional four slipways were laid out. At the same time the number and size of workshops also increased.

With this extra area now being laid out for shipbuilding it was only a matter of time until Harland and Wolff would have to construct larger offices for themselves and the growing numbers of white-collar workers that were being employed. Over the next few years designs were drawn up for a major new three-storey office block – the building that now fronts onto Queen's Road. Beginning in 1885, it was built in four separate stages, from sandstone and brick, and was completed around 1910. At the same time the yard also expanded across Queen's Road and there they set up many workshops, including boiler shops, an iron foundry and a pattern shop. Wood in large quantities was also stored at this side of the road. An early 1885 plan of the shipyard shows the office block with the 'U' shaped section at the rear which housed the drawing and accounts offices. The main entrance to these offices was later knocked down and replaced with what now exists. There was also a corridor which connected these two large offices at the shipyard end but this too has since been knocked down.

The second important happening in 1885 was that Sir Edward Harland began his design for two new ships that would nearly surpass the 10,000 ton barrier. The ships were eventually purchased by the White Star Line but were not to be constructed for another nine years. They would be called *Teutonic* and *Majestic*.

1885 was another special year for the shipyard. Firstly, Edward Harland was elected as Mayor for the town of Belfast. Secondly, the shipyard was included in the itinerary of the visit by the Prince and Princess of Wales, Edward and Alexandra, who were accompanied by their son Prince Albert Victor. The Royal party arrived at the shipyard around 6.00 pm in the early evening of 24 April. They were greeted by Edward Harland who, along with William Pirrie and Walter Wilson, would be their hosts for the tour.

Set out for the Royal party was a mini exhibition of the work of all the various crafts that were carried out at the yard. A foreman representing the particular trade was on hand to explain to the visitors the range of exhibitions. Among the displays laid out were views of riveting, boiler making, plate bending and plumbing. This exhibition and models occupied a space of around a mile, and the workmen who manned the stands were all given two tickets so they could bring family members along to witness the Royal Visit.

After the Royal Party had seen around the display of crafts, they moved to the main Queen's Road where they boarded a specially constructed Royal railway carriage that took them on a narrow gauge steam railway from the shipyard to the area where the new Alexandra Dry Dock was to be constructed. This railway system had been installed to assist with the reclamation work that was being carried out at the eastern end of Queen's Island. For the remaining members of the party other narrow gauge carriages were fitted out like Irish Jaunting carriages.

When they arrived at the site for the new Dry Dock, the 'Royal Train' steamed into a specially erected marquee, which was appropriately decorated. Belfast's mayor, Edward Harland, also in his capacity as president of the Belfast Harbour Commissioners, again welcomed the Royal Party. Mr W. Currie, the Secretary of the Harbour Commissioners offered Princess Alexandra a silver spade and a wheelbarrow, which were suitably engraved. Using the spade, the Princess then proceeded to lift the first sod and place it in the wheelbarrow. Quite surprisingly she then took the wheelbarrow and pushed it around the spectators to let them see the sod she had just cut. Edward Harland showed the Royal Party a model of the dock, which also contained a model of the *Britannic*. After a period of time the Prince and Princess of Wales, along with Prince Albert Victor, rejoined their 'Royal Train' which took them back to the main entrance of the shipyard, where they were met by a military escort for the journey back to the Royal yacht.

Some modern historians believed Harland and Wolff entered into 'an understanding' with the White Star Line, agreeing not to build ships for the shipping lines that were in direct competition with the White Star Line. However, this isn't true. The shipyard continued to accept orders from other shipping companies and constructed several ships for the Peninsular and Oriental Steam Navigation Company, more commonly known as P&O.

One such ship, the *Oceana* (yard number 201), was launched on Saturday 17 September 1887. The ship, at 6362 tons, was the largest vessel so far built at Queen's Island. A large crowd had gathered to witness the launching, something that was always a special sight to see. The ship was 466 ft long and her beam or width was 52 ft.

Shortly before 10 am the ship was launched. The ceremony was carried out by Miss Kendall, the daughter of Mr F. Kendall, the Belfast representative of the shipping line. The *Oceana* was built from Siemans-Martin steel and was classed as A1 at Lloyds and registered at Belfast. The vessel was destined for the Australia route and was fitted out to a very high standard. It accommodated over 300 first and second-class passengers, as well as 160 third class passengers. Another provision on the ship was the ability to convert the vessel to a troop carrier for the Admiralty if so required.

The *Oceana* sailed for the P&O Line for almost 25 years until she was lost after a collision in 1912 with a sailing barque, which was a month before the *Titanic* tragedy.

1889 was another very busy year for the shipyard, in which they launched 12 ships. The first, the *Runic* for the White Star Line, was launched on 1 January with the last, the *Nizam* for the Asiatic Steam Navigation Company, being sent down the ways on 21 December. At the end of May the newly completed Alexandra Dry Dock was opened.

On Saturday 19 January, *Teutonic* (ship number 208), which very nearly broke the 10,000 ton barrier, was launched. The launch from the Queen's yard was overseen by Alexander Carlisle, and took place at 11.25 am. It was noted that around 20,000 spectators turned up to witness the occasion. *Teutonic* and the sister ship *Majestic*, which was launched later in the year at the end of June, cost White Star around £700,000 for the pair. It is interesting to note that one newspaper, on reporting the launch, stated that this amount of money was almost equal to the amount of debt owed by Belfast city. During construction

SS Teutonic, *ship No. 208, launched January 1889* (A&C Black publishing)

the Admiralty approved, for the first time, the design of both ships. This meant that in the event of war they could be commandeered and fitted out as auxiliary cruisers, and in this case 12 large guns could be fitted within 48 hours to the strengthened decks. The ship was 582 ft long, with a breadth of almost 59 ft and a depth of nearly 40 ft. The hull was constructed from Siemens Martin steel. Two triple expansion engines served by a total of nine boilers propelled the ship at around 20 knots. Accommodation was provided for 300 first class, 150 second class and 850 steerage. After the launch the hull was towed to the Abercorn Basin for fitting out, with Gustav Wolff on board while Edward Harland, Walter Wilson and William Pirrie watched from the slipway accompanied by J. Bruce Ismay from the ship's owners.

The people who had come to see the launch used every vantage point that they could find. Some had gone near to the shipyard of Workman Clark, which was very close to the bottom of the slipway. At this point some of the spectators were balancing on logs, which were floating in the water. As the hull of *Teutonic* entered the water it set up a backwash, which hit the logs and unbalanced those standing on them. The lucky ones were just thrown into the water and got a good soaking, but some of the people fell between the logs as they moved and were to suffer serious injuries. Mary Nesbitt, a young 28 year old mother who came from Back Ship Street, had been standing on the logs holding her five year old son John. Both were thrown off the logs and fell between them. As the logs moved they suffered some serious injuries, including breaking their upper legs and were taken to the Royal Hospital for treatment.

The new Alexandra Dry Dock was officially opened on 21 May 1889, by Prince Albert Victor, the son of H.R.H. Alexandra, the Princess of Wales, who only four years previously had cut the first sod at the site of the dry dock. The Prince arrived in Belfast on board the Royal yacht *Osborne,* a paddle steamer that had sailed from Stranraer and anchored close to Carrickfergus. The Prince arrived at Donegall Quay around 12.00 noon, where he was met and welcomed by many dignitaries including the Belfast Harbour Commissioners. The Prince made his way to the Harbour Commissioners Office where a Royal Address was given to him. The party then made their way along crowded streets to the Alexandra Dry Dock on Queen's Road where there were a large number of specially invited people. On the way there were many banners displaying the words 'God save the Queen' and 'Céâd mile fâilté Prince Albert Victor'. At the dock the Second Royal Highlanders provided a guard of honour and a band. The whole area leading into the dock of Queen's Road had been decorated for the occasion, banners with 'Welcome' written in gold were hung up and large seven foot circular flower arrangements with the letters V and A picked out in contrasting flowers, were also displayed.

The new dry dock was at that time, the biggest dry dock in the United Kingdom. It was 800 ft in length, 50 ft wide and 25 ft deep, and could, when full, hold around 8.5 million gallons of water. The concrete floor was around 10 ft

A modern view of the pumping house that serviced both the Alexandra and Thompson Dry Docks.

thick in the centre. The design of the dock was extremely modern and it had been constructed by the firm of McCrea and McFarland with the works manager Mr T.R. Salmond in charge. The structure of the dock was unique as it could be sub-divided into three sections of 300 ft, 200 ft and 300 ft in order to accommodate ships of different sizes. The dock gate or caisson, while basically a large metal box, was designed with a water pump inside it. This meant the gate could be flooded, causing it to settle down quickly and seal the mouth of the dock. When the dock needed to be opened, the water inside the gate was pumped out, allowing the gate to float and making it easier to tow out of the way.

A new pump house was constructed at the east side of the dock. The building's design was Italian in style. The chimney serving the boilers was 120 ft high, and inside the pump house were pumps of around 7 ft in diameter, which could pump the dock dry in 2 ½ hours. Electric lighting around the dock was also installed, as was a steam crane that could lower items down into the dock. To finish the construction a tram system had been installed with track running all the way to the dock from the Engine Works at the Abercorn Basin. The cost of the dock was around £91,000.

A canopy and raised dais had been constructed on the Caisson gate, with a magnum bottle of champagne suspended above the raised platform, the Prince cut the cord on the bottle, which then fell and broke on the gate following which he named the dock the Alexandra Dry Dock. The sluice gates were opened below him and the dock rapidly filled up.

The Prince then proceeded to board the *Teutonic*, which was moored just outside the opening of the dock. At the gangway he was welcomed on board the ship by Sir Edward Harland who invited him to inspect the vessel. As he did so the ship was moved into position at the mouth of the dock. On board the ship, the Prince was introduced to Lady Harland and Mrs Ismay and finally, after walking around practically all of the ship, he made his way to the bridge where Walter Wilson was in charge of the moving of *Teutonic* into the dock. As the ship entered the dock the Prince declared the dock officially open. Following that the Prince and the numerous invited guests proceeded to a massive 130 ft by 40 ft specially constructed luncheon hall alongside the dock, where a rather large celebration luncheon was laid on. Later in the day the Prince had dinner with the Second Gordon Highlanders and in the evening he attended a ball in the Ulster Hall.

The shipyard continued to construct bigger and bigger ships and in June 1895 they broke yet another major milestone by building the 10,000 ton *Georgic*, a livestock carrier. The ship was launched on 22 June and it was engaged in transporting up to 900 cattle and a large number of horses between Liverpool and New York. There were two three cylinder triple expansion engines, which powered twin screws and could give an average speed of 13 knots. McBride and Company, photographers of High Street in Belfast, had been engaged to capture the launch for posterity. The ship, after being fitted out, was finally handed over to the White Star Line less than seven weeks later on 8 August.

All was going well for the shipyard. Since Edward Harland and Gustav Wolff had, in 1874, offered partnerships to Walter and Alexander Wilson and William Pirrie the shipyard had continued to push forward. In the 21 year period up to 1895 the yard constructed 213 ships, an average of just over ten ships being launched each year.

Alexander Wilson, as I have previously mentioned, had left the yard to take up employment elsewhere, and while Harland and Wolff had both taken a back seat in the business and had both entered politics, William Pirrie had been the one Partner to shine and was now in the position of being made Chairman of the board of Directors.

In 1895 the shipyard of Harland and Wolff was to be shaken nearly to its core, when there were two major tragedies. At around 5.30 pm on 16 April a fire was discovered in the shipyard's timber store on the Hamilton Road. As this happened during the Easter break most of the workforce were on holiday. Alexander Carlisle was in the yard at the time the fire was discovered and he and several employees, who had previously been trained as works firemen, tried to tackle the initial blaze. However, it proved too much for them and their limited equipment, and an emergency call was put through to the Belfast Fire Brigade. Chief Fire Officer Parker from Chichester Street Fire Station arrived first and very soon the initial attendance by the Brigade was increased to four horse drawn steamers (pumping appliances) from Whitla Street and the Albertbridge Road Fire Stations. The four steamers set in at the Abercorn Basin and were used to pump water to the 51 firemen that were fighting the fire.

By 7.00 pm thousands of spectators had gathered at the Queen's Roads to see what was happening. The Brigade decided to allow three massive stacks of wood to burn themselves out, because firstly there was a strong wind blowing up the river Lagan and secondly, the way in which the timber was stacked had made a roof over the rest of the wood and this in turn was actually increasing the ferocity of the fire. At around midnight, the wind died down and the firemen could then try to beat the fire down. By around 3.00 am on the following morning, the Fire Brigade had got to a position where they had stopped the fire spreading and could then concentrate on fully extinguishing it.

Apart from Carlisle, Walter Wilson, William Pirrie and Mr J.H. Chancellor the Assistant Manager of the yard were also present to see the devastation. Mr Allen from the shipyard of Workman Clark also came to see what was happening. The timber that had been involved in the fire had recently been landed from the *SS Kennebee* and included yellow pine, pitch pine, Oregan pine, teale wood, memal and spruce, and there was a feeling that the cause of the fire may have been spontaneous combustion as the wood had been tightly packed in the ship's hold for some time. However, one of the local Belfast newspapers stated that they considered that the fire was started by an incendiary device. It was later estimated that the value of the timber that was lost was around £40,000 and this sum was only partly covered by insurance.

The second major catastrophe occurred towards the end of the year in December. Edward Harland with his wife Rosa went to Glenfarne Hall in County Leitrim, which he had rented from Major Tottenham for many years. They arrived on Friday 21 December after Sir Edward had attended some important meetings at the shipyard in Belfast. He and Lady Rosa had arrived as usual and made themselves at home. On Sunday the weather was so bad that they decided not to travel the six miles to church but spent the day at home. As usual they had dinner at 8.00 pm. Later that evening before retiring Sir Edward said that he felt a slight cold coming on. On the following night, Monday 23 December, Sir Edward had a game of billiards after dinner and then at around 11.00 pm he decided to retire for the evening. While undressing and getting ready for bed he said to his wife that he felt faint, to which she replied that she would send for the doctor. Sir Edward then said, "It is no use Rosa"[1] and collapsed. Several guests assisted by lifting him unto the bed, and the local doctor from the village of Blacklion was sent for. He had to travel six miles to arrive at Glenfarne and on his arrival, after examining Sir Edward, Doctor Tate pronounced him dead. The cause of death was later given as heart failure. From very early on the following morning the 24th the local telegraph office at Blacklion was busy sending out telegrams announcing the death of Sir Edward Harland. The office was later inundated with messages of sympathy for Lady Rosa. Late in the evening of Christmas Eve, Sir Samuel Black, the Town Clerk of Belfast accompanied by William Pirrie arrived at Glenfarne.

The funeral of Sir Edward Harland took place on Saturday 28 December from First Presbyterian Church, Rosemary Street in Belfast. The service began at 8.45 am and there was a steady stream of carriages arriving at the church for

30 minutes prior to this. There was standing room only inside the church and thousands of people gathered outside had to wait in the rain and a biting cold wind. Following the playing of the 'Dead March' on the church organ, the Rev. Douglas Walmsley conducted the Funeral service.

The service was over shortly after 9.00 am and the cortege, with 500 workmen from the shipyard of Harland and Wolff at the head, walking four abreast, started the journey in the rain into Royal Avenue and Donegall Place. The glass covered hearse was drawn by four horses, with the Reverend Albert Harland (Sir Edward's brother) leading as Chief Mourner, walking with him were four nephews of Sir Edward, including Henry P. Harland.

As the funeral procession proceeded towards the Belfast City Cemetery, the bell on the Albert Clock tolled from 9.00 o'clock for an hour. Shops were closed and flags were at half-mast not only along the route but also throughout the City and harbour area. There were that many mourners and carriages present that it was estimated that it took the funeral procession a full hour to pass any given point. Included amongst those paying their last respects to the founder of the shipyard were representatives from the House of Commons in London; heads of industry and commerce including Thomas Ismay, the Chairman of the White Star Line; leaders from the local Churches; and members of the Orange Order, the local Unionist Associations and the Harbour Commissioners. Prominent in the procession, in the carriage behind Lady Harland, were Gustav Wolff, Walter Wilson, William Pirrie and Harland's private Secretary Sir James Douglas.

The headstone at the grave of Sir Edward Harland.

The cortege finally arrived at the Falls Road gates of the Belfast Cemetery at around 10.30 am, where several hundred people had gathered to pay their respects. The Rev. Douglas Walmsley again conducted the short service at the graveside. Finally Sir Edward Harland was laid to rest in his wife's family vault. There were no children from the marriage.

Many tributes were paid to Sir Edward. William Pirrie said of him:

> "Sir Edward Harland's death leaves a blank which will not be easily filled. He has done a great and lasting service to Ireland. My late partner's death to me is greater than to anybody. I was brought up with him since I was a boy of 15. I think he looked on me more as a son than as a partner; it is exceedingly trying to me. The loss to the city is something, which I think the citizens do not yet realise."[2]

Alexander Carlisle, the chief naval architect at the shipyard said of him, "Edward Harland was the only man I ever loved."[3]

Within a year of the death of Sir Edward, some of his very close friends got together to discuss the possibility of having some type of permanent memorial to him. In December 1897, the then Lord Mayor of Belfast, Sir William McCammond, chaired a meeting of specially invited people who all agreed with him that there should be a statue of Sir Edward Harland. They decided to ask the public to subscribe and set the minimum donation at 1 shilling (5 pence) and an upper limit of £10. Over £250 was raised at that initial meeting. The commission for the statue was given to Sir Thomas Brock, who was also to be responsible for the statue of Queen Victoria and also, many years later, the Belfast Titanic Memorial. The Belfast City Council granted a site in the grounds of the newly completed City Hall for the statue. The site at the junction of Donegal Square North and East is the closest space in the grounds to the shipyard at Queen's Island.

The statue is nine foot tall and carved from Sicilian marble, and stands on an 11 ft high granite pedestal. Sir Edward is depicted in morning clothes wearing a frock coat with the familiar type of tie that he always wore. To his left is a table with plans and sketches on it. Also sitting on the table is a model lifeboat similar to the one that Sir Edward designed in 1850. He is portrayed with his left hand resting on the bow of the lifeboat. In his right hand, he is holding a piece of chalk. This is a reference to his early days in Robert Hickson's yard when he used to walk around the shipyard marking any poor quality work with a chalk circle.

The memorial was finally unveiled on 23 June 1903. The Institute of Naval Architects were having a meeting in Belfast and as part of that its president, the Earl of Glasgow, was asked to unveil the statue. Among the many who attended the ceremony were Councilors such as the Lord Mayor Sir Daniel Dixon, Alexander Carlisle, William Pirrie and S. Shannon Mills, who would later write a highly acclaimed account of life in Belfast in his book *Sidelights on Belfast History*. Lady Harland was unable to attend.

Around 3.00 pm the Lord Mayor asked the Earl of Glasgow to perform the unveiling. In his speech the Earl said that Sir Edward Harland had, throughout his life, rendered inestimable services to the shipbuilding industry. He described him as an innovator, who successfully increased the length of new ships without increasing the beam or width, thus making a very streamlined shape of hull. Glasgow also acknowledged that Harland was responsible for the radical change of design when Harland and Wolff constructed ships with a flat bottom instead of the more traditional keel shaped hull.

The unveiling of the statue was captured on film by Belfast photographer Robert J. Welch who was the official photographer of the shipyard of Harland and Wolff.

The statue of Sir Edward Harland in the grounds of the Belfast City Hall.

The unveiling of the Sir Edward Harland statue in June 1903.

CHAPTER 12

Arising from the Ashes

Following the death of Sir Edward Harland, the shipyard reopened in 1896, and it was not really that unexpected that William Pirrie would take over as Chairman. He had become the major shareholder and over the years as both Harland and Wolff had taken more and more of a back seat Pirrie had asserted himself. The only other rivals for the Chairman's position were Gustav Wolff and Walter Wilson. Wolff, who by this stage was aged 62, had very much taken a back seat in the affairs of the shipyard and was pursuing other interests. Wilson, the other possible contender was happier working away in the background, so at the beginning of this New Year, William Pirrie became the new all controlling Chairman of the shipyard of Harland and Wolff.

Pirrie's first year in the driving seat was a memorable one, with the yard continuing to construct ships and 12 launches taking place that year. The shipyard was not just constructing ships, but by now they also had a profitable repair business. The Company was approached by the Union Steamship Company who owned a ship called the *SS Scot*. Discussions were entered into regarding the possibility of lengthening the ship. This would be a cheaper alternative to having a new vessel constructed. Harland and Wolff agreed to try and do this and put Thomas Andrews in charge of the operation.

A young Thomas Andrews.
(Thomas Andrews Collection)

Andrews had joined the shipyard as a gentleman apprentice in 1889 when he was just aged 16. His five year period of apprenticeship was now behind him and this operation was one of the first major responsibilities that he had been given.

The ship arrived in Belfast on Thursday 23 January and was docked in the Alexandra Graving Dock. It was to spend almost ten months in the shipyard. With the ship in the dock, the workmen and skilled craftsmen basically cut across the ship half way across its length. Large hydraulic rams and steam winches would have been used to gradually slide the two sections of hull apart. The distance the two sections of hull had to be pulled apart was exactly 54 ft. The new additional section of the hull was constructed within this space and once that was complete and watertight, the internal fittings were added. This by all accounts was a major technical achievement, even by today's standards. During this work a carpenter named James Crangle was killed when he fell from the orlop deck of the ship into the hold below.

The ship suffered a major embarrassment following completion of the work. When the *Scot* was leaving the harbour en route for Holyhead, it ran aground on the riverbed of the Lagan at Clarence Wharf, as the tide was not high enough to allow the ship to sail into the lough. The *Scot* had the indignity of having to sit grounded for nearly an hour until there was full tide to allow her to sail away.

The Union Steamship Company was delighted with their 'new' ship and very quickly word of Harland and Wolff's success spread. Nearing the end of the work on the *Scot*, the shipyard was approached by the Hamburg Amerika Line who wanted to do the same as the *Scot* to their vessel the *Augusta Victoria*. Thomas

107

Splitting the SS Scot to add a new section.
(© National Museums Northern Ireland, Collection Harland and Wolff, Ulster Folk and Transport Museum)

Andrews was again given charge of the project and started to discuss the matter with the draughtsmen and the ship's owners in early September. All was agreed and the ship arrived in Belfast on 23 November.

The *Augusta Victoria* was cut in half and separated on 9 January 1897. It was extended in length over the next five months finally leaving Belfast for Hamburg on 11 May with Andrews supervising the progress of work on the ship. So delighted were the Hamburg Amerika Line that they later presented a large silver cup to Thomas Andrews in appreciation for the work that he had done.

Perhaps the most annoying and embarrassing thing to happen at the yard in Pirrie's first year in charge occurred in July when another, and this time more damaging, fire occurred. At 11.29 pm on the evening of 26 July, the local Belfast Fire Brigade received a call stating that a fire had broken out in an Office building at the Harland and Wolff shipyard. Some workmen from the shipyard tried to fight the initial blaze, but quite swiftly the flames got out of their control. Immediately the Brigade dispatched two horse drawn hose carriages and one horse drawn steamer to the scene. On their arrival they found the Joiners shop well alight with the flames crossing Queen's Road. The workman's dinning room at the junction of Queen's Road and Hamilton Road was also well alight as was a large Engineering workshop belonging to the smaller shipyard of Workman Clark. Within 17 minutes of that initial call to the Fire Brigade the Chief Fire Officer, George Parker, who had just arrived to take command, sent back an assistance message to the Fire Station in Chichester Street, requesting that all available fire appliances and firemen in Belfast should be sent to the incident. By this stage the fire was advancing quicker than the firemen could walk and was heading towards the timber yard of Workman Clark. Quite quickly the fire took a firm hold in the timber yard of the 'wee yard'. The Brigade had by this time set up their steamers at the Abercorn Basin and were drawing water at a rate of around 1,600 gallons per minute from the river Lagan in their battle to subdue the flames.

By around midnight, it was estimated that around 4,000 people, mostly shipyard employees, had turned up to watch in horror as their jobs were going up in flames.

At one stage, the fire threatened to engulf oil storage tanks belonging to Harland and Wolff, which contained around 200,000 gallons of oil, but the quick and brave actions of the firemen stopped the fire getting near the tanks. Directors and managers starting arriving quite quickly, Chairman William Pirrie arrived just after midnight and stayed until nearly 4.00 am. By around 6.30 am the Brigade finally got to grips with the incident and began reducing the number of men and fire engines at the scene.

As daylight broke those present could clearly see what damage had been caused – it was massive. In Harland and Wolff's yard, major damage had been caused in the joiner's shop, the cabinetmakers and french polishers shops, the woodworking machinery shop, the sawmills, the mast and spar making shed, and the timber store drafting room. The estimated cost of the damage was around £42,000. Workman Clark also suffered major damage. Their Engineering Works, Engine shop, Pattern Shop, Smithy Engine Shop Stores and Time and Tool Offices were all badly damaged. Including damage at their south yard, Workman Clark's damage was estimated at around £25,000. They also lost timber to the value of £10,000, which was not covered by insurance.

The fire was totally extinguished by around 4.00 pm the following day, having burnt for just over 16 hours. One fire engine and a few firemen were left to check for any hot spots and extinguish these. During the height of the fire it was nearly impossible to walk down Queen's Road as the flames were crossing the road, one fireman had his fire tunic literally burnt off his back. One of the Brigade's horses, a gray called Tom, which had pulled steamers down to the fire, was returning to its station when he collapsed and died in Wellington Place in the centre of Belfast. Following the fires it was estimated that 2,000 men from Workman Clark and 5,000 from Harland and Wolff lost their jobs and, worse still, their sets of tools. Those men belonging to the Amalgamated Society of Engineers would receive £10 compensation for the loss of their tools.

Following the fire the Chief Fire Officer, Parker, made a very strong case to the Belfast City Council for the purchase of a floating Fire Tender. This was ignored at the time and it was around 103 years before Belfast finally had its first Fire Tender, the Tug, *Clandeboye*.

The yard again set a world record in tonnage with the launch of the *Pennsylvania*, a passenger cargo ship for the Hamburg Amerika Line. The ship, at 13,726 tons, was the largest ship yet to be constructed at the Queen's Island yard. The vessel was 585 ft long with a beam of 52 ft. The engines were quadruple expansion, rated at 6,000 horse power, which gave the ship a speed of around 14 knots. The ship's propeller shaft was a massive 230 ft long. There was accommodation for 200 first class, 150 second class and 1,000 steerage class passengers. 17 steam winches and four steam cranes were built into the ship to allow for cargo handling and it had the hold capacity for 20,000 tons of cargo. The *Pennsylvania* was launched on Thursday 10 September 1896 and the shipping line was represented by Mr Van der Smissin and Captain Kopff. The maiden voyage of the ship was on 30 January 1897 from Belfast to New York and the vessel was finally scrapped in 1924.

There was some thought that William Pirrie had considered expanding the shipyard prior to the destructive fire that occurred. This had already started a few years earlier, when in 1885 the initial shipyard, situated at the Abercorn Basin with its five slipways, had expanded and taken in land where the People's Park had been, with four slipways laid out at the newly named Queen's yard.

A massive three year reconstruction of the Harland and Wolff shipyard was undertaken. All new buildings were constructed with basic fire resistant materials, to avoid another serious fire. New equipment and machinery was bought including boring and drilling machines, new lathes, brass finishing machines and grinders. The Engine Works were also extended.

The Company also constructed a massive building on the east side of Queen's Road, opposite the Alexandra Dry Dock, which was used to build mock ups of the ships' internal passenger arrangements. This allowed potential new buyers to get an idea of the ships' interiors prior to them placing an order. A massive 700 ft gantry was built at the number two slipway at the Abercorn Basin, with moving cranes fitted on the top of the gantry to suspend the new hydraulic riveting machines. In total, over the three year period and not including the insurance money received after the fire, the expansion programme cost the shipyard in excess of £100,000.

1896 saw William Pirrie elected to and installed for a two-year period of Office as Lord Mayor of Belfast. The following year Pirrie hosted a Royal visit from the Duke and Duchess of York on 8 September. The Duke and Duchess visited both the shipyard and also William Pirrie's home at Ormiston in East Belfast. At noon on Wednesday 8 September their Royal Highnesses were welcomed at the Main office block of Harland and Wolff by Walter Wilson, accompanied by Alexander Carlisle. Wilson's daughter presented a bouquet of flowers to the Duchess who was accompanied by William Pirrie in his role as Lord Mayor of Belfast. The workforce in the yard had been given the day off while the Royal party were shown around the newly expanded yard, taking in the Engine Works, Fitting and Brass shops, where they saw engines which were ready to be fitted into a ship. After seeing some of the various foundries, they were shown the oak saloon that was being constructed to go onto the *Briton* which was being fitted out. Finally the Royal couple saw the new *Oceanic* that was still being constructed on the slipway.

Later that afternoon, at around 4.00 pm, the Royal couple arrived at Ormiston House where thousands of school children had been brought to welcome the Royal visitors. The procession had come from another event at the Ormeau Park and was accompanied by the Inniskilling Dragoons and around 150 policemen. On their arrival Miss Agnes Carlisle, the sister in law of William Pirrie, greeted them in the Dining Room of the house where there were about 300 invited guests. During the reception a string band played as well as the band of the second Kings Liverpool Regiment. The Duke and Duchess finally left Ormiston at around 6.15 pm.

By 1899 the shipyard was now employing almost 10,000 men, and this year again saw Harland and Wolff break barriers when they, for the White Star Line, launched *Oceanic*. At almost 705 ft long it was the largest ship launched up to that date. When completely fitted out *Oceanic* weighed 17,274 tons.

The ship was launched from slipway number 8 at the Queen's yard, roughly about where the *Titanic* would later be built. The keel of the ship had previously been laid on 12 March 1897 and the ship had been the last one that had been designed by Sir Edward Harland before his death. Work on the ship was postponed until April 1898 due to the erection of the new gantry over the slipway. Harland's design was to make the ship 20 ft longer than Brunel's *Great Eastern* but by using the tried and tested 'Belfast Bottom' shape the hull would be 15 ft narrower and her depth nine feet less. The ship had over 1,500 ft of promenade decking and was designed to use around 700 tons of coal in her 96 furnaces, which fed the 15 boilers. 800 tons of steel alone was used for the construction of those boilers. It was calculated that the hull weighted 11,000 tons as it rested on the slipway and that 1323 shell plates had been riveted into place to make that hull. These plates were 28 ft long and 4½ ft wide. 1,704,000 rivets were used in this ship, the first in Ireland to be hydraulically riveted. It was stated that around 1,500 men had been engaged on her construction and fitting out. *Oceanic* had seven decks and space for 410, 200 second class and 1,000 steerage passengers, and 394 crew. Her first Captain was John Cameron.

The *Oceanic* was launched on Saturday 14 January 1899. Preparations for the launch had gone on for many weeks prior to that date. This was the first ship launched with the assistance of a hydraulic launch trigger. Under the direct supervision of Alexander Carlisle, a massive hydraulic ram was pushed into position under the bow of the hull, and the ram slotted into a shoulder that was specifically constructed in the hull. The ram exerted a force of 500 tons per square inch to stop the hull from moving until the actual launching. This was critically important, because workmen had to go under the hull and knock out all the keel blocks and prop shafts that were holding the hull in place.

The day of the launch turned out to be a beautiful sunny one, and draped over the gantry was the Union Jack alongside the American flag. A massive grandstand had been erected on the Victoria Wharf with seating for around 2,000 people. There was space for another 3,000 to stand and watch the launch. The shipyard took the decision to sell tickets, with the monies raised being given to the local Royal Victoria Hospital. All around the banks of the river Lagan people clambered for the best vantage point to witness the launch. It was estimated that somewhere between 25,000 and 150,000 people saw the *Oceanic* being launched. The press had been invited and came from all corners of the globe to report on the event. Management in the shipyard had made a very shrewd decision, to have the hull painted in a light colour, to make it stand out and look even bigger and more impressive for the Press. Her upper hull was later painted black. This launch was so special that six 'cinematographic artists' (camera crews) would record the scene for posterity. Thomas H. Ismay, Owner of the White Star Line and his wife had come over from England and stayed with the Pirrie's at Ormiston, before coming to see the launch. Gustav Wolff, Bruce and James Ismay, the Duke and Duchess of Ava, The Earl of Shaftsbury, Mr W.S. Graves of Ismay and Imrie, and many of the Belfast Harbour Commissioners joined them. James Henderson, the Lord Mayor of Belfast also attended, accompanied by several of the Belfast City Councilors.

A signal gun was fired to warn all the tugs and small boats in the river that the launch was about to happen and a further two signals were fired at 11.27

am when Mr Alexander M. Carlisle gave the go-ahead to begin the launching procedure. The hydraulic ram was released and the hull of the *Oceanic* slid down the slipway and into the water in less than a minute. As the hull entered the water it set up a larger than expected wash which surged towards where the spectators were standing at the grandstand – quite a few got wet feet! Sadly just as the hull was entering the water, a spectator called Mr William Rennie, a well know local engineer from the Malone area of Belfast, who was present with his daughter, collapsed and died from a heart attack. This death was a sad end to the day as the shipyard proudly boasted that the *Oceanic* was the first ship constructed in quite a long period of time in which no one was killed.

The nineteenth century was fast drawing to a close. The shipyard that Edward Harland started was now almost 39 years old. The yard had built and handed over 328 ships, averaging at just over eight ships a year. But by now the mastermind behind the shipyard Sir Edward Harland was dead, his financial backer Gustav Schwabe was also dead, and Thomas Ismay, one of Harland's best customers was seriously ill and died in November of 1899. In fact the White Star Line, under the leadership of Bruce Ismay, had to cancel an order to Harland and Wolff for the *Olympic*, which was destined to be the sister ship of the recently completed *Oceanic*. The order was cancelled as the shipping line, following the death of Thomas Ismay, was preparing themselves to pay the recently introduced death duties, a new form of taxation introduced by the Government.

The new century that was fast approaching would bring much hope for orders and prosperity. New men were replacing the old, productivity was high, the shipyard had been expanded, the workforce were now working 24 hours a day in eight hour shifts and surely in the coming years only good times could be ahead for this the biggest shipyard in Great Britain. Surely nothing could happen that would dent the confidence that was felt on the Queen's Island …

SS Oceanic *at the out fitting wharf.*
(© National Museums Northern Ireland, Collection Harland and Wolff, Ulster Folk and Transport Museum)

CHAPTER 13

The New Century

The Twentieth century got off to a great start, the shipyard had several orders on their books and they continued to amaze the public with the ships that they were building. Before the end of 1898, when Thomas Ismay was still alive, the yard had entered into a contract with him and his White Star Line to build ship number 335, the *Celtic*, which at 20,904 tons would be the largest ship in the world. The ship was constructed in the Queen's yard on slipway Number 2, the same one that was used for the *Oceanic*.

The *Celtic* was launched from Queen's Island on Thursday 4 April 1901. The shipyard continued with the policy of giving out free launch tickets to the Heads of Departments and the Foremen in the shipyard, while the general public could buy a ticket giving them access to the various vantage points. These public tickets were sold for one shilling (five pence) with all the proceeds being given over to the Queen Victoria Memorial Statue Fund. A souvenir programme was on sale for 3d (about 1 new penny). Strangely the workforce who actually built the ship were not allowed time off to see the launch. If a workman wished to see the launch he had to get permission from his Foreman, and then the workman had his wages docked by a half day's pay. There really weren't too many men in the yard who could afford to loose that amount of money from their pay packet, so it was most likely that the general productivity of the workforce dropped during the launch as they clambered for a suitable unseen vantage point from which to view the proceedings.

The specially invited guests at the launch included The Lord Mayor Sir Daniel Dixon and the

SS Celtic, *the largest ship in the world at its launch.*
(A&C Black publishing)

Lady Mayoress, Sir Otto Jaffe, the High Sheriff of Belfast, members of Belfast City Council and the Harbour Commissioners. As they arrived Gustav Wolff, William Pirrie and Walter Wilson greeted them at the main entrance. Bruce Ismay, his family and Officials of the White Star Line had arrived the previous evening in Belfast by ferry. Included amongst the dignitaries was Mr T. Moriarty the Chief Commissioner of the local police and from Comber, Mr Thomas Andrews senior, no doubt there to inspect the work of his brother in law William Pirrie and his son Thomas.

William and Margaret Pirrie made their way to the York Street railway station where they formally welcomed the Countess of Cadogan and her party who had travelled from England to witness the event. After taking the party to the Royal Hotel they were escorted by mounted police to the shipyard and to their seats in the specially constructed grandstand.

Again Alexander M. Carlisle was in charge of the launching operation, assisted by Head Foreman Mr Robert Keith.[1] There had been some concern that the launch should go well, because on the previous day, even though the hydraulic trigger was fully engaged under the hull, the *Celtic* had moved ½ inch down the slipway on its own, but then settled. Above the ship, flying from the gantry were the Union Jack, the Stars and Stripes and the flag of the White Star Line.

Prior to the launch there were three rockets fired, the first was to warn all ships in the river that the launch was imminent, the second was to warn all the tug boats and essential staff to be in place, and at 10.15 am the final rocket was fired which signalled that the hydraulic ram had been released and the ship allowed to slide down the ways. The launch took just over two minutes, from the moment the ram was released until the hull of the *Celtic* had stopped in the river. As usual and in keeping with White Star Line tradition there was no formal christening ceremony.

Following the launch the principal guests, including the Countess, were escorted to Pirrie's home at Ormiston where a luncheon was laid on. After the function William Pirrie escorted the Countess and her party to Great Victoria Street railway station, where she boarded the train for Dublin. Other guests were entertained in the Drawing Office in the Office Block in the shipyard. Later that evening Mr Williamson, 'a cinematographer' who had filmed the launch on behalf of local Belfast company, Erskine Mayne's, had his film publicly shown at the Ulster Hall, a ticket costing one shilling (5 pence) and all proceeds being given to the Queen Victoria Memorial Statue Fund.

The *Celtic* was a massive ship at 700 ft long, with a breadth of 75 ft and nine decks. The ship, as I have already said, was the last White Star Liner to be ordered by Thomas Ismay prior to his death, and the first of four new ships that the White Star Line were to use on the Liverpool to New York route, the other three being the *Cedric, Baltic* and *Adriatic*.

While the shipyard was continuing to attract orders, these new bigger and bigger ships that they were building were beginning to become too large for the two existing dry docks available on Queen's Island. The *Celtic* that had just been launched was close to the maximum length that could be accommodated in the Alexandra Dock and at the rate at which the shipyard was increasing the size of their ships it wouldn't be long before that dock would no longer be able to cope. Happily for the shipyard, the Belfast Harbour Commissioners, in the closing months of the old century, agreed to build a new dry dock adjacent to the Alexandra dock and the plans were that this new dock would be almost 900 ft long. To save costs it was decided to build the dock adjacent to the Alexandra dock so that it would share the same pump house. The pump house would have to be extended to cope with both docks, but this was a cheaper option than having to build a new pump house. As mentioned previously, the initial plans for the dock were decided in the last few months of 1899. The plans were confirmed, finally drawn up and a contract with Messers Walter Scott and Middleton of Westminster was signed in 1903.

With this contract in place and the work being paid for by the Belfast Harbour Commissioners, William Pirrie was now in a position to have the shipyard build massive ships up to 887½ ft long. The seed had been planted that would see the Olympic class ships being built. Work commenced on the construction of the Dock in 1904. The main contractor was Messers Walter Scott and Middleton of Westminister. The Chief Engineer was Mr W. Redfern Kelly J.P. M.Inst C.E. and the resident Engineer was Mr T.S. Gilbert M.Inst C.E.

The total cost of the seven year contract was in the region of £350,000, with 500 men being employed in the construction. Some idea of the sheer size of the dock can be seen in the amount of material excavated. Over 300,000 cubic yards of sand and clay were removed while 76,000 cubic yards of concrete, 24,000 cubic yards of brickwork and 36,000 cubic feet of granite stonework were all built into the structure.

It was originally envisaged that the work would take about three and a half years, but, due to unforeseen circumstances, this period of time was nearly doubled. One of the main reasons for the delay was the subsidence or collapse of the adjacent Alexandra dry dock on 4 October 1905. The Alexandra dock had to be closed for nearly two years to allow for repairs.

The new dock was able to accommodate ships up to 887 ft 6 inches. A detailed look at the dimensions gives a view of the enormous size of this structure:

Width at coping level	128 ft
Depth of floor below high tide level	32 ft 9 inches
Thickness of floor at centre	17 ft 6 inches
Thickness of walls at base	18 ft 9 inches
Volume of water when full	23 million gallons (aprox.)

When the project was first considered, plans were submitted for three sizes of dock, the first 750 ft, the second 800 ft and the third 850 ft in length. Eventually it was decided to build the largest. It was indeed fortunate that the Commissioners decided on this size or there would have been no dry dock large enough to accommodate the new breed of 'super ships' being planned by the shipyard. It should be pointed out that the length of the dock could be increased by another 37½ ft by placing the caisson (the water tight gate arrangement) on the outer face of the dock gate.

Three pumping engines, each of 1,000 horse power, were installed to pump the water out. An extra powerful pump was provided as a leakage engine for removing drainage water. The three pumps could drain the dock, when completely full of water in about 100 minutes. The volume of water contained in the dock when full was in the region of 23 million gallons or over 100 million litres. Normally only two pumps would work together with the third being held as an emergency standby. Four boilers were provided to power the pumps.

Two capstans with a 30 ton capacity and three with a 11 ton capacity were also provided. At no other dry dock in the world in 1911 were such large capacity capstans found. Even those in Admiralty yards would normally only be rated at about 16 tons. The entrance to the dock was closed by a large rectangular steel gate called the caisson, which was carried on two lines of heavy rollers. When the dock was flooded, the railings on top of the gate collapsed in on themselves and the whole structure, under hydraulic pressure, slid to the side to allow access. The capstans, the caisson (the main gate structure) and the water inlet sluices all worked by hydraulic power generated by two engines of 155 horse power with a working pressure of 750 psi or 51 bar. On the floor of the dock were laid 332 massive keel blocks of cast iron with timber capping pieces. On top of these blocks would rest the keel of the ship.

The Harbour Commissioners had also constructed a new large outfitting wharf close to the graving dock. Queen's Road had to be extended by over 300 ft and a new road 1,150 ft in length had to be built to allow access. A tramway was also laid, which could accommodate rolling loads of up to 150 tons.

A view from inside the Thompson Dock of the main cassion gate. To the left is one of the openings used to flood the dock.

The Commissioners had the channel at West Twin Island widened to allow the proposed new ships to turn, instead of having to turn in Belfast Lough. This work cost in the region of £9,400.

The river opposite the new timber outfitting wharf and the approaches to the entrance of the dry dock were dredged to a depth of 32 ft. Other contractors involved were the Belfast firms of McLaughlin and Harvey, who were responsible for the Pumping house and W.J. Campbell, who laid the brickwork and reinforced concrete.

It was decided that the new dock would be named the Thompson Dry Dock, after the then Chairman of the Belfast Harbour Commissioners, Robert Thompson. He was born in Ballylesson, County Down in 1839 and was named after his father who was a very successful linen manufacturer. After his formal education he entered the family business of Lindsay Thompson and Co. Ltd., where he eventually rose to be Chairman of the firm. Thompson was also involved in public life, he was Member of Parliament for Edward Harland's old constituency of North Belfast and was President of the Belfast Chamber of Commerce and the Flax Spinner's Association, Chairman of the Board of Governors of Campbell College, a Deputy Lieutenant for County Down and for 11 years he was Chairman of the Belfast Harbour Commissioners. He died in 1918.

Sir Robert Thompson, Chairman of the Belfast Harbour Commissioners, after who the dry dock was named.

(Courtesy of the Belfast Harbour Commissioners)

Whilst the Thompson Dock was being built the shipyard continued to produce bigger and bigger ships, but the rival shipping line Cunard had, for the first time, surpassed the White Star Line by having the *Lusitania* of 31,550 tons, built by Brown's shipyard on the Clyde in June 1906.

The *Adriatic,* which was launched at Queen's Island on 20 September 1906, was the last of four ships (the *Celtic, Cedric, Baltic* and *Adriatic*) that lovingly became known as the 'Big Four'. The shipyard had issued 10,000 invitations to the launch and spectators crowded around both sides of the river Lagan. Amongst the VIPs were the Dowager Marchioness of Dufferin and Ava, the Rt. Hon. Sir Antony MacDonnell, representatives of the Belfast City Council and the ship's owners the White Star Line. Suspended over the gantry and above the hull of the ship was the White Star Line flag, the Union Jack and the Stars and Stripes. While it was a dull and overcast day, this did not diminish the excitement of the crowd when, at 11.15 am, the signal was given to launch the hull. Under the supervision of Mr Alexander M. Carlisle, the hydraulic ram was released and the hull took only 45 seconds to enter the water, accompanied by much cheering from the spectators. No sooner had the ship been launched when a workman came to the end of the gantry and put up a notice that the next ship to be built in this the number 3 slipway would be ship number 390, the *Rotterdam* for the Holland America Line.

Once the hull was stopped in the river, three tugs, the *Jackal, Musgrave* and *Despatch*, towed the hull to the Alexandra wharf for fitting out. When completed the ship had nine decks, 11 watertight bulkheads, seven cargo holds and a refrigeration system for some cargo. There was accommodation for around 3,000 passengers and 350 Officers and crew. After the launch the guests were taken to Ormiston House and entertained with a luncheon which had been laid on by Chairman William Pirrie.

On this same day the Swan Hunter shipyard on the Tyne launched a new Cunarder, the *Mauretania,* a sister ship to the *Lusitania.* After its launch, Swan Hunter entertained their guests with refreshments in the rather dowdy surroundings of their moulding loft. Not a pick on Pirrie's good Belfast hospitality!

Now, in those first few years of the twentieth century, after William Pirrie had convinced the Harbour Commissioners to build the massive new Thompson Dry Dock, he was now able to continue his quest to have his shipyard build bigger and bigger ships. All he now had to do was to get a shipping line to sign up to buy this new super ship, and who better, than Bruce Ismay and his White Star Line.

CHAPTER 14

The Olympic Class Liners
The Beloved, the Dammed and the Forgotten

It has for a long time been felt that the decision to build the Olympic Class ships was made after dinner at William Pirrie's London home, Downshire House. The story goes that Pirrie and his wife Margaret had been entertaining the Ismay's, Bruce and Florence. After the meal, and no doubt after the two ladies had withdrawn, it was said that the two men discussed the building of this new class of ship and there and then drew out designs on the back of a serviette. There is no evidence to support this story, but it is in keeping with the way that business was conducted in those days. However, what can be proved is that on that evening, if William Pirrie had been playing a game of poker he had the deck well and truly stacked in his favour.

Pirrie later made a speech in Glasgow, in September 1922, at the Annual Dinner of The Clyde Trust. He spoke of the co-operation between the Harbour Commissioners and Harland and Wolff:

> "We have never built a ship that the Harbour Commissioners of Belfast had not built a graving dock ready to accommodate that vessel the day we launched her."[1]

As a member of the Harbour Commissioners, Pirrie used his position to ensure that the Commissioners made the correct decision regarding the new dock; it would be built to look after his and Harland's best interests. In his speech he said that Belfast had taken the lead in building big ships because the required dry dock space was available. He also disagreed with the suggestion that graving docks did not pay because no return was visible and asked the question could any profit from roads be seen? These docks, he concluded, were absolutely necessary appliances if they were to carry out, to their utmost degree, the building of ships.

On that night when Bruce Ismay had dinner with Pirrie, and then subsequently agreed to purchase two massive new ships, he was agreeing to do something that Pirrie had been scheming at since the Thompson Dry dock was first thought about; to build the Olympic class ships, which would be the biggest ships in the world.

All the pieces of the Olympic class jigsaw were falling into place, Pirrie had the Belfast Harbour Commissioners agree to build a dry dock to accommodate the increased size of the ships and Bruce Ismay had agreed to purchase the ships. Only one slight problem remained, where would Pirrie build them? Obviously the ships would be built in Belfast, but, and it was a big but, there were no slipways in the Harland and Wolff shipyard that could accommodate construction of the Olympic class. The shipyard in the early 1900s had nine slipways on which they could build ships. In the original Abercorn yard there were five slipways but the longest, number 6, could only accommodate the construction of a ship up to 698 ft long. There was another problem at the Abercorn yard, in that the number of buildings and workshops that had been constructed there would now make it impossible to extend any of the slipways to the length that would be required for the new ships. It would also have been nearly impossible to launch a ship of this proposed size in the limited space of the Abercorn basin.

A solution presented itself within the four slipways of Queen's yard. Number 2 was 706 ft long but also had the space to extend the slipways there to the required length. It was on this slip that the *Oceanic* had recently been built. However, there was a problem with this. Ship number 358, the *Adriatic,* was at that moment undergoing construction on this slip. The shipyard would thus have to wait until the ship was launched on the 20 September 1906 before work could commence on the next expansion.

Clearing of the other three slipways started before the *Adriatic* was launched and, once the number 2 slipway was clear, work began on digging up the old slips. Surprisingly, all the slipways in the Harland and Wolff yard had been built on hardcore that had only been compacted or flattened. This may not, by today's standards, seem much of a firm foundation, but they had been able to construct the hulls of larger and larger ships on them. However, now looking to the future and the probability of even heavier ships, they realised that they would need a far more substantial base on which to construct their slipways. Once the existing hard core was removed the workmen set about driving hundreds and hundreds of oak poles up to 40 ft in length into the soft muddy ground. On top of this was poured concrete to a depth of 4–4 ½ ft. This was the first time that concrete had been used as the base for a slipway. Also included into the slipway was a mini railway system, the tracks of which were also laid into the concrete. This mini railway system would later be used to transport equipment and material up to the gantry with horses pulling small bogies. The whole slipway was laid at an angle, sloping down towards to the water, for every foot travelled there was a drop of 3/8 of an inch. This would then give the slipway a drop from the head to the water of around 28 ft (8.53 m).

The plan to build these large ships would call for some new thinking in their construction. One thing that was decided was that the ship should be built under a large permanent gantry. Built into this new structure would be cranes that could lift parts and material up to where they were needed. It was also decided that there would be three slipways under this new gantry and they would be numbered 1–3.

An approach was made to the Glasgow firm of Sir William Arrol and Company. They were contracted to supply the gantry, which cost in the region of £100,000. Sir William Arrol (1839–1913) had previously built some massive steel structures, including the replacement bridge over the Tay River in Scotland after the previous one had collapsed in 1879 and the 1890 Forth rail Bridge at Edinburgh. The company was also involved with the construction of Tower Bridge over the Thames.

The new gantry that the Scottish company constructed became a massive landmark in the harbour area of Belfast. It was 840 ft long, 270 ft wide and 230 ft in height (256 m × 82 m × 70 m). There were three rows of towers, each spaced 120 ft (36.5 m) apart. The base of each tower was anchored into the concrete slipway and at the top steel girders were attached and locked the whole structure together. Built into the main gantry that straddled slipway numbers 2 and 3 were four electric lifts and ramps that would give the workforce access to the whole structure. On the very top was a massive crane with a jib 135 ft (41 m) long that could lift weights of up to five tons. A further ten cranes (five at each side) with a lifting capacity of five tons and six travelling cranes (three at each berth) with a lifting capacity of ten tons were incorporated in the design. Both number 2 and 3 slipways were able to construct ships up to 990 ft (301 m) long.

To the side of the main gantry and attached to it was the smaller number 1 slipway, which was 670 ft (204 m) long. This slipway was fitted with three travelling cranes, which again had a lifting capacity of ten tons. The whole structure was completed in early 1908.

With the order for two ships now confirmed, William Pirrie had briefed his design staff on what was required for the Olympic class ships. Before work commenced on the actual ship, a model of the proposed vessel had been created and was shown to the owners. Only then could work begin. On 16 December 1908, on the new number 2 slipway under the Arrol Gantry, workmen started to lay the keel of ship number 400, the *Olympic*. Building commenced on the *Olympic* and within three months the double bottom was complete. The hull had all the ribs attached and was fully framed on 20 November 1909. The riveters, caulkers and platers were extremely busy for the next four months, and by 15 April 1910, they had the ship's hull now fully plated and finished.

Throughout the construction of the *Olympic*, there were continuous meetings between the owners and the shipyard to decide on colour schemes or to make changes as construction continued. Alexander Carlisle, who at that time was the Chief Naval Architect and therefore responsible to Pirrie for the design of the ship, later recalled a meeting that he attended, in October 1909, less than a year after the keel was laid.

J. Bruce Ismay, Chairman of the White Star Line.
(© National Museums Northern Ireland, Collection Harland and Wolff, Ulster Folk and Transport Museum)

■ 122

Titanic *and* Olympic *in Arrol Gantry.*

(© National Museums Northern Ireland, Collection Hogg, Ulster Museum Belfast)

Present at the meeting were J. Bruce Ismay and Mr Harold Saunderson for the White Star Line, Carlisle and William Pirrie. The meeting lasted around four hours and Carlisle pointed out to those present, that there were not enough lifeboats being provided in the design. He some time previously had done the very simple sum of comparing the number of passengers and crew with the planned lifeboat capacity, which showed even then that there was not enough space for all the people who could be accommodated on this new ship. From memory he said that out of the four hours duration of the meeting, there was only a discussion for a matter of 5–10 minutes regarding the number of the lifeboats to be supplied and fitted, the rest of the meeting he recalled was given over to what the internal decorations of the ship would be. He also came up with a plan to be able to place four lifeboats at each davit, if the Board of Trade agreed, but this was also dismissed by the other three men at the meeting.[2]

The hull of *Olympic* was launched on Thursday 20 October 1910, and when fully fitted out the ship was the largest ship in the world. This was to be a momentous day for William Pirrie and his shipyard. The Cunard Line had taken the lead by

having the *Lusitania* and *Mauretania* built, but on this day, here in Belfast, Pirrie and the White Star Line were about to make a very bold gesture with the launch of the first of two ships that would make up the Olympic Class liners. In order to emphasise this point, Harland and Wolff went to the additional expense of painting the entire *Olympic* hull white, in order to make it stand out, look even bigger and more impressive than it was.

For weeks prior to the launch date, the shipyard was preparing itself. Special grandstands were erected, one for the ship's owners, the White Star Line, and their visitors; another for the guests of Harland and Wolff; and of course one for the members of the Press who were coming to record the launch. Over 100 reporters came, representing newspapers in the United Kingdom, Europe and America. All of these grandstands were decorated with white and crimson cloth. Special permission was sought from the neighbouring shipyard of Workman Clark to set up staging for a local photographer to record a 'cinematographic' record of the launch. For some time prior to the launch it was possible to purchase a ticket which gave access to a special enclosure from which the ceremony could be seen from close quarters. Around 5,000 tickets were made available for public sale, raising £435, which was donated to the local Royal Victoria Hospital.

To ensure that the hull of the vessel would not foul on the riverbed during launch, the Belfast Harbour Commissioners had decided to deepen the River Lagan at the Queen's yard. For almost a week prior to launch they dredged the river to a depth of around 50 ft.

From very early in the morning crowds of spectators starting arriving at both sides of the Lagan. The Lord Lieutenant of Ireland and the Countess of Aberdeen had been specially invited and travelled by special train from Dublin to the railway station at Great Victoria Street in Belfast, where William Pirrie welcomed them, before travelling by carriage to the shipyard at Queen's Island. Over 300 men from the Royal Irish Constabulary were on duty, mainly engaged in the role of crowd control due to the large numbers that were expected to attend. Also present were the Lord and Lady Mayor of Belfast, Mr and Mrs R.J. McMordie, many Officials from the Belfast City Council and Miss Asquith, the daughter of Prime Minister Herbert Asquith. The Officials from the Belfast Harbour Commissioners had gone on board the *SS Musgrave* in order to get a better view. The overnight steamer from Fleetwood also arrived early in the morning with J. Bruce Ismay, the Directors of the White Star Line and their special guests on board.

However, while all the invited guests and spectators were gathering in eager anticipation of the launch, there was an amount of grumbling going on in the shipyard because a few days previously an instruction banning all the workforce from having time off to witness the launch had been typed up and was displayed throughout the shipyard. It stated, that any workman found 'downing tools' to catch a glimpse of the proceedings, could face dismissal, even if he had previously worked on or in the hull. The workforce, however, would have been pretty sure that, at the moment the largest hull in the world slid down the slipway, all Foremen's eyes would be watching the hull and that they would not be in a position to see any workmen 'sneaking a quick look'.

The Union Jack, the Stars and Stripes, the house flag of Harland and Wolff and the White Star Line Flag were flown high above on the Arrol Gantry, and coded flags spelt out the words Good Luck.

For the first time in many years, Alexander Carlisle did not oversee the launch. He had been off work for sometime and was said to be resting prior to coming back to the shipyard. In his absence, the responsibility for supervising the launch was entrusted to Mr Charles Payne, a Director of the yard. In this position he had a responsibility for over 100 men, who since early morning had been undertaking the dangerous task of removing the keel blocks under the hull. In this role Payne was assisted by Mr R.F. Keith, who was the head Foreman Carpenter and who had previously assisted Alexander Carlisle in the same role for many previous launches. Payne also had to keep a very careful watch on the pressure for the hydraulic rams as any sudden drop in pressure could result in the ram failing and the hull launching before its time.

Launch of Olympic.
(© National Museums Northern Ireland, Collection Hogg, Ulster Museum Belfast)

The White Star Line had a very clear policy with regard to the launching of their ships. They, unlike other shipping lines, did not believe in a christening ceremony and, apart from the first two ships launched, no other White Star Line ship launched from Harland and Wolff ever had a bottle of champagne broken over its bows nor ever had the words "I name this ship *Olympic*, may God bless her, and all who sail in her" spoken during a launch.

At 10.50 am two rockets were fired and their exploding signalled that the launch was imminent. At exactly 11.00 am a further single rocket was fired and over the noise of it exploding could be heard the voice of William Pirrie shouting from the grandstand "Now".[3] From this signal Charles Payne then released the launch trigger. For just a second or two nothing happened and then the hull, which weighted around 27,000 tons, started down the slipway. It took only 62 seconds for the hull to enter the water and a further 45 seconds before the 80 tons of drag chains and six anchors brought the hull to a complete stop in the water.

In keeping with tradition, the shipyard, prior to the launch, referred to the ship as *SS 400*, the number that the vessel was given when it was ordered. It was only when the launch took place and the vessel was in the water that it would be called by its name, so whether the White Star Line knew it or not, at just after 11.01 am on 20 October 1910, the *SS Olympic* was traditionally named. The ship would later lovingly be given the nickname of the 'Beloved', as she gave 25 years service before being scrapped.

Workmen rowed out to the hull, removed the wooden launch cradle and then towed it to the newly completed outfitting wharf adjacent to the new Thompson Dry Dock. It was here that the shipyard had a floating crane, purchased second hand, that was capable of lifting weights of around 150 tons.

A special luncheon was hosted by William Pirrie at the shipyard at Queen's Island for the V.I.P. guests, which included the Lord Lieutenant and the Countess of Aberdeen, and the Lord Mayor and Lady Mayoress. The press were transported to the Grand Central Hotel in Royal Avenue in Belfast and there Mr Saxon J. Payne, a Director of the shipbuilders, and Mr R. Sherry, representing the owners, hosted a luncheon for the reporters and photographers.

While the launch of the *Olympic* was happening, work had been suspended on the two adjacent slipways, under the Arrol Gantry. In slipway number 1 was ship number 422, the *Nomadic*, the 1,260 ton passenger tender that would be required to serve the Olympic class ships at Cherbourg in France. The problem that faced the White Star Line was that these new ships were too big to bring into the French harbour, so to solve the problem, it was decided that two tenders would be built and that they would ferry the passengers from the harbour out to the ships as they were moored in the bay. The second tender *Traffic* was at the same time being constructed at number 7 slipway in the older Abercorn yard at the Abercorn Basin. In the number 3 slipway beside Olympic was the *Titanic*, which by now had its hull just one day away from being fully plated.

Titanic was finally ready for launch on 31 May 1911 and that day was selected for a couple of reasons. Firstly it was the joint birthday of William and Margaret Pirrie and also the *Olympic, Nomadic* and *Traffic* were all ready for handing over to the White Star Line.

Prior to the launch, the Directors of the Shipyard met and it was agreed that the launching of the *Titanic* would follow the same pattern as that of the *Olympic*. To make the launch go smoothly was a compliment to the organisation within the yard. Careful prior planning had been going on for several months before the actual launch date and many things required meticulous attention to detail:

- The owners of the vessel were written to about 10 days before the launch informing them of the proposed date and time of the proceedings. They were asked to specify whether any guests would be crossing to Belfast. Arrangements were then made for seating in the grandstands for those invited guests.
- Soundings were taken in the channel at the bottom of the slip, and the Belfast Harbour Commissioners made arrangements to have the area dredged. There would be nothing more embarrassing than to send the vessel down the slip only to see it run aground if the channel was not deep enough.
- Various local groups were informed of the proceedings, including The Belfast Harbour Commissioners, The Board of Trade, Lloyds of London and The Belfast Harbour Master.
- Any buoys in the water in the line of the launch had to be removed.
- Mooring ropes had to be provided.
- A flag pole was to be placed at the stern of the vessel and flags supplied and placed on board in good time.
- Ladders and fenders were placed on the vessel's side.
- A check was made to ensure that the derricks and any other guys were clear of the launch area.
- The boom at the end of the slip had to be hauled away in good time prior to the launch.
- A fitter was to ensure that the Ballast tank manholes were closed. After the launch, a caulker was to inspect the Peaks and Hold tanks to ensure they were dry.
- Two flag boats and tugs with a number of men had to be organised and in position to move the vessel after launch and have it towed to the fitting out wharf.
- Steam apparatus that was needed to assist with the launch had to be ordered and in place and got up to working pressure.
- A large notice was to be placed adjacent to the hull of the vessel stopping men working on board.
- A few days before the launch meetings were organised with the yard foremen and the Captain of the Tug to finalise last minute problems.
- Provision needed made for a cable to be sent to the owners advising them that

the vessel had been safely launched.

The final checks were completed long before Lord Pirrie and the other Directors arrived at the slipway.

On the day of the launch, Pirrie, the professional businessman with a broad Belfast accent that never left him, gave everything a final look over. This firm of his was the number one ship building yard in Britain, and it was important for Pirrie and Harland and Wolff that all went well at the launch. That was why the long and detailed checks were made, so that Pirrie could make the launching ceremony look easy. It had to look as if they 'just shoved 'er in', and with the yard's dedication and sheer professionalism it just seemed like that.

Just like previous launches, the shipyard offered tickets for sale, allowing members of the public to gain access to a special enclosure to witness the ceremony. All monies raised were given to local hospitals.

Extra trams were laid on by the Belfast Corporation starting at 10.30 am, and leaving from Castle Junction to Pilot Street, opposite the Queen's Quay, to accommodate the thousands of spectators that were expected to watch the launch. Extra ferries crossing the river were also provided from the Abercorn and Milewater Basin.

The Managing Directors issued another instruction in May 1910 in connection with any future launchings.

NOTICE

After this date any of the staff or their friends wishing to witness a launch must send in an application on a Question and Answer reply form, the day prior to the launch to his Superior, unless he has an actual duty to perform in connection with the said launch and has instructions either from his Superior or from one of the Managing Directors.

Any violation of this rule will mean dismissal.
26th May 1910 [4]

This was a major change from the instruction that was given at the launch of *Olympic,* where no one was allowed time off to see the launch. However, what the new instruction failed to mention was that if you did take time off, it was with no pay, so maybe not too many men would take up the offer.

Launch day for *Titanic* on 31 May 1911 was a glorious one. The list of distinguished guests included Chairman William Pirrie and his wife Margaret; J. Peirpoint Morgan, the American owner of the International Mercantile Marine Company which had taken over the White Star Line in 1902; and J. Bruce Ismay, the Chairman of the White Star Line, along with members of his family and fellow

Directors Mr Sanderson and Mr Graves. Also present for the first time was the new Chief Designer of Harland and Wolff, Thomas Andrews. The Lord and Lady Mayor of Belfast, Mr and Mrs McMordie, who had also been present at *Olympic's* launch, were also special guests. Mrs McMordie was later to be responsible for starting a fund to provide money for the Belfast Titanic Memorial.

The owner's gallery had been set up at the port side of *Titanic*, and was draped in white and crimson. Three other stands had been erected at the end of the yard opposite the bows of the ship. One was reserved for the hundreds of Pressmen who had travelled from as far as London and America to report on the event. The other two stands were for V.I.P. ticket holders who had to be seated by noon (the gates to the stands were opened at 11.00 am).

During the morning, gangs of men were busy removing the wooden props which supported the ship. A heavy clanging was heard all around the ship. Just before noon William Pirrie left the owners stand to make a last inspection of the ship and the launching equipment. Over the bow of the ship flew the White Star flag and a coded signal spelling the word 'SUCCESS'.

At 12.05 a red flag was hoisted at the stern. Five minutes later two rockets were fired and shortly afterwards a third rocket was also released. As usual, no one broke a bottle of champagne over the ship's bow nor did anyone utter the words "May God bless her ..." However, there was a report in one of the local papers that quietly from her seat in the spectators stand, Mrs Bruce Ismay said the words "I name this ship *Titanic* and may God bless her and all who sail in her."

At 13 minutes past midday ship number 401 started her way down the slipway and took only 60 seconds to enter the water. Large anchors had been driven into the bed of the river, with steel hawsers fastened to eye plates on board *Titanic,* so the hull was pulled to a halt in the water in less than one half of her own length.

The men watching the ceremony took off their caps and hats and cheered, while the large number of ladies waved their handkerchiefs excitedly. The men shouted themselves hoarse. Gradually the cheering stopped and within 15 minutes of *Titanic* coming to a stop in the water, the crowds of many thousands had dwindled away.

The launch weight of *Titanic* was around 26,000 tons and, within one hour of the launch, *Titanic* had been towed to and berthed at the outfitting Wharf. A special celebration luncheon hosted by William Pirrie was provided for the distinguished guests at Queen's Island, while the Press and other guests, would dine at the Grand Central Hotel in Royal Avenue, Belfast.

The hull of *Titanic* had been safely launched and the *Olympic, Nomadic* and *Traffic* were now completed and ready to be handed over to their owners, the White Star Line. However, it was not just quite as simple as that. For weeks clerks and managers in the shipyard had been busy making the final preparations for this special hand over of not one ship but three. Just as there was a lengthy checklist to be gone through before a vessel was launched, so too there was a

comprehensive checklist to be completed before a ship departed from the works at Queen's Island. This included a check on the freeboard and final check on the tonnage; the passenger certificate was inspected; and all tanks were filled. Tests were also run on the following:

Weather decks	Electric lights
Tunnels	Electric heaters
Derricks	Electric searchlights
Cargo cranes	Masthead lights
Steering gear and winches	Sidelights
Steam fans	Freshwater system
Watertight doors	Refrigeration system
Fire extinguishers	Sanitary system
Galley ranges	Ballast system
Telephone systems	Steam heaters and winches[5]

The shipyard also ensured that ropes, flags, charts, compasses and parallel

Titanic in slipway prior to launch. This photograph is unusual in that it shows women walking near to the ship in the gantry, while a workman is shown in the foreground.

(© National Museums Northern Ireland, Collection Harland and Wolff, Ulster Folk and Transport Museum)

rulers for the bridge were on board. The office staff sent orders to the various departments in the shipyard to ensure that the following preparations were made for departure day:

- Steam was provided for the fitted ships winches.
- Tugs were provided to assist the ship's passage down the lough.
- Compasses were adjusted.
- A request was made for a boat and pilot for the tow ropes.
- The crew that would man the vessel was assembled.
- Riggers and labourers were assembled to see the vessel safely down the lough.
- Provisions for the vessel were ordered.
- Meals for the departing crew were arranged; they would be supplied by the shipyard's dining room.
- A telegram was to be sent to Lord Pirrie, informing him when the vessel was safely down the lough and when it safely reached its destination.
- The owners were notified of the time of departure.[6]

Later in the afternoon of 31 May the *Olympic* set sail, heading for her registered port of Liverpool. On arrival, the ship was opened to the public to allow them to marvel at the style and interior decorations incorporated in this new ship. *Nomadic* and *Traffic* made their respective ways to Cherbourg in France, where they were placed into service to ferry passengers to the ships when they called at the French port.

The fitting out of *Titanic* then began at the outfitting wharf just vacated by the *Olympic*. This new class of ships were to have the most luxurious fittings provided for the comfort of the passengers.

In June 1912, just eight weeks after the loss of the *Titanic*, Saxon J. Payne, a Managing Director of the shipyard wrote to John Andrews telling him what news the shipyard had received about his brother Thomas. Also in the letter he gave quite a detailed description of the *Titanic*. This was intended for Shan Bullock, who was preparing to write his biography on Thomas Andrews:

> "Whilst Mr Andrews had had an important and leading share in the design and construction of numerous large steamers and at the time of his death had many large shipbuilding projects in hands, his most important work was in connection with the two White Star liners – the *Olympic* and the sister ship in which he unfortunately lost his life.
>
> These two vessels by universal consent represented the highest skill and perfection yet reached in Naval architecture. They were replete with every modern contrivance for efficiency combined with the latest developments in the art of shipbuilding and marine engineering, and the character and luxury of their appointments will probably never be surpassed. Costing about £1,500,000 each the two ships represented a capital of three million stg.
>
> The *Titanic* was 882.7 ft in length overall and 92.5 ft extreme breadth. The

depth of the Hold 59.58, the nett registered tonnage was about 21,831 and the gross tonnage 46,329 – the displacement at load draft being 52,310 tons. The length of the Engine Room was 123 ft. The depth from the keel to the Navigating Bridge was about 96'-8" and the depth from the bottom of the keel to the top of the funnels about 173 ft. As conveying some idea of the spacious character of the internal arrangements, the height between the Saloon and Shelter decks was 10'-6" amidships – an extraordinary height in a ship. The boat deck was nearly 500'-0" long and the Promenade deck which was the deck below was over 500'-0" in length.

The passenger accommodation was arranged for the following persons:-

1st	Class passengers		1034
2nd	"	"	510
3rd	"	"	1022
		Total	2,566

A grand total of 3,510 souls as the full compliment of passengers and crew could be carried.

The structure of the vessel was an exceedingly strong one, she was built throughout of steel and had a cellular double bottom with a floor at every frame, its depth at the centre line being 63" for the most part, but 78" in way of the main reciprocating engines. For about half of the length of the vessel, this double bottom extended high enough up the ship's side to protect the bilges, and the bilge plating was doubled. Forward and aft of the machinery space the construction was of the usual type where it extended from bilge to bilge, it was so divided that there were four separate tanks athwartships, before and abaft the machinery space it was divided by a watertight division at the centre line except in the foremost and aftermost tanks. This part of the vessel's structure was all exceptionally well strengthened, also being hydraulic riveted throughout, including the shell plating for the half length in way of the machinery space. Above the double bottom the vessel was constructed on the usual web frame system, some of the web frames extending to the highest decks.

Beams were fitted on every frame at all decks, from the Boat Deck downwards, to ensure the maximum strength and freedom from vibration, and also a bilge keel about 300 ft long, and 25" deep, was fitted along the bilge amidships, this materially stiffening the bilge plating.

The heavy ship's side plating was carried right up to the Bridge Deck, and between the Shelter and Bridge deck was doubled, and the stringer or edge plate of the Bridge Deck was also doubled, and these doubled plates were hydraulic riveted so as to provide ample strength. All decks were steel plated throughout.

The ship was further considerably strengthened by 15 transverse watertight bulkheads which were specially stiffened and strengthened to enable them to stand considerable pressure in the event of accident, and also were very strongly connected by large double angles to decks, inner bottom, and shell plating, with the same object.

Five of the decks were continuous all fore and aft, and there were ten decks in all. In connection with the watertight sub-division there were a number of watertight doors for access from one space to another, these doors being electrically controlled from the Captain's Bridge, and when the accident happened these were duly closed but unfortunately so many compartments had been ripped open by the iceberg that Mr Andrews appeared to have realised the ship was doomed, and whilst judiciously avoiding any panic, did everything possible to induce the passengers to take to the boats while he with his staff and the engineers of the ship heroically endeavoured to keep the ship afloat as long as possible.

The pumping arrangements in the ship were more complete than fitted in any other vessel except the *Olympic*, and all the other auxiliary machinery such as Telegraphs, Steering Gear, Winches, Hoists, Refrigerating Plant, electrical Installation, fans, etc, were of the most advanced type.

The first class Public rooms such as Dining Saloon, Restaurant, Lounge, reception Room, Smoke Room, Reading and Writing Room, etc, were unusually spacious, the Dining Saloon extending the full width of the ship and seating 500 people, the Restaurant also seating a large number, and the size and magnificence of the other rooms being in keeping therewith.

The first class staterooms were most luxuriously furnished and decorated in different styles, Louis XIV, Adams, Georgian, Louis XV, Queen Anne, Louis VXI and Italian Renaissance.

The first class accommodation included a Gymnasium, Swimming Bath, and Squash Racquets Court. It is impossible to indeed adequately describe the decorations in the first class Passenger Accommodation, they were on a scale of unprecedented magnificence. Even in second class the accommodation was unusually fine and the Dining Saloon also extended the full breadth of the ship and seated 400 people. The third class accommodation in its turn was of a superior character, equal to Saloon accommodation of an earlier period in Ocean ships.

The staircases in the ship constituted one of the principal features and the various decks served by spacious electric elevators were reached without physical exertion.

The vessel had a most imposing yet withal graceful appearance, with her four funnels, two masts towering superstructure and fine lines."[7]

The latter part of 1911 was a busy time. Fitting out was proceeding on the *Titanic*, when, in September, the *Olympic* had a serious collision in Southampton water with *HMS Hawke*, a Royal Naval cruiser. The *Olympic*'s hull was quite seriously damaged on the starboard side and it was decided that the ship would have to come back to Belfast to facilitate repairs. She required being dry docked and therefore her repair work could not be carried out at the works at Southampton. The following month the White Star Line signed a contract for the third of the Olympic class ships, the *Britannic*.

Olympic arrived back in Belfast on 6 October and, following an extensive survey on her damaged hull, it was agreed that the *Titanic* should be moved out of the Thompson Dry Dock to allow the *Olympic* to have the repair work carried out on her hull. During the repair work on the *Olympic* a very curious incident

THE OLYMPIC CLASS LINERS

occurred when Joseph Sharpe, a leading hand boilermaker, was shot three times in the leg in the boiler room of the ship. Even stranger yet, Sharpe was shot by a good friend of his called Edward John Wilson.

Due to the amount of repair work that had to be undertaken, the shipyard had decided that the best thing to do was to offer overtime to the workforce, in order to get the work done in as short a time as possible. It appeared that Sharpe as the charge hand was being offered the overtime, while Wilson, as a boilermaker wasn't. Wilson at that time was having major personal problems at home, his wife and youngest child were seriously ill and he needed every penny he could get for the Doctors bill. He complained that he thought it unfair that Sharpe should get the overtime and he didn't, and the Foreman promptly sacked Wilson for insubordination. This, of course, did not go down well with Wilson. Not only did he lose out on the overtime but now he also lost his job as well. Wilson, who was described by his work mates as a quiet and decent man, seemingly couldn't take this extra strain. He decided that it was all Sharpe's fault and that he would get even with him.

We will never know how he procured the revolver, but armed with it, Wilson set off looking for his revenge. In the late evening of 18 November 1911 the sacked Wilson walked down Queen's Road, getting more and more agitated with every step he was taking. He came across James Stewart, a Foreman, and asked him if he knew where Sharpe was. Stewart told him that he was in the boiler room of the *Olympic*. As he made off Wilson showed Stewart the revolver and told him that he was going to blow Sharpe's brains out. Stewart took a short cut to the ship in a bid to warn Sharpe about what was happening. Wilson eventually found Joseph Sharpe in the boiler room, went up to him and told him to come out of the boiler room as he had something he wanted to say. Sharpe replied that, if he had anything to say, he should say it now. Wilson then put his hand in his pocket and pulled out the gun, Sharpe jumped at him and both men fell on the floor, then Wilson fired the gun, which hit Sharpe in the left thigh. Wilson got up and shot again this time hitting Sharpe just below the right knee. Wilson managed to get off a third shot again, hitting Sharpe in the right leg before he was overpowered by workmen and handed over to the Harbour Police. As he was led away in handcuffs, he said, "I am sorry for what I did, is the injured man dead?"[8]

On 14 March 1912 at a Belfast Court, Edward John Wilson was charged that he feloniously, unlawfully and maliciously did shoot at one Joseph Sharpe to do grievous bodily harm. He pleaded guilty and the verdict of the Court was that he be bound over with a surety of £20 to be forfeited if he did not keep the peace and be of good behaviour for the next two years. This he did. The Court did not appear to be too concerned from where Wilson had obtained the handgun. At that particular period of time, with the Home Rule debate and the general feeling, it would not have been too difficult to acquire a gun at the right price.

Repair work was completed on the *Olympic* and the ship departed Belfast on

20 November 1911 to resume service with the White Star Line. Just ten days later at slipway number two, where *Olympic* had been constructed, quietly and without ceremony the keel for ship number 433, the *Britannic*, was laid down. Since that time there has been much debate as to how the name of this third ship in the Olympic Class came about. Several sources have claimed that the ship was to be called *Gigantic*, but that following the sinking of the *Titanic* and the large loss of life incurred in April 1912, it was then felt that this was unsuitable. There may be some truth in this when you consider that the first two ships' names were drawn from the Greek Olympus and the Titans. The *Gigantic* may well have been named after the Gigantes, the Greek giants. However, from my research into the surviving Harland and Wolff documents in Belfast, I can find no evidence anywhere that states that the name was ever anything but *Britannic*. Then again, as I explained in the Introduction, many of the records of the shipyard were lost in the 1922 fire in Public Record Office in Dublin and also as a result of the bombing of Belfast in the Second World War.

Prior to the fitting out of *Olympic*, the shipyard had installed many new workshops at the outfitting wharf to accommodate the additional workmen that were needed. This allowed the fitting out to continue promptly on *Titanic*. The Harbour Commissioners had also arranged for a new electrical sub station to be built because of the additional demand for electricity. By the end of February 1912, the *Titanic* had her radio installed and the 16 lifeboats and four collapsible Engelhard lifeboats had been placed on board. All of this work had to be stopped

Arrol Gantry from Queen's Road.

(Courtesy of the *Belfast Newsletter*)

when *Olympic* returned to Belfast on 1 March, for a second occasion, this time to replace a blade that had fallen off one of her propellers in the mid Atlantic. The *Titanic* had to be moved out of the Dry Dock and tied up at the outfitting wharf while the *Olympic's* replacement blade was fitted. In just under a week the work on *Olympic* was complete and, on 7 March, the two ships parted company for the very last time.

The *Olympic's* repair slowed the final fitting out of the *Titanic*, consequently delaying both its departure date from Belfast and its maiden voyage. There are many 'what if's in the tale of the *Titanic* but perhaps if the *Olympic* had not had the accident with *HMS Hawke*, *Titanic* might not have been delayed by *Olympic's* repairs, might have left Belfast on time, set out on her maiden voyage earlier and might never have even seen, let alone hit an iceberg.

Edward Smith, the Captain of the new *Titanic* arrived in Belfast along with his senior Officers at the beginning of the last week in March. In Southampton, Captain H.J. Haddock, a Captain with the White Star Line, assembled 16 crew members, amongst them a Frederick Fleet, the lookout who would first spot the fatal iceberg. These men all signed the ship's Articles in Southampton, with Haddock signing first and giving his position as Master, thereby making him the

135

Plans of the Harland and Wolff shipyard in 1912.

(*Shipbuilder Magazine*, 1912)

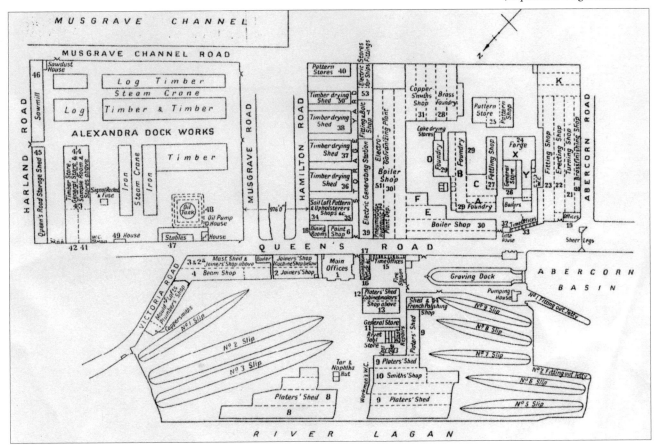

first Captain of the *Titanic*. When they arrived in Belfast, Smith and his senior Officers signed on, followed by the crew that would take over the ship.

During that week there were many meetings between the senior crew and officials of Harland and Wolff. Charles Lightoller, the ship's eventual Second Officer, witnessed a demonstration of lowering of the lifeboats which was overseen by Francis Carruthers, the Board of Trade Surveyor. The two Marconi operators, Jack Philips and Harold Bride, set about testing the new radio equipment and sending and receiving messages.

Rather strangely, Harland and Wolff (at that time) considered the sea trials of a new ship to be somewhat a waste of time. This originated from an idea held by Edward Harland that sea trials, no matter how long or short they were, would only give a snap shot view of a ship and its system's performance. He argued that the maiden voyage at sea would give a more balanced picture of how the vessel was working. This view of Harland's was implemented for many years and consequently all sea trials only lasted for a maximum of one day.

The *Titanic*'s sea trials were originally set for 1 April 1912, but when the day came there were high winds and the weather was bad. The Captain and the Harland and Wolff officials constantly monitored the situation, hoping for a break in the poor conditions, but by mid afternoon it was obvious that the weather was not going to change. A decision was taken to cancel the trials and put them back to the following day. Some of the crew had been on board since 4.00 am, and when they were dismissed they were paid an additional 25p per day detention pay.

As the second of April dawned the weather was much improved and the decision was made to conduct the sea trials. On board for the trials was the representative of the Board of Trade, Mr Francis Carruthers, as well as Edward Wilding from Harland and Wolff. Also on board was Thomas Andrews with the local members of the guarantee group: William Parr, Roderick Chisholm, Artie Frost, Robert Knight, William Campbell, Ennis Watson, Francis Parkes and Alfie Cunningham. These men formed a group of assorted trades employed in the yard and were selected to sail on the maiden voyage of the ship to correct any small faults that may occur. They were picked because of their skills and dedication to their work and selection was seen as a feather in their cap, with the very strong possibility of promotion on return to Belfast.

Before the *Titanic* set sail, Mr Carruthers carried out a full inspection of the ship. He and Second Officer Charles Lightoller examined the lifeboats, all of which were swung out and lowered. Fifth Officer Harold Lowe and Sixth Officer James Moody took an inventory of the lifeboats and their contents on the port side, and Third Officer Herbert Pitman and Fourth Officer Joseph Boxhall did the same for those on the starboard side. Mr Carruthers then had one of the anchors lowered and rehoused, and he and Lightoller also inspected the bulkheads and the watertight doors.

The *Titanic*'s sea trials got under way at 6.00 am and lasted for just over 12 hours. She sailed out of Belfast Lough and headed south into the Irish Sea, passing the Copeland Islands and Donaghadee. The *Titanic* was set for various tests – she went from slow speed to full speed; she was put astern – this would fully test the engines; she was put through a series of circling trials; she was tested with her port propeller going full astern while the starboard propeller was set full ahead. A speed run, where she reached speeds of up to 21 knots, and a full stop test were also carried out. At around 6.00 pm she returned to Belfast Lough for the short journey back to Belfast, arriving at about 7.00 pm. Mr Carruthers then completed his 'Report of Survey' for the ship.

The normal procedure for the sea trials was to steam north out of Belfast Lough and sail towards Glasgow. Such trials would normally last for a complete day, but due to the bad weather on 1 April this northern route was dropped for the quicker southerly route.

Before the *Titanic* set sail for Southampton, Harland and Wolff handed over plans and relevant documents to the crew.

Captain Smith was issued with the following set of plans:

Water Tight Doors	Cargo Capacity
Fire Connections	Ballast Tank Board
Plugs in Ship's Bottom	Fresh Water Tank Scales
Displacement Scale	Stability Curves
Docking Outline Plans	Rigging Plans
General Arrangement Plans	

Chief Officer Joseph Bell was issued with the following set of plans:

Water Tight Doors	Discharges Through Ships Side
Fire Connections	Ventilation Plans
Ballast Tank Board	Pipe Plan Arrangement
Plugs in Ships Bottom	Telemotor Instructions
Fresh Water Tank Scales	Steam Steering Gear House
Bunker Capacity Plan	Bilge and Tank Suction Plans[9]

Finally, White Star Line were presented with a complete set of all plans of their new vessel. It was also the policy of Harland and Wolff to make a small payment to the Captain and Chief Officer of each new ship that they handed over. The shipyard hoped that the recipient would be able to purchase a small souvenir of their visit to Belfast.

At 8.00 pm on Tuesday 2 April, the *Titanic* left Belfast and set out on the short voyage to Southampton.

On board also were over 400 crew, including 107 Firemen, 12 Greasers, one Storekeeper, two Room Attendants, 53 Trimmers, 12 Stokers and 29 Able Seamen as well as one Boatswain, six Lookouts and six Quarter Masters.

Among these there were quite a few Ulster men, some of whom were:

Joseph Beattie	Stoker, but later engaged as a Greaser
Hugh Calderwood	Trimmer
Thomas Graham	Fireman
John Haggan	Fireman
Robert Hopkins	Able Seaman
William McQuillan	Fireman
Patrick Morgan	Fireman
William Murdoch	Fireman
Richard Turley	Fireman

Construction on ship number 433, the *Britannic*, the third sister continued. By the time *Titanic* had left Belfast, the double bottom of the *Britannic* was completed. The vessel was fully framed by 27 February 1913 and fully plated (the hull completed) by 20 September in the same year.

However, the loss of the *Titanic* was to have a major impact on the construction of the *Britannic*. Immediately following the tragic loss, all work was scaled down until the shipyard could consider the outcome of the public inquiry held in London by Lord Mersey. There were several major changes incorporated into the design of the ship. The hull was constructed with a double skin, which ran right up to the top of the watertight bulkheads. The existing double bottom, which was 5 ft deep, was increased in size to 6 ft. The watertight bulkheads were also increased in height and new arrangements put in place for pumping out water.

For the first time in the construction of the three Olympic class ships, the *Britannic* had 'plumbed in' hot water to the suites as well as having the sewage from all over the ship pumped out. The Marconi radio mast was extended to 200 ft, allowing the ship to transmit radio signals up to 2,000 miles. Also included were standby batteries in case of a power failure. Pneumatic pipe work was fitted between the Radio room and the Bridge to speed up the transfer of messages. A brand new type of davit was added whereby the ship could be fitted with 48 lifeboats, two of which had independent engines. The davits were designed to allow those in the spaces between the funnels to extend their arms across the deck of the ship and, if necessary, pick up a lifeboat from the opposite side. The new davits also had lights fitted to them and a further design change allowed for the lifeboat to be lowered level, even if, like *Titanic,* the ship were sinking by the head. There were to be eight sets of these new davits but in the end, due to time constraints, the ship was only fitted with six sets.

Britannic was launched on Thursday 26 February 1914. The local paper announced the launch of the "Largest British Built Vessel" and, not surprisingly, nowhere in the report was *Titanic* mentioned.

The morning started off with drizzling rain, which kept up all morning. Like the previous two launches thousands of people turned up, either buying tickets or just looking for a vantage point to witness the launch. The Press representing newspapers from all over Europe and America were on hand, occupying one of the four specially built grandstands. Amongst those occupying the other grandstands were the Lord and Lady Mayor R.J. McMordie; Sir Robert Thompson, the past Chairman of the Belfast Harbour Commissioners, after whom the Thompson Dry Dock was named; Miss Carlisle, the sister in law of William Pirrie; the Rev. A. Harland, the brother of Sir Edward Harland; the Recorder of Belfast, Judge J. Walker Craig; Sir William Whitla; and the American Consul. The adjoining shipyard of Workman Clark even allowed the construction of grandstands for the public to get a view of the proccedings.

For one man sitting in the grandstand, however, the launch must have revisited some painful emotions. That man was Thomas Andrews senior, the father of Thomas Andrews who was one of the *Titanic's* designers that was lost along with the ship. Although saddened that his son was not there to see the launch he must also have been extremely proud of Thomas Andrews junior and his contribution to the shipyard.

Again, like the previous launches, there was no ceremony but only a simple display of the Harland and Wolff house flag flying along side the Union Jack and the Stars and Stripes. Just prior to the launch William Pirrie made his customary inspection of the ship accompanied by Harold A. Saunderson, the new Chairman of the White Star Line, who had taken over from J. Bruce Ismay.

Thomas Andrews Senior
(Thomas Andrews Collection)

In keeping with launching tradition, a rocket was fired at 11.10 am to warn everyone that the launch was about to happen. Out on the river, the Belfast Harbour Commissioners had an incredible view as they watched from the tug *Musgrave*. Underneath the hull workmen were knocking away the final props, and as they were being pulled away painters were applying red paint to the bare parts of the hull. Again Charles Payne and Foreman Mr Keith were responsible for the launch. Just as the time approached 11.14 am a whistle sounded and all the workmen who had been busy under the hull quickly scrambled to safety. Just at that moment a young telegram boy arrived at the owners' grandstand with a telegram for William Pirrie. Pirrie told the boy to be quiet and allowed him to stay and watch the launch.

At precisely 11.15 am a second rocket was fired, and under the ship Charles Payne gave the signal to release the hydraulic launch trigger. Slowly at first, the hull, weighing in the region of 24,800 tons, started down the slipway. It took only 81 seconds for the drag chains and anchors to bring the *Britannic* to a dead stop in the water, amid the cheering and hat waving that was going on at both sides of the river. Four tugs made their way to the vessel and the hull was towed to the outfitting wharf.

No sooner had the launch taken place than the *Britannic's* name board was removed from the Arrol Gantry and replaced with a new one marked ship number 469, the *Nederland*. This had been designed as a passenger liner for the Red Star

Line, but shortly afterwards the order for the vessel was cancelled.

Luncheon for the very special guests was as usual provided at Queen's Island, while the Press were entertained at the Grand Central Hotel in Royal Avenue.

By August 1914, Britain had declared war on Germany and the country was now entering the First World War. In Belfast, fitting out was steadily progressing on *Britannic* when, in November 1915, the ship was officially requisitioned by the British Government, with instructions that she was to be completed as a hospital ship.

The first class dining room was fitted out as an intensive care ward while the Grand Reception room was turned into an operating theatre. There was accommodation for 3,300 patients, 52 Doctors, 437 nurses and attendants, and 675 crew.

The ship's sea trials were carried out in Belfast Lough and the Irish Sea on 8 December 1915. The ship, now called His Majesty's Hospital Ship *Britannic*, was handed over to the Admiralty on 12 December 1915.

It was always intended that only three Olympic class liners would be built and on 8 December 1915 the *Britannic*, the 'Forgotten' one of the three, joined her elder sisters, the 'Beloved' *Olympic* and the 'Dammed' *Titanic*, as she left Belfast or the last time. For the *Britannic*, like the *Titanic*, this was to be a one-way journey, as in less than a year, on 21 November 1916, the ship sank in the Aegean Sea. She either hit a submerged mine or was torpedoed (the cause is still hotly disputed even today), with the loss of 28 lives.

From those three ships, each the biggest in the world at their launch and handing over, sadly only one would remain, the *Olympic*. She was the favoured ship of William Pirrie and would continue to sail until scrapped on 19 September 1937.

CHAPTER 15

The League of Gentlemen

Herbert Jefferson in his biography of William Pirrie, the Chairman of the shipyard of Harland and Wolff, stated that:

> "Directors and Managers are only one side of a firm's success, what of the tens of thousands of loyal, devoted pride taking workmen in the Belfast yard. The worth of these great men must not be overlooked. Take them away, and men at the top are helpless, and up may go the shutters. Fortunately these men, generations of them from early days, have been dependable and trustworthy. They have always been as keen as the very Directors for a finely finished and superb ship; the Belfast shipyard workers have been, and are still unsurpassed as the most competent and best trained shipbuilders and engineers in the world."[1]

Jefferson is right in what he says, the shipbuilders of Belfast have always been a hard-working and dedicated workforce. However, in a context like the industry that we have been examining, there usually is one person who stands taller than the rest, has a wider vision of where they are going, and who has the strength of character to lead those around him and have them all contribute towards the greater goal that he has set in his mind.

The rise of shipbuilding in Belfast Lough has seen its fair share of those who had such a vision and were prepared to battle for it. This is why they would, for many years, make the small town of Belfast the centre of the shipbuilding world.

This, as has already been mentioned, started with William Ritchie and his brothers, and progressed until the arrival of Edward Harland. Previous chapters looked at their contribution in detail, and following after these two men came others who would assist and ultimately take control of shipbuilding in Belfast. I would like to look at the lives of four of them, who, with their own individual contributions, shaped the future of the shipyards in Belfast and, in my opinion, played a major role in creating an industry that was the envy of the world. These men were Gustav W. Wolff, the business partner of Edward Harland; Walter Wilson, who started as an apprentice with Robert Hickson in his fledgling shipyard; Alexander M. Carlisle, the brother in law of Pirrie, who rose to be Chief Naval Architect and Director of the Harland and Wolff shipyard; and Thomas

The Directors of Harland and Wolff. From left to right: Gustav Wolff, Walter Wilson, William Pirrie and Sir Edward Harland.

(© National Museums Northern Ireland, Collection Harland and Wolff, Ulster Folk and Transport Museum)

Andrews, the nephew of Pirrie who also became Chief Naval Architect, as well as Director and Personnel Assistant to Pirrie.

Gustav Wilhelm Wolff
1834–1913

Gustav Wilhelm Wolff was born in Hamburg, Germany on 10 November 1834. His parents were Moritz and Fanny Maria. His mother Fanny was the sister of Gustav C. Schwabe, who was very strongly associated with many aspects of early shipbuilding. Schwabe was responsible for bringing Harland and Wolff together and financing their initial purchase of the shipyard in Belfast. He also introduced Thomas Ismay's White Star Line to their fledgling shipyard.

At the age of 14, Wolff left Germany and moved to Liverpool, where his uncle Gustav Schwabe was living. He was enrolled at Liverpool College and stayed there until he turned 16. At this point his father Moritz decided that the young Wolff should be trained in engineering and, to further that, he was apprenticed for the next five years to Joseph Whitworth and Company, tool and machinery manufacturers of Manchester. While employed by Whitworth's, a 21 year old Wolff, was sent by the firm to represent them at an exhibition being held in Paris in 1855. Following this he left Whitworth's and joined Goodfellow and Company as a draughtsman. Around 1857 Wolff was engaged as a draughtsman by Robert Hickson at his newly established shipyard on Queen's Island in Belfast. Edward Harland was engaged at that time as the Manager of Hickson's shipyard and this would have been the first time that the two met.

It is interesting to note that Harland and Wolff were both quite distantly related. Wolff's uncle, Gustav Schwabe, was married to Helen Dugdale and a relative of hers, Mary Dugdale, married Thomas Harland, who was the uncle of Edward Harland. This made them distant cousins to some degree. Also common to both of them and waiting in the background was Gustav Schwabe.

Wolff then went to sea as an engineer. In 1858 Edward Harland purchased Hickson's yard with the financial assistance of Gustav Schwabe. Schwabe suggested that Harland might consider bringing Wolff back from sea to work at his new yard and Harland did just that. Wolff accepted and was looked after by the Jewish community upon his arrival in Belfast, living with the Jaffe family for a period. Within a year Harland took him on as a full Partner, and he managed the yard and oversaw the Drawing Office. He then took up residence in Strandtown, within sight of the shipyard, at a large detached house that, with his usual good humour and wit, he would refer to as 'The Den'. In fact he was reported as penning the following rhyme, which I think is best repeated, if possible, with a German accent:

"You may talk of your Edinburgh and the beauties of Perth,
And all the large cities famed on the earth,
But give me my house, though it be in a garret,
In the pleasant surroundings of Ballymacarrett."[2]

In 1873 he branched out from the shipyard and, along with William Smiles, he was one of the founders of the Belfast Rope Works, based at Connswater in East Belfast. This was a shrewd business move by Wolff, as the company became one of the biggest such works in the world. As Chairman of the works Wolff was also guaranteed a continuous source of rope for the shipyard.

By 1892, he and Edward Harland had made a conscious decision to take a back seat with regard to the shipyard. Wolff was approached by some prominent Belfast businessmen and asked to consider the possibility of standing for election as a Conservative at the vacant East Belfast constituency. Many years later, recalling that offer he stated, "perhaps it would be a pleasant way of spending one's time." The election was held on 9 March 1892 and his opponent was Sir William Charley, who by all accounts put up a good fight for the seat. However, in the end Wolff polled 4,743 votes, 2,136 ahead of his rival's 2,607 votes.[3]

Rope Walk
(¼ mile long)

Top: *A bird's eye view of the East Belfast Rope Works.*

Above: *A drawing depicting the rope walk in the Rope Works.*

(Both: *The Pictorial World*, Linen Hall Library)

For the next 18 years Wolff represented the voters of East Belfast and such was his popularity that for all those years he was returned unopposed. Of his time in the House of Commons, he was very proud that he never neglected the interests of the people of Belfast. Wolff was not the type to try and gain press attention by continually making speeches and was happier addressing the House with speeches that were to the point. On a personal note he said that nicest place in the Commons was the smoking room, he always felt that there were some lovely people there. On one occasion near the end of his tenure, he was in discussion with the Head Waiter in the smoking room and commented, "That this is not like the place it used to be." "No", said the Waiter, "It is not, in fact you would hardly believe it, but the whole consumption of whisky in this smoke room is only one bottle a day, apart that is from when two Conservative members, who I will not name, come in and then the consumption goes up to two bottles."[4]

Wolff's humorous style could always be counted on have an audience laughing. After the launch of one ship from the Belfast shipyard, a lunch was being held on board for the new owners and their party. After the meal various dignitaries rose to their feet and gave speeches praising the new vessel, her owners and no doubt her builders. Gustav Wolff then rose to his feet, cigar in hand, and began, "Mr Chairman," between puffs of the cigar, "Sir Edward Harland builds the ships for our firm; Mr Pirrie makes the speeches, and as for me I smoke the cigars for the firm," and then promptly sat down.[5] Perhaps he had the best job in the shipyard! By the year 1908 Gustav Wolff was now aged 74 and he finally took the major decision to break all connections with the shipyard, allowing William Pirrie virtually a free hand in the control of the yard.

Three years later, in February 1911, just 15 months before the loss of *Titanic*, Belfast City Council honoured Wolff by electing him as the fourteenth Honorary Burgess (or Freeman) of the City of Belfast. On Thursday 20 April 1911, a Luncheon was held in the Banqueting Hall of the City Hall at which Gustav Wolff was officially honoured.

It was hosted by the Lord Mayor Mr R.J. McMordie and over 300 guests were invited. Seated at the top table, along with the Lord Mayor and Wolff, were the High Sheriff of Belfast Crawford McCullough, His Grace the Primate of all Ireland, the most Reverend Dr Crozier, The Earl of Shaftsbury, the Right Hon. Thomas Andrews DL Snr., Sir Otto Jaffe, Sir William Whitla and Mr Meyer the Town Clerk. It was Mr Meyer who stood and read the Council resolution:

> "That Gustav Willhelm Wolff of 'The Den', Belfast and 42 Park Lane, London W.2., be and is hereby elected and admitted an honorary Burgess of the city of Belfast in recognition of his services to the city, to the phenomenal growth of which the great shipbuilding and engine works of Harland and Wolff, established by Mr Wolff and the late Sir Edward Harland, Bart., in the year 1860, have so largely contributed.*
> In recognition also of the fact that he represented the material interests of the city in the Imperial Parliament from 1892 till 1910, inclusive, having been four times re-elected as member of Parliament for the East Belfast Division without opposition. In recognition also of the deep interest he had in the welfare of the city, and of his noble benefactions to her charitable institutions, and that he now retires from public life in the enjoyment of the affectionate regard of all those who have the honour of knowing him."[6]
>
> *Wolff contributed to and supported many local charitable institutions including the Ulster Hospital for Woman and Children.*

The illuminated certificate was presented in a silver casket, measured 20 inches by 8 inches and was engraved with Wolff's initials. The front of the casket was engraved with views of the Houses of Parliament and an enamelled view of the Belfast City Hall, while the reverse had a view of a launching from the Queen's Island shipyard. The other sides contained other views of the shipyard. The guests enjoyed a lavish meal at which was served consume, followed by filet of sole, roast beef, peach soufflé, green figs and coffee. Music throughout the meal was provided by Mr Wright's bijou orchestra.

After the meal there were numerous speeches, but finally Mr Wolff addressed the guests and thanked them for the honour that the City Council had bestowed upon him. In a witty address he explained that he never hankered after a title "perhaps, because there is no Mrs Wolff." He said that he had lived in Belfast for well on 50 years and now considered it as home. Looking back on his time in the shipyard he recalled an evening when some people were stranded on the People's Park on Queen's Island having missed the last ferryboat. They came to Harland and Wolff looking for help, which was given, to get them home. He also talked about the time when Edward Harland asked him to go to Liverpool to look at land where Harland though that they could together open a shipyard. This was before the Hickson buyout and it was only, Wolff said, when Liverpool turned down their request to set up their own business, that they looked to doing something in Belfast instead.

Later that evening there was another function, this time held by the East Belfast Unionists in the Y.M.C.A. in Wellington Place, where a presentation of four drawings of the City Hall, the Shipyard, the Rope Works and the Houses of Parliament were made to him. In another amusing speech Wolff commented on the earlier event at the City Hall and said that he wasn't really sure what was meant by the granting of the Freedom of the City, but that he had a Rates bill at home and maybe he should return it to the Lord Mayor. He also wondered if he now would be allowed to travel free on the trams. Referring to the wonderful casket and certificate, he said that he had no son to pass it to but he might have a nephew or two who would be interested in it.

He moved to London and spent most of his time at his residence at Mayfair. For sometime his health had been declining, and, on 15 April 1913, he underwent surgery for a serious internal complaint, but died two days later on 17 April. The flag at the City Hall in Belfast was flown at half-mast as a mark of respect and Wolff was buried at Brompton Cemetery in London.

He had also been a Director of the Union Castle Steamship Company, served for several years as a member of Belfast Harbour Commissioners, and he had been a past President of the Belfast Chamber of Commerce. He had been a member of Carlton, Junior Carlton and Garrick Clubs in London, and the Ulster Reform Club in Belfast. His other interests included shooting and fishing, and he was a Partner with Walter Wilson in a salmon fishery on the North Antrim coast. In his will he left legacies of over £800,000.

Grave of Gustav Wolff,
Brompton Cemetery, London.

(Courtesy of the David Mann Collection)

Walter Henry Wilson M.I.N.A. M.I.C.E.
1839–1904

Walter Wilson was born in Maryville, in the Malone area of Belfast on 15 November 1839. He was educated at the Moravian College at Gracehill near Ballymena in County Antrim and then at Chester College in England. In 1856, when he was aged just 17, his father died and his mother, due to her financial situation, was forced to move out of the family home with her two boys, Walter and Alexander.

They took rooms at 245 York Street, Belfast. It is interesting to note that this area of Belfast had major connections with the shipyards at Queen's Island. When Edward Harland arrived in Belfast in 1854 to manage Robert Hickson's shipyard he took rooms at 305 York Street. Similarly Gustav Wolff resided at Mrs Salters' house at 20 Brougham Street, which was just off York Street. William Pirrie also resided in the area for a short while, before he moved across the Lagan to Bridge End. The earliest maritime related resident in the York Street area was William Dargan when he was straightening the river Lagan.

Wilson from an early age was interested in all things mechanical. He even made a one foot high working steam engine from spare parts in his father's workshop. When his mother moved to York Street, he and his younger brother Alexander were apprenticed to the new shipyard that had just been opened by Robert Hickson. They were the first and second such apprentices, and both of them worked under the new manager Edward Harland. Walter progressed through the Hickson's shipyard becoming a skilled draughtsman. When Harland and Wolff formed their partnership, Wilson was placed in charge of the design of the earlier ships constructed by the shipyard.

He was an extremely practical man, who was happiest standing in front of a group of people on the slipway, with a piece of chalk in hand, drawing or outlining plans of the greatest detail. His mental capacity was such that he could calculate a fraction to four or five decimal places. One report noted that he was able to calculate the amount of energy that a small piece of coal could provide. However, ask him to address a public group, present a paper or talk and Walter Wilson would run the proverbial mile.

While with Harland and Wolff he was responsible for introducing many new ideas to assist with the construction of ships. He was responsible for the design and construction of a single plate rudder and also for the creation of a lap tied butt for joining the plates on a ship's hull. He was a great innovator and solved a major problem associated with shipbuilding; corrosion of the hull of a ship near the propeller blades. The problem was that as the massive blades turned in the water they set up an electrical current, which resulted in the corrosion. Wilson proposed that by incorporating zinc plates in the area of the bronze propellers during the hull's construction it would act as a shield. This idea was quite inexpensive but had the desired effect of cutting down corrosion to the costly blades.

In 1874 he was offered a full partnership with a position on the Board of the shipyard. In 1882 the 150th ship was built at the Belfast yard, a 2,500 ton sailing ship commissioned by Samuel Lawther. It was named the *Walter H. Wilson* in honour of Wilson's service to the shipbuilding world. In the same year he held shares in the company to the value of almost £38,000.

When Edward Harland and Gustav Wolff both decided to stand down and have less involvement in the shipyard, they took the decision to place Walter Wilson and William Pirrie as joint managers of the yard. For this joint service they were

Walter H Wilson
(© National Museums Northern Ireland, Collection Harland and Wolff, Ulster Folk and Transport Museum)

Figure head on the W.H. Wilson sailing ship built by Harland and Wolff.

(Courtesy of the *Belfast Newsletter*)

paid the sum of £4,500 per year. On 30 September 1875 Walter Wilson married Sarah Elizabeth Wynne and following their wedding they lived for a while at 1 Botanic Avenue in Belfast. They then moved further up the Stranmillis Road and, in 1890, took up a house that stood where the current Stranmillis Training College is today. During all these moves, Walter and Lill, as he affectionately called his wife, managed to have four daughters and one son. As an interesting aside, his mother lived to the ripe old age of 100. Apparently even at that age, she still called him "her boy".

Walter Wilson retired from his position as a Director of the shipyard of Harland and Wolff in 1901, aged 62. Following his retirement, he moved his family to Deramore House at Newtownbreda on the outskirts of Belfast, which he rented from Lord Deramore. He spent his retirement yachting and angling, was a member of the Royal Ulster Yacht Club and President of the Belfast Anglers Association, and he and Gustav Wolff also rented a salmon fishery on the river Bann at Kilrea. He also found time to be the President of the Cross Country Association, served as a member of the Midlands Railway Northern Counties Committee and, as a Justice of the Peace for County Down, he sat quite regularly at Newtownbreda Petty sessions. As a churchgoer he put much effort into developing a scheme to encourage church extension in Belfast.

Walter Wilson died on 4 May 1904 while travelling on the train between Kilrea and Portrush. He had left his home at Newtownbreda with the intention of visiting his salmon fishery in Kilrea. While there he decided to take a trip to Portrush and boarded the 8.59 am train to Coleraine. The train arrived at Coleraine at 9.45 am and he transferred to the 9.50 am train for Portrush. The train stopped at Portstewart at 10.00 am, to enable the Ticket Collector, Mr Kennedy to inspect the tickets of the passengers. Mr Kennedy reported that he saw Walter Wilson sitting alone in a first class compartment smoking a cigarette and, as Wilson was a Director of the Railway Company, he decided not to bother inspecting his ticket, but did state that Walter Wilson spoke out to him. The train departed and arrived at Portrush just ten minutes later, where the dead but still warm body of Wilson was discovered, sitting upright in the compartment, the cigarette that he been holding in his hand still alight. His body was removed to the Northern Counties Hotel in the seaside town, where the local police contacted the local Coroner, Dr Woodside, who arrived promptly and pronounced Walter Wilson dead. It was thought that he died of heart failure. He was 65 years of age and Lill his wife, who was 15 years younger than Walter, lived for another 35 years.

Alexander Montgomery Carlisle
1854–1926

Alexander Montgomery Carlisle was born in Ballymena, County Antrim on 8 July 1854. He had two brothers and two sisters. One of his sisters was Margaret, who married William Pirrie. His father was John Carlisle and his mother was

Catherine Montgomery, whose sister Eliza had previously married James A.M. Pirrie. From that marriage came William Pirrie and his sister Eliza who would be the mother of Thomas Andrews Jnr. of *Titanic* fame.

Before Carlisle was seven years old, his father had been appointed Head Master of the English Department of the Belfast Academical Institution, which eventually became the Royal Belfast Academical Institution. The family moved to their new residence in the school and it was there that Carlisle received his education. When he was sixteen, in August 1870, Carlisle was apprenticed to the shipyard of Harland and Wolff as a gentleman pupil. William Pirrie who had been appointed a draughtsman in the yard in the previous year, when he had just completed his five year pupilage or apprenticeship, no doubt encouraged this placement.

For five years, Carlisle underwent his training as a gentleman apprentice, travelling the two miles from his home at Inst in College Square to the shipyard on Queen's Island. Surprisingly, and to his credit, during that five year period, when he had to report for work at 6.00 am, Carlisle was never once late. When he completed his apprenticeship Harland and Wolff took the unprecedented step of presenting him with a gold watch with the following inscribed on it:

> "Presented to Alexander M. Carlisle by Messers. Harland and Wolff, in recognition of his rare achievement of never being late at his work during the five years of his apprenticeship."[7]

Alexander M. Carlisle
(Hobart family collection)

Shortly after completing the apprenticeship Carlisle was placed in the Drawing Office. He was soon put in charge and given the title of Chief Confidential Naval Architect. He was later promoted to General Manager of the yard, then made a Director of the firm and appointed Chairman of the Board of Directors. He held the position of responsibility for the safe and efficient launch of each ship built by the shipyard. As Chief Naval Architect he was also responsible for the design of all Queen's Island ships, including the Olympic Class Liners.

So great was his standing in the shipbuilding world that there were several occasions when other shipyards tried, unsuccessfully, to tempt Carlisle to leave Harland and Wolff. One other shipbuilder was quoted as saying that Carlisle "was not only a great manager: he was the greatest shipbuilding manager in Europe". Praise indeed.

Carlisle, who throughout his entire life said that he had only ever read one book, *The History of Elmwood Presbyterian Church,* and who also had taken no interest whatsoever in public matters, decided that he was going to stand as an independent candidate for the West Belfast constituency in the General Election of 1906. For the previous 20 years local Unionists had continuously held the seat. As well as Carlisle, there were two other candidates, Joseph Devlin, a Nationalist and Captain J.R. Smiley, a Liberal Unionist. When the votes were counted Carlisle had succeeded in splitting the Unionist vote and allowing the Nationalist to win, the number of votes cast were:

Joseph Devlin	4,138
Captain J.R. Smiley	4,122
A.M. Carlisle	153[8]

The local unionists were beside themselves with rage and anger towards him. As a result of him standing he had allowed the Nationalist to win by just 16 votes and break the Unionist dominance of the seat for 20 years. This began the break down in relations between Carlisle and his brother in law, William Pirrie.

In 1907 Carlisle was appointed as a member of His Majesty's Privy Council in Ireland. This gave him the opportunity to stand on the steps of the Throne during a sitting of the House of Lords. This he did some years later, on 9 August 1920, when, during the debate on the Restoration of Order in Ireland Bill, he shouted to the members present, "My Lords, if you pass this Bill, you may kill England, not Ireland." These 13 words were to land him in all sorts of trouble, with a Bench Warrant being raised by Parliament for his arrest. Finally things calmed down.

In 1910, at the age of 56, he retired from Harland and Wolff and moved from his Belfast home at Elmwood Avenue, to live in London at 7 Orme Square, along with his wife Edith Wooster. Edith was an American from San Francisco, whom Carlisle had married there in 1880. They had one son and two daughters. The son, Ralph, fought in the First World War and was captured by the Germans. Following his repatriation, he later married a lady from London.

Carlisle's early retirement was right in the middle of the fitting out of *Olympic*, and the continuing construction of *Titanic* and the tenders *Nomadic* and *Traffic*. No explanation for this move was ever officially given. There were many reasons offered as to why Carlisle retired, but while working on the Olympic class liners he, as chief designer, had clashed with the White Star Line regarding the number of lifeboats that should be carried. In the end his advice was ignored and the ships were initially fitted out with the regulation number of lifeboats, which was not enough for the total number of people that could be carried. White Star Line's decision to install only the minimum number of lifeboats placed Carlisle in a difficult position, as this conflicted with him sitting on the Committee that was then reporting to the Board of Trade on Live Saving Appliances. This conflict of interest may well have been the main reason why Carlisle left the shipyard.

Edith Carlisle
(Hobart family collection)

Another reason why Carlisle may have retired was his deteriorating relationship with his brother in law, William Pirrie. Carlisle was not afraid to speak his mind and it is generally considered that he and Pirrie did not agree on a number of matters. Carlisle was also all the things that Pirrie was not. He was considered by many as a 'Captain of Industry', he was Privy Councillor, mixed in the right circles and included the Kaiser of Germany as a friend. He was also able to influence important events. For example, on one occasion during the First World

War he wrote a scathing letter to the *Times*, insisting that the Government split the construction of merchant shipping and naval ships, and reorganise the British shipyards accordingly. Four days later the First Lord of the Admiralty announced that a Controller General for Merchant Shipping was being appointed, and named William Pirrie as the person to take the position.

Carlisle spent much of his time as a member of many clubs and official bodies, including the Committee on Accidents in Factories and Workshops; the Merchant Shipping Advisory Committee, which made a report to the Board of Trade on Life Saving Appliances; and the Royal Thames Yacht Club. He was also an avid autograph collector. At the beginning of this interest, it seemed just a good idea to have people sign his autograph book, but after a period he had amassed quite a collection, including King Edward VII, the Kaiser of Germany, the Duke of Windsor and Caruso the famous Italian opera tenor. His autograph book became one of his proudest possessions. Shortly before he died, a burglar stole some lead from the bird bath at his London home. Carlisle was most annoyed about this and was reported as saying that he was sorry for the little bird that could no longer get a drink. However, he also added that if the thief did not want to return the lead, then maybe he might send his autograph so that it could be added to his collection.[9]

Alexander Montgomery Carlisle died Friday 5 March 1926. A few weeks prior to his death, with his usual witty style, he planned and made arrangements for his own funeral service. The service took place at Golders Green Crematorium. As the coffin was moving out of the chapel, following the instructions left by Carlisle, the organist started to play The Merry Widow Waltz, much to the amusement of the mourners. Finally his ashes were scattered in the Garden of Remembrance.

William Pirrie, who reportedly never wasted many words in public speeches, did utter a few in his eulogy of his brother in law when he said:

> "… very soon his thorough mastery of work and management of men, and many other sterling qualities, were so evident that he became General Manager, and to his great success in that capacity the growth and present state of perfection of the shipyard are, no doubt, largely due."[10]

Thomas Andrews Junior
1873–1912

Thomas, or Tommie as the family called him, was born in Comber, County Down on 7 February 1873. His father was Thomas Andrews and his mother was Eliza Pirrie, the sister of William Pirrie, which made Andrews the nephew of William Pirrie. The Andrews family had a long established line and are one of very few families that can trace their ancestry back to before the battle of the Boyne in 1690. They were involved in the production of linen and, for many years, the

Andrews mill dominated the Comber landscape and had connections to many local families over the years.

Thomas Andrews was the second of six children, born at Ardara in Comber. His elder brother John eventually became the second Prime Minister of Northern Ireland, holding Office during the Second World War. Another brother, James, practiced law and was in due course appointed as the Lord Chief Justice for Northern Ireland. His sister Eliza married a Lieutenant Colonel Hind, while his youngest brother William stayed in Comber at the Mill.

Thomas was educated at home until he was eleven years of age, when he was placed as a boarder at the Royal Belfast Academical Institution, where his family had all been educated. Throughout his time at Inst it was reported that he was fonder of games than lessons but he applied himself well to his studies. On his sixteenth birthday Andrews left the school and was immediately engaged as a gentleman apprentice in the shipyard at Harland and Wolff. On the surface this would appear to be quite a strange move by the Andrews family but Andrews' uncle, William Pirrie, was by now climbing the promotion ladder in the shipyard. With no children of his own after ten years of marriage to his cousin, Margaret Carlise, he may have been happy to take the young Andrews under his wing. He may also have considered Andrews to be a personal and confidential assistant for himself in the future.

Thomas Andrews
(Thomas Andrews Collection)

The Andrews family. From left to right, Front: Eliza, William and Thomas Junior. Back: James, Thomas Senior, Lizzi and John.

(Courtesy of the The Deputy Keeper of the Records, Public Record Office of Northern Ireland)

Andrews boys. From left to right, Thomas, James, John (lying) and William.

(V. Morrison Collection)

After his five year apprenticeship, during which he only missed one day's training, Andrews continued with his studies after work in the Municipal Technical College in Belfast. He resided in Belfast during his apprenticeship, as the daily journey from Comber to Belfast and back would have been impossible due to the poor roads, the lack of public transport and his 6.30 am start. Where he stayed may never be known but it is possible that he resided with his uncle, William Pirrie, at his home at Schomberg Terrace at Bridge End in East Belfast. When he had completed his time, he rented rooms at 33 Wellington Place in the centre of Belfast, from which it was a quick half hour walk to the shipyard.

Like his uncle Pirrie he was to travel widely for the Company and in doing so make a study of the design of hotels, ships and ports that could later be used in the internal layout of new ships. One such trip was to view the ports and facilities of the west coast of Ireland. The Company was interested to see if it would be possible to open up new routes from this part of Ireland to America. While on this trip he wrote a letter to his mother from a hotel in Westport. In the letter he tells her of the places he had visited, which included Sligo and Buncranna. He writes that while in Galway he saw an interesting sight:

33 Wellington Place Belfast, where Andrews rented rooms. This is now the location of H.M.R.C.

(© National Museums Northern Ireland, Collection Green)

> "In the old part of the town the window in a house where the Mayor, a Major Lynch, hung his own son who had shot another fellow because they both loved + courted the same girl. The poor Father had to hang his own son because he could get no one else to do it."[11]

The murdered man was a Spaniard who had been visiting Galway and had fallen for the young Lynch's girlfriend. The young man decided that he was not going to tolerate the prospect of his girlfriend falling for the charms of the foreigner and promptly, in cold blood, killed the interloper. This then placed his father in a terrible position in which he had to execute his own son. Some think that this is where the phrase 'lynch mob' emanated from.

Quickly Andrews rose through the yard, starting as an Outside Manager and finally, in 1907, he was appointed as a Managing Director and personal assistant to the Chairman, William Pirrie. After some discussion by the Board of Directors a decision was taken that Thomas Andrews should represent the firm and travel on the maiden voyage of all newly constructed ships leaving Belfast.

On Tuesday, 23 June 1908 Thomas Andrews married Helen Reilly Barbour of the Barbour family of Lisburn, County Antrim. Her family owned a thread and cotton mill so the families would have known each other, with both being in the textile business.

Thomas had proposed marriage to Helen on the Friday night of 24 March 1905. It would seem that he did not get the immediate response that he had hoped for, because the following day he wrote to her apologising for the fright and annoyance that he had given her the previous evening:

> "Had I for one moment thought that we did not understand each other all these years, since we first meet, + that you did not love me, as I felt sure, and was lead to believe you did by both your + my friends and relations, I would never have placed you in such an awkward position as I did."

After this apology he restates his love for her, and hopes that she may still accept his offer by adding: "as it would have been awful to have been refused by the one I love so much." He asks her to think over his offer of marriage and tells her, that if she only wants his friendship to never reply to his letter, for what he calls his "ideal dream." He continues by telling her, that he is not disappointed or annoyed for not giving him an answer and states that "I am alone to blame" for the position that she is now in. He concludes the letter by stating:

> "God bless you dear, + don't do anything that you think your Mother, sister + brothers, would not approve of, otherwise I could never look them straight in the face again.
>
> Your ever affectionate + loving friend
>
> Thomas Andrews Jnr."[12]

Helen Reilly Barbour
(V. Morrison collection)

There was a bit of a problem, which Thomas was unaware of, in that Helen was also quite keen on another young man by the name of Henry Harland, a nephew of Sir Edward. Young Harland was supposedly also keen on the idea of marrying Helen. Apparently after Thomas made his proposal, Helen's mother locked the young girl in her bedroom at Conway House and told her that she would not be let out of the room until she had made her mind up regarding which of her two suitors she would marry. What is not known or recorded is how long she was held 'captive', but obviously she was released from her torment when she told her mother that she was to accept the marriage proposal from Thomas Andrews. Henry Harland was no doubt bitterly disappointed at his rejection in favour of the young man from Comber, but as we shall see Henry Harland came back into Helen's life at a later stage.

The wedding was held at Lambeg Parish Church and the guest list read like a 'who's who' of the shipping world, including Gustav Wolff, Mr Imrie (Messers Ismay, Imrie and Co.), Mr Henry Harland, Commander H.J. Haddock, Commodore of the White Star Line, and Mr and Mrs William Pirrie. The reception was held at the Barbour family home at Conway House, Dunmurry. On arrival the guests were greeted by the newly married couple, who stood beneath a large bell made up of white lilies and asters, and received congratulations. The bride's mother also received guests in the drawing room.

The house was filled with the smell of fragrant flowers that adorned the rooms. In one room the numerous wedding gifts were displayed, and in another was the wedding cake that was decorated with bells. It was reported that the guests almost expected the bells to chime. In another room dainty refreshments were served, and out on the magnificent lawns tables were also laid out for guests, so that they could enjoy the beautiful surroundings of the house.

The band of the Royal Irish Constabulary played a selection of music including tender solos from 'Bohemian Girl'. The 'Lady Correspondent' in the *Belfast Newsletter* stated that "The scene was one of happiness and the guests laughter and chatter filled the air." By late afternoon the time had come for the young couple to depart. At around 4.30 pm guests lined the large oak panelled hall, which was adorned with glittering swords and armour, to say farewell to the departing Mr and Mrs Thomas Andrews Jnr. The bride wore a travelling dress of blue souple cloth, her cutaway coat was adorned with soutache, and its vest and cuffs were of cream Shantung silk. She wore a picture hat of white chip, which was lined with blue silk and wreathed in wisteria roses and grey tulle. Their honeymoon was spent in Switzerland.

On their return from honeymoon the Andrews took up residence in a house called Dunallen in Windsor Avenue along with five servants. Andrews returned to the shipyard and the construction of the Olympic class liners. Their only child, Elizabeth Law Barbour Andrews, was born on 27 November 1910. The child was given the family pet name of Elba due to her initials.

Andrews wedding.
(Thomas Andrews Collection)

Thomas went on the sea trials of *Nomadic, Traffic* and *Olympic* before they were handed over. He then left Belfast on *Titanic* with a group of workmen from the shipyard. These men were referred to as the Guarantee Group and their job was to travel with a ship on its maiden voyage and be responsible for fixing any defects or snags. To be selected to be a part of this group was not only an honour, but also a sign from the yard that promotion may follow.

Immediately after the ship struck the iceberg, Captain Edward Smith asked Andrews to check out the ship and give a report on its condition. Andrews reported back that *Titanic* was doomed and had only a couple of hours before she would sink. Reports from survivors said he acted heroically and helped passengers put on lifejackets and get into the lifeboats. His body was never recovered.

Five years later his widow Helen married Henry Harland, nephew of the late Sir Edward Harland and Helen's earlier suitor. Helen and Henry were to have three girls and one boy. Henry Harland became an MP for Belfast and died 22 August 1945, Helen also died on the 22 August but 21 years later, in 1966. She is buried in the Barbour family grave at Lambeg Parish Church.

Elba, never married and spent a large amount of time travelling. She was returning from the Guinness family home near Slane, Ireland, on 1 November 1973, when she was involved in a fatal road traffic accident. She was cremated at Roselawn Crematorium outside Belfast.

Henry Harland, second husband of Helen Andrews.
(V. Morrison collection)

CHAPTER 16

William Pirrie
1st Viscount of Belfast

Willilliam James Pirrie, contrary to popular belief, was a Canadian rather than an Irish man. Born in 1847 he was the second child to James and Eliza Pirrie. James Alexander Pirrie (1821–1849) was the son of Captain William Pirrie, who eventually resided in Conlig, County Down. James wanted to start a new life for himself and decided to move to Canada. He arrived in Quebec in 1844, aged 23, and married Eliza Swann Montgomery (1820–1895) on 28 June that same year. She was the daughter of Alexander Montgomery of Dundesart, County Antrim.

The couple were to have two children, a daughter Eliza Morrison who was born 17 December 1845 and a son William James, born in Quebec, 24 May 1847. (Subsequent records of Pirrie's birth would give his date of birth, not as 24 May, but rather 31 May.) The eldest child, Eliza, would later go on to marry Thomas Andrews of Comber and together they would have six children, including Thomas Andrews Junior who would perish on the *Titanic*. When William was just over two years of age, his father died from cholera whilst in New York and was buried in Greenwood Cemetery in that city. After the funeral, Eliza took the decision that she would leave America and return to Ireland to the family she had left just a few years before. She and the two children left behind them a husband and father. On his headstone she had the following inscription carved:

"Farewell
We cherish your loving memory in your native land
and pray that we meet again in Heaven."[1]

William J Pirrie
(V. Morrison collection)

When Eliza returned to Ireland she moved into the house of her father in law, Captain William Pirrie. She felt that Conlig, a small village that is situated mid way between Bangor and Newtownards, was a safe place to raise her two children. In her spare time Eliza was a great collector, especially of famous sayings and quotations, and she passed her passion for these onto to her son William. One favourite that he used to quote was "Respect your parents' wisdom and good advice." She later presented him with his own little book full of these maxims, which William kept with him wherever he went.

■ 158

Captain Pirrie, the grandfather, was to play a very important role in the life of the young Pirrie. He was to become almost a father to the boy and his thoughts and dreams would be passed down. He was the person who would spark the maritime interest in the growing child, recounting the adventures and stories of his own colourful past. The young Pirrie, like most middle class children at that time, was educated at home until 11 years of age. He was then enrolled at the Royal Belfast Academical Institution in Belfast in 1858. Sadly there are very few records of that period that survive today and little is known of his time at the school, but he did shine at mathematics. Most probably he would have been a boarder at the school. Today to travel from Conlig to Belfast would take about 30 minutes, but in 1858 public transport was poor and the same journey would have taken several hours, making it impractical for the young Pirrie to travel daily.

He grew up surrounded by relatives who were involved in shipping to some extent or another. An aunt called Eliza was married to John Sinclair, who had established a shipping business in Belfast, while another aunt, Letitia, married into the Heyn shipping Company. It thus came as no great surprise that the young Willie's career was to have something to do with the sea.

Eliza Pirrie, William Pirrie's mother.

(Jefferson, Herbert, Viscount Pirrie of Belfast, WM. Mullan & Son Ltd, Belfast: 1948)

When he completed his studies at the school and no doubt also influenced by his grandfather, he pleaded with his mother to be allowed to join the shipyard of Harland and Wolff. With Captain Pirrie's connections and through knowing both Harland and Wolff this was arranged. On 23 June 1862, William Pirrie entered the shipyard as a gentleman apprentice.

For the next five years he was placed in many of the departments in the yard, experiencing how each of them operated and contributed to the construction of the ship. During this period, again due to travel arrangements, Pirrie lodged in a boarding house at Bridge End in East Belfast. The story goes that also lodging there were two Bank officials who complained about Pirrie wearing his working clothes around the house, which they said lowered the standard of the home. They asked the landlady to evict Pirrie but she refused and the two Bankers then promptly vacated the house.

When his apprenticeship period was up he was placed in the Drawing Office, quickly promoted to Assistant manager, then Sub Manager and finally to the role of Works Manager. It was obvious to all concerned that Pirrie, a young man now aged 21, was showing great promise. Edward Harland would later say of him, "Pirrie won his place in the firm by dint of merit alone, by character, perseverance and ability." To further his training he was sent to the shipbuilding yards of MacNab and Company in Greenock, Scotland. On his return to Belfast he showed a great talent for ship design and construction. He also applied himself to learn as much as possible about the finance of the yard from Gustav Wolff and the yard's bookkeeper John Bailey.

Now firmly established in the shipyard, William's fancy turned to affairs of the heart. He wrote to his mother telling her about his new found love, Margaret Carlisle, who was his cousin. He asked his mother to accept Maggie, as he referred to her, as a daughter and said that he had been fortunate to secure her love. He told his mother in the letter that he had been spoilt by having such a mother and sister and that his intended bride was the only girl he could compare with them. His mother did accept Maggie into the family and, on 17 April 1879, they were married. The wedding took place at the bride's father's home at Inst school and was conducted by the Rev. Alexander Gordon. Strangely Pirrie's address was given as Comber. His bride was described as being strikingly good looking and had a forceful and dynamic personality.

From the beginning of their marriage she made it plain that she wished to share fully in her husband's business life and William was soon to rely on and respect her judgement and advice. However, shortly after their marriage she arrived at the yard demanding that he withdraw some of their capital from the Firm. He took her out to the yard and showed her a large machine that had recently been purchased and told his wife that she could have it if she arranged to take it away. It was also around this time that many thought Mrs Pirrie was behind the idea of purchasing an ambulance to take injured workmen in the yard to the Royal Victoria Hospital.

With the Partners now watching Pirrie, they decided that he should be allowed to travel on behalf of the firm and see what other shipyards were up to, as well as studying foreign ports and the facilities that they offered. In those early years he travelled widely for the firm, visiting Boston, Portland, Montreal and Buenos Aires. In 1899 his wife joined him to travel around more of the ports of America and Canada. One wonders if, while in America, he took time to visit his father's grave in New York.

Pirrie worked hard to become the leading light on the Board of Directors of the yard, so it is perhaps not that surprising that he took the lead in the Company following the death of Sir Edward Harland.

Apart from the shipyard, Pirrie also served as a Commissioner with the Belfast Harbour Commissioners, for 13 years from 1893–1906. However, he did not always have a happy relationship with them and if decisions taken by the Commissioners didn't go his way he could always be counted on to play the "I'll move the shipyard away" card. This happened in 1897 when he threatened to relocate the shipyard to either Scotland or England if the Commissioners would not build him a new 900 ft dry dock. He won the argument and the Thompson Dry Dock was constructed.

In 1893, Pirrie became involved with politics and was elected as a Councillor to the Belfast City Council where, over many years, he represented the Cromac and then Victoria wards.

In 1896 he was honoured by being elected as Lord Mayor of Belfast, a position that he held for two years. During this period in Office he worked hard to try and bring all sections of political opinion together. He also put forward the idea that the local population should be interested in all aspects relating to Ireland as a whole and not just what was effecting the north east of the island. In Office he tried very hard to ensure that he represented all the people of Belfast and not just the Unionist community. One of his last functions as Lord Mayor was to attend a large bazaar in a Nationalist area of the City.

In his first year in Office a child of a friend of his died in a local hospital from a cross infection. Pirrie and his wife both decided that something had to be done to help the local hospitals and he called a meeting to consider the possibility of having a new hospital constructed on the Falls Road in Belfast. The Pirrie's contributed £5,000 and within six months £100,000 had been donated. The contract for the new hospital, to be called the Royal Victoria, was awarded to McLaughlin and Harvey, a firm of local builders. The contract cost £111,000, and on being told of the additional cost Pirrie immediately wrote a cheque for the extra £11,000.

The Royal Victoria Hospital was opened by King Edward VII and Queen Alexandra on 28 July 1903. There was space for 300 beds. Margaret Pirrie herself raised another £100,000 as an Endowment Fund and two of the wards were named after the Pirrie's. At the Official opening ceremony the Pirrie's were presented to His Majesty. The King said, "And so Mr Pirrie, this magnificent hospital is all your great work," Pirrie bowed and before he could rise, another guest replied, "Yes, his wife collected the money."[2]

After Pirrie had completed his second term of Office as Lord Mayor he was made a Privy Councillor for Ireland. In 1898 he was made the first Honorary Burgess or Freeman of Belfast. To celebrate this honour, a special dinner was held on 21 July, when over 150 guests attended the function at William and Margaret's Belfast home, Ormiston House. They had taken up residence at the East Belfast home in 1895 following the death of Sir Edward Harland. Included among the special invited guests were the Lord and Lady Mayoress of Belfast, the Bishop of Down and Connor, and the Moderator of the General Assembly. Also seated at the top table was Pirrie's sister, Eliza Andrews.

After dinner, the Lord Mayor presented a special casket made by W. Gibson and Company, which was made from gold and fashioned in the Renaissance style. In the centre of the front panel was the Shield of the City of Belfast and also depicted were the SS Oceanic and the Harland and Wolff shipyard. The side panels had views of the Royal Victoria Hospital and Belfast Lough. Inside the casket was an illuminated vellum scroll with the wording:

> "This is to certify that Alderman, The Right Honourable William James Pirrie C.E., J.P., of 'Ormiston' in the County of Down and the Queen's Island, Belfast, Lord Mayor of the City of Belfast 1896–1897, High Sheriff for the County of

Antrim was, on the first day of January one thousand eight hundred and ninety eight, elected and admitted by the Lord Mayor, Aldermen and Citizens of the City of Belfast an Honorary Burgess of the City.

James Henderson, Lord Mayor
Samuel Black, Town Clerk, Belfast."[3]

In his acceptance speech Pirrie said that it had been his ambition both in his business career and in his public life to emulate the example of those who had gone before in striving to promote the interests of all classes in Belfast. He also said that he believed Belfast was "destined to occupy a still more important place in the commercial world." He thanked all those present for the special honour of having his name enrolled as the first Freeman of the City and said that now that his name had been entered on the new Roll, he hoped that with time it would become an illustrious one.

It is interesting to note that in 1904, the name of Margaret Pirrie was added to the Roll as the first female Honorary Burgess of the City, Gustav Wolff, on the other hand would have to wait a further seven years before he was likewise honoured.

As mentioned previously Pirrie had taken up residence in Ormiston House, following the death of Sir Edward Harland. It is a beautiful large house built in the Scottish Baronial style and occupying a delightful setting in large secluded grounds in the heart of East Belfast. The house was originally built in Glasgow in

Ormiston House.

Scotland in 1867 and brought over to its present site by Coombe Reed, a wealthy Scotsman who was associated with shipping in Belfast's early history.

From the roof the panoramic view takes in nearly all of Belfast, spreading out to the Cave Hill in the north of the City. Quite easily picked out above the rows of trees in the gardens are the gantries and cranes of the Harland and Wolff shipyard.

Entry to the house and gardens is along a short driveway from the Wandsworth Road. The private grounds radiate out from the house with the lawns laid out with bushes and trees. Any visitors to the estate may give little thought to the previous owners or history of Ormiston, but if the walls could talk, what a story they would tell. When Pirrie occupied the house he used it as his Belfast base for himself and his wife. In his time the entrance to the house and grounds was via a long private avenue, which ran up through the lawns from the Belmont Road. The gatehouse is still in use today as a private dwelling. The Gardener, Thomas Griffin, who occupied the front lodge, did not have his skills tested too much, as Pirrie had the lawns laid out without a single flower or flowerbed present. The whole of the grounds were given over to wide stretches of grass with the driveway bordered with rows of fir trees.

Throughout his life Lord Pirrie always carried the little book of maxims given to him by his mother Eliza. He would have no doubt been fond of the various sayings that were fixed to the walls of the house. "Truth will Prevail", "What shall be shall", "Do right and trust in God" and "He that thoules overcomes". One

162

Belfast from the roof of Ormiston House.

wonders if these were added to his collection.

To enter the house today is like stepping back in time. As the main door is approached, there is a strong feeling of déjà vu.

The entrance hall and stairway are finished in fine oak panelling, and the ceilings are of intricate plasterwork. The dog-leg staircase rises from the entrance hall with its welcoming marble fireplace; the workmanship and finishing of the newel posts, spandrels and banister rails are of the highest standard. At the head of the staircase is a beautiful bowed, three panelled, leaded window, with various mottoes engraved, including 'Dieu et Mon Droit' and 'Nemo me Impune Lacessit'.

While some of the rooms have been divided, the character of the house is still there, in details such as the fine carving in some of the wooden surrounds to the fireplaces. One of the toilets still holds the original Shanks wash-hand basin and toilet, complete with wooden seat and lid. Behind the house are outbuildings that were once used as stables, and a secluded door leading to what was probably a kitchen garden.

On 8 September 1897 the house was visited by Royalty: The Duke and Duchess of York, who later became King George V and Queen Mary. Lord Pirrie, who was in his second year of Office as Belfast Lord Mayor, invited 10,000 Sunday School children to meet with the Duke and Duchess. During their visit, the Duke and Duchess planted two cypress trees, which still stand behind the house a century later.

Following Lord Pirrie's death, the house was occupied for a short time by George Cumming of Harland and Wolff, and then it was placed for sale on the open market. Pirrie had stipulated in his will that the house, if possible, should be used for educational purposes and in 1927 it was bought for use as a preparatory school for Campbell College. In 1975 it was purchased by the Police Authority for Northern Ireland, who occupied the building until 1996. The Northern Ireland Assembly, with a view to using it as office space, then purchased the building. This option was never followed up and the building is being considered for a change of use to apartments, with housing being built in the grounds.

To ensure that Harland and Wolff would be major players in the shipbuilding industry worldwide, Pirrie felt he also needed a London base and in 1898 he bought Downshire House at number 24 Belgrave

163

'Truth will Prevail', the wall above the doorstep of Ormiston house today.

The main staircase at Ormiston House.

Witley Park, Godalming, Surrey.

Witley Court, the Surrey seat of Lord and Lady Pirrie.
(A. Hobart collection)

Square in London. The large house contained a ballroom, library, large dinning room with 11 guest bedrooms and accommodation for staff and servants. Today the house is home to the Spanish Embassy.

In a bid to become accepted by 'London Society' he purchased the greater part of the estate of Witley Court in Godalming, Surrey, in 1909. It was rumoured that the purchase price was around £200,000. The estate covered 2,800 acres, was spread across the counties of Surrey and Sussex, and at one time was Queen Elizabeth I's deer forest. The grounds contained three lakes and under one of them a ballroom with a glass ceiling was constructed. Marjorie Wood McCormick, the daughter of Artie Frost of the Guarantee Group on *Titanic* and late President of the Ulster Titanic Society, remembered being taken to the estate and into the room under the lake as a young girl, after her father was lost on *Titanic*. There was also an observatory and a theatre in the grounds. Internally the house was also massive. There was a Palm House, an elegant staircase, dining rooms, a morning room, business rooms, a library and a billiard room.

William Pirrie's views on politics were to change over the years and he classed himself as Liberal Unionist. In 1899, there was a by election for a seat on Belfast City Council and Pirrie threw his support for the son of the Unionist Councillor who had died. However, the Conservative party chose another candidate and throughout the election period there was a lot of mud slinging going on. The Conservative leadership publicly spoke out against Pirrie, attempting to undermine his position to try and alienate his shipyard workforce, upon whom Pirrie would hope to draw support. The Conservative candidate won and this was to be the beginning of bad feelings between Pirrie and the Unionists. In 1902, Pirrie was asked by friends to put his name forward as a candidate for the South Belfast constituency in that year's General Election. Again the Conservatives decided to stand against him and put forward a Mr Dunbar-Buller, who came from Millisle on the Ards Peninsula and who had no connections with Belfast. Pirrie decided not to allow his name to go forward and on Election Day there were only two candidates. Mr Thomas H. Sloan, an Independent, won the seat by a majority of 826 votes. Pirrie and a large number of Unionists were outraged at how he had been ignored after all that he had done for the city of Belfast.

Pirrie took a stand against Home Rule in the ongoing debate. He believed that its introduction would mean financial ruin for Ireland and that it would be more prudent to be aligned with a stronger partner, which would give security and financial stability. It was also rumoured that Pirrie was prepared to move Harland and Wolff 'lock, stock and barrel' to a site in Glasgow should Home Rule succeed. In fact Thomas Andrews wrote to his mother in 1905, telling her how advanced Pirrie's plans for a move were. In the letter he tells her:

> "I suppose you were surprised to see we have bought a yard on the Clyde. I will be interested to see what the Belfast papers will say and how the Harbour Board will explain our extension outside Belfast. Well as I have respectively said they have only themselves to blame and the pity is the rate payers don't know how their interests are abused by a narrow minded lot of old women."[5]

Trying to show that he was not a traditional Unionist but a Liberal one, Pirrie organised for Winston Churchill to come to Belfast to speak at a rally in the Ulster Hall, to try to show the local Unionists that their views on Home Rule were wrong. In reality Pirrie really misjudged public opinion. The Unionists were furious and all sorts of threats against him were used. They staged their own event at the Ulster Hall the night before the Pirrie rally, so that the Unionists would then have to be evicted before the Pirrie/Churchill rally could start. Pirrie hastily decided to reschedule the rally at Celtic Park. The Authorities were so worried about civil unrest that 3,500 men of the 15 Infantry Brigade were placed on stand-by in case of trouble. As Churchill arrived a large number of protesters starting signing the National Anthem. Churchill had to be secretly whisked away after the event to the York Street railway station to catch the boat train to Larne.

Pirrie became seriously ill not long after this, suffering with prostrate cancer. He underwent surgery and spent the greater part of the year convalescing. He also lost both his nephew, Thomas Andrews, and the *Titanic* in that year. Pirrie had been due to sail on the ship's maiden voyage but following the advise of his Doctors the arrangements for the trip were cancelled.

At the end of 1912, he, along with six other prominent men, issued a statement in which they felt that some form of Home Rule was "the only feasible method of removing … the anomalous relations between Great Britain and Ireland."

Previous to this, in 1906, he had been created Baron Pirrie and during the First World War he was appointed Controller of Merchant Shipping. In 1910 he had been appointed Deputy Lieutenant for the City of Belfast and on 13 July

1921 he was elevated to Viscount Pirrie of Belfast. With the creation of Northern Ireland in 1922, Lord Pirrie was selected to sit as a member in the new Senate at Stormont. He held this position until his death.

Lord and Lady Pirrie left Southampton on 21 March 1924 to undertake a three month sea trip, firstly to Buenos Aires and then on to New York. His private secretary, Mr A. Marshall and his private physician, Doctor Morrow, accompanied them. At Buenos Aires they transferred to the *SS Ebro*, which, incidentally, had been built by Workman Clark. It was sailing to Chile where

Lord and Lady Pirrie.
(Millin, S., *Sidelights on Belfast History*, W&G Baird, Belfast: 1938)

Pirrie had some business connections. Pirrie had taken a chill, which was first diagnosed on 23 May and quickly turned into double pneumonia. The ship continued north and then proceeded through the Panama Canal, which Pirrie wished to see and he was brought on deck while passing through a section of it. As *SS Ebro* sailed out of the Canal towards Cuba on 7 June, William Pirrie passed away, aged 78, at around 11.30 pm. The ship made for New York, where his embalmed body was transferred onto the *Olympic*, his favoured ship.

The remains of the Chairman of the largest shipyard in the world were then returned to Ormiston, his East Belfast home. Tributes poured in from around the world and messages of sympathy were received from King George V and Queen Mary, Queen Alexandra and the Prime Minister Ramsay MacDonald. Mr H.M Pollock the Northern Ireland Minister of Finance said of him, "A great Ulsterman has fallen, we only realise his greatness."[6]

Monday 23 June 1924 was a beautiful sunny morning and gathered at Ormiston were many of the most prominent citizens of Belfast and the surrounding district, who had come to pay their last respects to this giant of the shipbuilding world. The Governor of Northern Ireland, His Grace The Duke of Abercorn, represented the newly constituted Government, Mr Wm. Turner, the Lord Mayor of Belfast, was also present as were the Marquis of Londonderry, the Right Hon. John and Mrs Andrews, Lord Chief Justice Mr James and Mrs Andrews, and Mr Blackmore, representing James Craig the Prime Minister of Northern Ireland.

A service was conducted at the house by 79 year old Rev. Thomas Dunkerly of Comber. The coffin, with the inscription "Deeds not words", then made its way out of Ormiston for the last time. It was accompanied by 15 carriages carrying the mourners and proceeded down the Belmont Road, where children from Belmont National School stood to watch its passing. From there the cortege proceeded down the Newtownards Road and turned right into Dee Street, pausing at the main gates of the shipyard before heading towards the City Hall. There, thousands of people had gathered to catch a view of the funeral. In the background the Albert Clock tolled minute chimes as the procession made its way towards the Grovesnor Road where, again, there was a pause at the main gates of the

The funeral cortege passing the Belfast City Hall.
(Courtesy of the *Belfast Newsletter*)

Royal Victoria Hospital before it made its way up the Falls Road to the Belfast Cemetery. At the graveside the choir of Harland and Wolff sang the hymn 'Now the Labourer's task is over'. The Reverend Rossington of First Belfast Presbyterian Church conducted the Committal service. Finally William Pirrie, a Canadian by birth, was interred in the city of Belfast that he adored.

In his Will, Pirrie stipulated that Lady Pirrie should enjoy an income and the use of the property of his estate for the rest of her life. Annuities were to be paid annually to the following:

Pirrie grave.

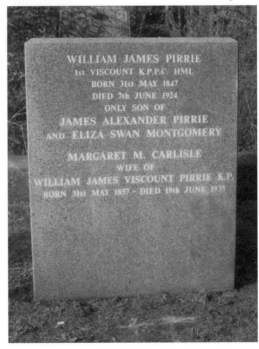

WILLIAM JAMES PIRRIE
1st VISCOUNT K.P.P.C. HML
BORN 31st MAY 1847
DIED 7th JUNE 1924
ONLY SON OF
JAMES ALEXANDER PIRRIE
AND ELIZA SWAN MONTGOMERY

MARGARET M. CARLISLE
WIFE OF
WILLIAM JAMES VISCOUNT PIRRIE K.P.
BORN 31st MAY 1857 - DIED 19th JUNE 1935

- £500 to John Philips for as long as he kept the accounts for Harland and Wolff.
- £300 to Saxon Payne.
- £300 to his secretary Iris Edmiston.
- £1,000 to Mrs E. Hind, his niece and sister to Thomas Andrews.
- £500 to Elizabeth Andrews, the daughter of Thomas Andrews.

However, when the Directors of Harland and Wolff held their first meeting after his death they were to find out that there no new orders for ships and virtually no funds available to them. They even had to ask prominent businessmen for financial assistance to help lady Pirrie.

The death of William Pirrie was in some ways the beginning of the end of that golden era of shipbuilding.

CHAPTER 17

The End of an Era

You may have heard of the joke that starts, "There was an Irish man, a Scots man and an English man." Well the development of shipbuilding that happened in Belfast was no joke and it involved a German, a Canadian, a Welshman and quite a few thousand Irish men. Belfast is a small place, with none of the raw materials necessary to support shipbuilding, yet a massive industry grew here and, at one point in history, established itself as the world leaders and innovators in shipbuilding. As Michael Moss and John Hume describe in their exceptional in-depth study of the shipyard, Harland and Wolff's shipyard became *Shipbuilders to the World,* which at its height employed over 35,000 people.

However, for us today, entering the second decade of the twenty-first century, it can be somewhat difficult to imagine that the largest shipyard in the world was established in East Belfast. There are many tours to Queen's shipyard, some of the best allowing you to walk around what is left of the yard, such as Belfast City Council's tour during its 'Titanic 100' event. It can be quite disconcerting to walk down Queen's Road and see a barren wasteland. Most of Harland and Wolff and Workman Clark's massive buildings are gone and although Titanic Quarter Limited have begun restoration on the Office block, the hub of Pirrie's empire, including its Drawing Offices, is currently falling apart. Gone forever are all the ancillary buildings, including the Mould Loft and the Time Offices, and the slipways have been half in-filled many years ago to make a car park. Where there was once an army of men working, there are now weeds and open mussel shells, dropped from a height by seagulls which have plucked them from the banks of the

Derelict building on Sydenham Road prior to development in the Titanic Quarter.

(Wesley Johnston)

The Drawing office today.
(© Ross McDonald)

river Lagan. However, there is some regeneration going on in this wasteland, with building work well underway in an area adjacent to the *Titanic* skipway and the impressive 'Titanic Belfast' structure now erected, to tell the story of the famous ship.

Take a walk around Belfast and there is little in the way of statues, memorials or plaques to tell visitors of the city's shipbuilding past. The Belfast that saw the 1630s departure of the *Eagle Wing* is a far cry from the city of today. Then Belfast was little more than a few streets, if indeed they could even be classed as such. There was no organised shipbuilding and the construction of the vessel that attempted to cross the Atlantic was undertaken by a handful of men using the local oak.

It was to be many years before the town of Belfast would see a properly organised shipbuilding yard, when the Ritchie family left their home in Scotland in 1791 and came to Belfast. William Ritchie wrote many years later that when he arrived in Belfast with a group of his skilled craftsmen, there were only a few ships' carpenters who were working on their own initiative. It is recorded that Belfast businessmen had approached Ritchie with the suggestion that he relocate his shipbuilding business to Belfast. What Ritchie saw, when he first visited Belfast, was a fragmented 'shipbuilding industry', situated on the shores of the river Lagan at Belfast. He immediately saw the potential of setting himself up in business with no formal or organised opposition from a rival shipbuilder. He hoped to dominate and prosper from the construction of ships, and that is in fact what he did. In a 19 year period from his arrival, William and his brother John built 40 vessels ranging in size from 50 tons to a massive 450 tons. Ritchie also gave much back to the town that he adopted. He was a member of the Academical Institution, on the organising Committee for the General Hospital, as well as being Chairman of the Charitable Society, and, most importantly, he and his brothers were to lay the foundation stone for what would eventually put Belfast at the centre of the world's shipbuilders.

By the year 1820, William Ritchie, who was then aged 60, decided to retire from the business. The industry that he had established started to expand, with others seeing the opportunity to start their own businesses. One such man was Charles Connell, who had managed Ritchie's yard for many years. Throughout that time he learned the art of ship construction, no doubt waiting for an opportunity to open his own shipyard. Ritchie's yard was bought over and renamed Charles Connell and Sons and, at the same time, Hugh Ritchie and another brother, John, also set up in partnership.

There is a direct link from that first shipyard of the Ritchie's to the massive Harland and Wolff yard on Queen's Island. This was accomplished through buy-outs, partnerships and takeovers. Sadly, however, the contribution made by William Ritchie and his family has all but been forgotten. There is only one official portrait of him, which is in the safe care of the Belfast Harbour Commissioners, but there is no statue or work of art (apart from a very worn tablet secured to a wall over his grave in Clifton Street) to show the world where, when and why this Scottish man made Belfast his home.

A modern view of the Thompson Dry Dock.

In those early days, the Belfast Ballast Board finally saw the need to make major improvements to the port and facilities at Belfast for both shipping, ship repair and construction. Civil engineer William Dargan made massive improvements to the approaches to Belfast when he undertook the task of both straightening and deepening the river Lagan. In doing so, he accidentally created the location for the world's largest shipyards, then known as Dargan's Island. Sadly, yet again, apart from a few roads in the harbour estate being named after him, any visitors to Belfast today would have a hard time finding any other information about him. Nowhere is there a mention of this man, who along with his workforce reshaped the heart of East Belfast, built the Lagan canal and was responsible for the construction of most of the railways still in existence the greater Belfast area today. Dargan sadly has even been written out of the history books, following the decision by the Belfast fathers to rename *his* island in favour of Her Majesty Queen Victoria.

It was on this island, now named Queen's Island, that Robert Hickson set out an iron shipbuilding yard. Hickson, who was born in 1815 in County Kerry, arrived in Belfast to try his hand at running an iron foundry. The Hickson family, who lived in Tralee, owned ships and also ran a timber importing business. They probably would have had contact with the wooden ship *Jeannie Johnston*, which transported many emigrants to the new world in America during the Irish Famine. To its credit the ship never lost one passenger on any of its voyages and was also engaged in importing timber to Ireland. Hickson's venture into the world of iron production was to fail miserably. His purchase of the iron foundry off Cromac Street was really doomed from the outset, when it became clear that the area didn't actually have any of the raw materials needed to produce iron in a profitable manner. Undaunted by this down turn, Hickson tried to salvage something from the situation and came up with the idea of building iron ships on Queen's Island, something that was already happening in the shipyards of England. He wrote to the Harbour Commissioners, proposing to lease a plot of land for his new shipbuilding venture and they agreed. He quickly received an order from Edward Bates of Liverpool. It's not surprising that his first order came from this seafaring city, as he had connections there.

Hickson had a family background in timber business and may have been fairly competent in the world of buying and selling, but he was certainly not an engineer. He was also let down badly by the local Belfast work force, particularly his first manager, Mr Jordan. By all accounts Jordan was happier being 'one of the boys' than managing the shipyard and ensuring that targets were met. Due to the inexperience of Hickson and Jordan's poor supervision things rapidly went down hill. In September 1854, just before the launch of his first ship, Hickson had to intervene to save its construction. Jordan was sacked and the whole fiasco left Hickson all too aware of his own limitations and inexperience in shipbuilding. He needed a replacement manager, quickly, so placed an advertisement in the national press.

A couple of months later a young Edward Harland decided to cross the Irish Sea from England and take up this job. Harland, with his previous experience in the shipbuilding on the Clyde and the Tyne, was the right person to help Hickson turn around his yard, but it was an uphill battle. After three years of working in Belfast Harland began to consider opening his own yard and looked around various locations in England and Ireland. However, he could see the potential of Hickson's small yard and its situation on an island in the river Lagan. Hickson, sensing that Harland was searching for new horizons, offered his yard to him as the sale would solve Hickson's financial problems. Harland's only problem was that he didn't have the money available to finalise the purchase. Financial backing came from Harland's uncle through marriage, Gustav Schwabe. Hickson was quite delighted to offer Edward Harland the yard for £5,000 and he generously included a hundred pound discount in the deal if payment was made in cash.

With this family and financial backing, Edward Harland's shipyard started off heading in the right direction. Schwabe suggested that Harland consider taking his true nephew, Gustav Wolff, into the business and Harland agreed. With Schwabe investing such a large amount of money (several million pounds by today's standards) into this small shipbuilding yard, he needed to ensure that the venture was economically successful. He called on the 'old boy' network to secure as many orders for Harland as possible. Schwabe was heavily involved in the Bibby Shipping Line and, over a period of around 11 years, he arranged for the Bibby Line to have 18 ships constructed, each one an improvement on the last. New radical designs were used and many of the 'old breed' of sailors called these new ships names such as 'Belfast Bottom' and 'coffin ships'.

The fortunes of the new Belfast yard were to take a massive boost, when Schwabe played a masterstroke by introducing his friend Thomas Henry Ismay to Harland and Wolff. Ismay had just bought the bankrupt White Star Line and needed to update his fleet. The building of the *SS Oceanic* was the start of a long and generally quite happy relationship between the two firms. The ship, with its first class accommodation placed amidships and palatial interiors, was rightly deemed to be the first modern Atlantic Liner ever built. Fine praise indeed not only for the ship but the Belfast workforce who built it.

Over the years that followed, both the White Star Line and the shipyard grew together and profited out of their mutual understanding and agreement. Harland and Wolff set a standard in not only the design of the ship but also the interior fixtures and fittings. Edward Harland, with his engineering background, naturally ran the construction side of the business, while at the beginning Gustav Wolff designed not only the ships but also the internal fittings and accommodation. He also was responsible for keeping a watchful eye on the firm's accounts. When Wolff, later in his career, made that famous speech, "Sir Edward Harland builds the ships for our firm; Mr Pirrie makes the speeches, and as for me I smoke the cigars for the firm", he was clearly massively underplaying his role in the company.

Harland and Wolff engaged local workmen who, although not experienced master craftsmen, were willing to quickly learn the skills needed for this new and growing industry. They also continued with Hickson's 'gentlemen apprentice scheme' to fill the management positions within the firm. This was a two-tier

system of entry for young men into the shipyard. Apprentices were engaged in the usual way but to ensure that there was always a good supply of well-qualified and motivated middle and senior management, the gentlemen (or premium) apprentice system was used. Harland and Wolff were also very good at spotting potential in the young men training in the shipyard and, more importantly, they were not afraid to let the men prove themselves. If the young men succeeded they were quickly promoted up the management chain, taking on more important responsibilities. Some of those who quickly rose to positions of authority were Walter Wilson, William Pirrie, Alexander M. Carlisle, Thomas Andrews, Saxon Payne and Charles Payne (no relation). All of these men moved up through the yard to sit around the Directors' table.

Harland and Wolff were also considerate and not afraid to be of assistance to others. Consider Frank Workman and George Clark, two young apprentices who went through the accelerated apprentice scheme. When these men had completed their time, not only did they both leave the shipyard where they had learnt their skills, but they then went about setting up their own shipyard just a few hundred yards across the river. Harland and Wolff would have been forgiven if they had started a 'dirty tricks campaign' against these two men whom they had trained, but they didn't, even when some customers moved to the new yard. Luckily for Harland and Wolff, it quickly became obvious that Workman Clark were to specialise and would not really be in direct competition with their former employers. Indeed some company records show that at times communication between them was "quite friendly".

However, Harland and Wolff must have been a little concerned about the competition from Workman Clark when they decided to re-establish the firm in 1874 and admit some of the younger men onto the Board as Directors. This was a shrewd move in a couple of ways. Firstly, it provided extra capital for the shipyard. Secondly and more importantly, it would ensure loyalty to the firm.

The Wilson brothers and William Pirrie were the first to be invited onto the Board. In later years they would be followed by Alexander Carlisle, Thomas Andrews, Saxon Payne and Charles Payne. All of these men had joined the shipyard under the premium apprentice scheme and had progressed on to management. Pirrie emerged as the main contender to run the Board of Directors and in the closing years of the nineteenth century he was poised to take control of the yard. By then both Harland and Wolff had taken a back seat in the affairs of their shipyard and entered politics, but it was the sudden death of Sir Edward Harland that allowed Pirrie to take command of the shipyard.

An examination of the life and times of William James Pirrie, 1st Viscount K.P., P.C., H.M.L. is not something that I ever intended to undertake in this book. His life and his wheeling and dealing are something that could fill many, many pages of print but I have tried to show something of his manner. When he staked his claim as the next Chairman of the shipyard, to lead the Board of Directors, he was, I believe, doing it for all the right reasons. His major problem was that he was not the same type of businessman as Edward Harland had been. Where Harland was open to fresh ideas and allowed those young men who were progressing through the shipyard to have their say, Pirrie would become quite the reverse. Over the years he became very secretive and would only ever fully discuss his business matters with his wife Margaret or his trusted bookkeeper John Philips. However, despite Pirrie's manner, his business sense was not to be underestimated:

> "Those who met Lord Pirrie for the first time were quite confident that they would have no difficulty in besting (beating or out doing) the apparently guileless innocent gentleman who ushered them into his office. But no matter who they were, they all came out shorn."[1]

Pirrie has been accused of not planning for the future of the shipyard, as he never announced who his chosen successor was to be upon retirement. It is thought that he had hoped his nephew, Thomas Andrews, would succeed him but this was never made publicly known to his fellow Directors. This theory is supported in one of the many letters written by Saxon Payne, a fellow Managing Director of the yard, and sent to the Andrews family after the loss of *Titanic*. Regarding Andrews, Payne writes that with his knowledge and capacity so abundantly proved, Thomas was regarded by all the staff as "the coming man of the establishment".

> "His position in the Shipping and Shipbuilding World was a most important and promising one, probably no other Naval Architect had equal experience in the construction and working of large steamers."

Finally, Payne explained that the assumption was that Andrews was being groomed to succeed Pirrie, as Chairman of the shipyard of Harland and Wolff:

> "Closely associated as he had been for a number of years past with his Uncle, Lord Pirrie, the Chairman of Harland and Wolff Ltd., it was the general expectation of the prophets that he would succeed and worthily maintain the traditions of that great shipbuilder."[2]

William Pirrie had married his cousin Margaret Carlisle and they were to have no children. Thomas Andrews was the second closest male heir to Pirrie. If left in Comber, Andrews would either have joined the flax mill or have read law like his siblings, but Pirrie's unexpected move to train him as a shipbuilder in the shipyard was undertaken without upsetting the Andrews' family business. The elder brother John was already working at the mill so there was no issue with taking Thomas away to the Belfast yard at the early age of 16. The problem for the shipyard was that, following the devastating loss of the *Titanic* in 1912, which claimed the lives of Andrews and the entire Harland and Wolff Guarantee Group, Pirrie never made any alternative arrangements for who should succeed him.

Towards the beginning of the twentieth century, things began to go wrong for the shipyard and Pirrie in particular. Harland died in 1895, Walter Wilson retired in 1901 and died in 1904, and Director Alexander M. Carlisle parted company with Pirrie, his brother in law, in 1910, after many heated arguments. Thomas Andrews, the much relied upon heir apparent, perished in 1912, and finally Pirrie's good friend and early mentor Gustav Wolff died in 1913.

Pirrie then became obsessed with trying to eradicate the name of Harland or anyone or anything associated with it. Denis Rebbeck, in his unpublished 1950 thesis, *The history of iron shipbuilding on the Queen's Island up to July 1874*, states "that Pirrie was responsible for sending Sir Edward Harland's nephew (Henry Harland) as far away from Belfast as possible after Sir Edward's death, so that the name of Harland should be dulled, forgotten and outshone by the increasing brilliance of the name of Pirrie." Henry Harland was quickly dispatched to China.

Pirrie also became more and more secretive with the firm's accounts and following a meeting with him, the Chairman of the firm's Bank said that he found it difficult to understand the accounts. To raise extra cash Pirrie even had the audacity to sell his Board of Directors extra shares in the Company. They thought they were getting voting rights but in fact they were just handing money over to their Chairman and getting nothing in return. When Pirrie died and the Directors finally opened the accounts, there was little left in the company's coffers. Pirrie had surrounded himself with a group men who would agree with all his decisions, yet none of them would be prepared to stand up to his bullish ways, and it was this lack of trust and faith in others that was to be his downfall.

Shipbuilding in Belfast carried on and was extremely busy during the First World War, with the continuous demand to replace ships that had been sunk. However, it suffered during the slump in the 1930s and Belfast didn't launch a single ship between 1932 and 1933. In 1935 Harland and Wolff bought over the 'wee yard' of Workman Clark and again, during the Second World War, the shipbuilding fortunes improved. Sadly, this was short lived and after the war it became clear that British shipbuilding was in terminal decline. Harland and Wolff decided to specialise and moved away from ocean liners to designing and constructing bulk oil carriers. To assist with this they constructed the massive building dock at the Musgrave Channel, where the yard had expanded to in June 1916. The dock was surmounted by Samson and Goliath, the two yellow cranes that have now become an iconic part of the Belfast skyline. Here they built many supertankers, including the 1970, 126,538 ton *Esso Ulidia*.

World shipping continued to decline and, although they clung on for many years, finally in 2003, the last ship to be built at Harland and Wolff (the *Anvil Point*) was floated out from the building dock. However, Harland and Wolff are still a going concern today. The company reinvented itself and is currently at the forefront of massive wind and wave turbine construction, with the repair side of the firm kept busy as well.

The Anvil Point. The last ship to be built at Harland and Wolff.
(E. Gregory Collection)

At the beginning of this chapter I asked if you had heard the joke that starts with, "There was an Irish man, a Scots man and an English man"? Well, the punch line is that out of virtually nothing, they managed to firmly place Belfast at the centre of the shipbuilding world. All those men with a vision, combined with the thousands who laboured through difficult conditions, created a success story unmatched anywhere else in the world. Their efforts put Belfast well and truly on the map, and her ships, built on a mud flat to the east of the city, were fitted with a maker's plaque to recognise this achievement. It was thus with a sense of pride that men spoke of working on Belfast-built ships, while seafarers boasted of sailing upon them.

Today, in the second decade of the twenty-first century, there is very little left standing to show the visitor any of Belfast's shipbuilding history. In the grounds of Belfast City Hall there is a statue of Sir Edward Harland, a bronze bust of William Pirrie and the *Titanic* memorial. But where is the public acknowledgment of all those other influential figures in shipbuilding, such as the Ritchie brothers, Paul Rodgers, William Dargan, Robert Hickson, Walter Wilson, Gustav Wolff, Frank Workman, Ernest Clark, Alexander M. Carlisle, and Thomas Andrews? It's strange that there isn't a fitting sculpture to honour all those who contributed to the success of the industry but, as mentioned earlier, the 'Titanic Belfast' building is nearing completion at Queen's Island. This building will give the visitor a 'Titanic' experience and perhaps this public display is what is needed for Belfast to take full ownership of the history of its past. The thousands of local people, both men and women, who worked, and sadly those who died, in our shipyards must never be forgotten. We must be proud of the achievements of those who went before us and made Belfast the only place to "have her built."

Opposite: Titanic *memorial in the grounds of the City Hall.*
(Peter Clarke)

Did you know…?

Some interesting facts about the shipyards of Belfast

- The Arrol Gantry constructed at the Queens shipyard in Belfast was in later years costing Harland and Wolff around £40,000 per year to maintain. Having been a landmark in the shipyard for almost sixty years, it was demolished in the mid 1960s.

- Messers Stothert and Pitt supplied the cranes that straddled the Arrol Gantry.

- A hydraulic riveting machine weighted around 7 tons.

- The bronze centre propeller on the *Olympic* weighted 22 tons.

- There were over 2,000 windows and side lights (port holes) on *Olympic*.

- Following the death of Thomas Andrews on *Titanic*, Edward Wilding was promoted to the position of Head of the Designing Department. A perk of the job was that he could now lunch in the Company's subsidised Dining Room.

- In 1912, Samuel Morrow, a riveter in Harland and Wolff, died after working in the yard for 43 years. The Directors decided to give his widow a one off gratuity of five pounds.

- Women were employed in manual work in the shipyard in the Upholstering shop.

- In 1900 women were employed as Tracers or Secretaries in the Office Block.

- The families of the Harland and Wolff staff that were lost on the *Titanic* received their wages until the 30 June 1912.

- A £15 grant was given for the education of the children of Roderick Chisholm, Anthony Wood Frost and Robert McKnight. They were members of the Harland and Wolff Guarantee Group that were lost.

- In June 1916, Harland and Wolff leased land from the Belfast Harbour Commissioners and set up the Musgrave, or East, Yard. Ships with diesel engines could be built there, on one of the six slipways.

- The *War Riddle*, No. 565, was the first ship launched from the new yard on November 1919.

- In 1859 Harland and Wolff shipyard covered an area of 1¾ acres and employed 100 men. By 1917 the site covered 135 acres and over 15,000 were employed.

- Sir Edward Harland had a vision of constructing a ship 1,000 ft long, Lord Pirrie wanted to create a 1,500 ft vessel.

- Sir Edward only wore the best of clothes, and his shirts were made from the finest linen. He had a short neck and set a design for the shirt maker to follow. He was obviously very proud of the shirts and wrote to Walter Wilson telling him of the design and sending him one of his old shirts to try on. He added a note explaining the design and suggested that Wilson try the shirt for a day or two and finished his note by saying, "don't return it".

- Lady Rosa Harland died on 21 October 1911 at the home of her niece, in Tunbridge Wells, Kent. She was laid to rest beside her husband at the Belfast City Cemetery.

- Lady Pirrie died in her London home on 17 June 1935. She was laid to rest with her husband at the Belfast City Cemetery.

- Thomas Andrews lived at 12 Windsor Avenue, Belfast, with his wife, daughter and five female servants.

- J.C. White and Co. of Belfast were the solicitors for Harland and Wolff.

- A rivet could be anything in diameter between 1¼–2 inches. The hydraulic rivet machine exerted a pressure of 40–55 psi when operated.

- R.J. Welch, the official Harland and Wolff photographer lived at Longsdale Street in Belfast and died in 1939.

- William Pirrie was 5'9" tall and had grey eyes; Lady Pirrie was 5'6" with blue eyes; Thomas Andrews was 6'0" and had brown eyes; Helen Andrews was 5'2" and had hazel eyes; while Alexander Carlisle was 5'11" and had blue eyes.

- Harland and Wolff also had a small shipbuilding yard on the river Foyle at Londonderry.

- The maximum length that a wooden ship could be was around 300 ft.

- Sailing ships were constructed at Carrickfergus between 1874 and 1893.

- In 1888 Walter Wilson and William Pirrie had a joint annual salary from the shipyard of £4,500.

- Harland and Wolff always considered that the sea trials of their new ships was "a useless and expensive amusement" and that the best and only true test of a ships performance was while at sea during the first voyage.

- Thomas H. Ismay gave a donation of £2,000 to Liverpool University for the creation of a scholarship in the name of E.J. Harland.

Belfast Shipbuilding Chronology

1538	Queen Elizabeth received a report that Belfast seemed a suitable place for shipbuilding.
1613	Belfast declared a free port in the Charter of Belfast.
circa 1636	The 150 ton *Eagle Wing* built in Belfast.
1662	Government declared Belfast as a landing place.
1663	Small vessels ranging from 12 - 20 tons built in or near Belfast, including a barque of 25 tons.
1669	250 ton *Loyal Charles* built in Belfast.
1675	Belfast Town Council agreed to enlarge quay facilities in High Street.
1751	John Ritchie born in Scotland.
1755	William Ritchie born in Scotland.
1767	Hugh Ritchie born in Scotland.
1775	William Ritchie established a shipyard in Saltcoates, Ayrshire, Scotland.
1780	*January* William Pirrie Senior born in Fortwilliam.
1791	*March* William Ritchie first visited Belfast. *3 July* William Ritchie set up shipyard in Belfast, in partnership with his brother Hugh.
1792	*7 July* William Ritchie built and launched 300 ton *Hibernia*.
1793	William Ritchie dissolved partnership with his brother Hugh.
1796	Construction of the first Dry Dock in Belfast, built by William Ritchie.
1798	Hugh Ritchie sets up his own shipyard with his brother John.
1799	*February* William Dargan born in County Carlow.
1807	Hugh Ritchie died, he was succeeded by his brother John.
1811	John Ritchie took Alexander McLaine as a partner to found Ritchie & McLaine.
1820	William Ritchie retired at the age of 60, allowing Charles Connell to manage his shipyard.
1824	Charles Connell purchased William Ritchie's shipyard and renamed it Charles Connell & Sons.
1826	Steamboat *The Chieftain* built by Ritchie and McIlwaine. Second dry dock called No. 2 Claredon Dry Dock opened.
1828	John Ritchie died at the age of 77. His shipyard taken over by Alexander McLaine who renamed the yard Alexander McLaine & Sons.
1831	*May* Edward J. Harland born in Yorkshire. River Lagan deepened by the Belfast Ballast Board.
1834	*January* William Ritchie died. *November* Gustav Wilhelm Wolff born in Hamburg.
1837	Belfast Ballast Board by Act of Parliament empowered to create a new channel in the Lagan.
1838	Another shipyard established under the name of Kirwan & McCune. Coates & Young of the Lagan Foundry launched an iron ship the *Countess of Caledon*.
1839	*November* Walter Henry Wilson born in Belfast.
1840	Belfast Ballast Board engaged William Dargan to straighten the Lagan, the spoil to be deposited at the east side of the river, eventually to be known as Dargan's Island.
1845	Belfast Ballast Board purchased all the land of the shipbuilding yards and virtually closed them down. A Pond for holding timber was cut at Dargan's Island but permission was withheld for shipyards to operate there.
1847	*May* William James Pirrie born in Canada. Belfast Harbour Commissioners constituted.
1849	Second cut to river Lagan completed by William Dargan. Victoria Channel officially opened by Captain William Pirrie. Queen Victoria visits Belfast, in her honour Dargan's Island is renamed Queen's Island. Belfast Ballast Board purchased a patent slip on Dargan's Island to haul ships out of the water.
1850	Edward Harland employed by J & G Thompson,

Marine Engineers on the Clyde, in Scotland. Gustav W. Wolff apprenticed to Joseph Whitworth & Co., Manchester.

1851   Belfast Ballast Board laid out a slip for Thompson & Kirwan (formerly Kirwan & McCune) on Queen's Island.
Slipway also laid out for Charles Connell adjacent to Ritchies' Dry Dock on the County Antrim side of the river Lagan.

1853   Belfast Harbour Commissioners build a four acre shipyard for Robert Hickson on Queen's Island at a cost of £1116 17s 6p. Hickson had taken over the Belfast Iron Works.

1854   Alexander Montgomery Carlisle born in Ballymena.
September Robert Hickson launched his first ship the *Silistra*. Hickson's manager, Mr J. Jordan, sacked prior to launch. Advertisement placed for new Manager.
Christmas Edward Harland engaged as Manager in Hickson's shipyard.

1857   *May* Margaret Montgomery Carlisle born in Ballymena.
Sinclair Seamans Church in Belfast constructed. Walter H. and Alexander Wilson engaged as gentleman apprentices by Robert Hickson.

1858   *June* William Pirrie Senior died.
21 September Edward Harland buys Hickson's shipyard for £5,000 minus a £100 discount.
1 November Firm of Edward Harland & Company established. Harland purchased the semi-derelict yard of Thompson & Kirwan.

1859   *July* Edward Harland launches his first ship, the *Venetian*, for Bibby Line.

1860   *January* Edward Harland marries Rosa Wann Approximately 100 men employed at the Harland shipyard.

1861   *11 April* Gustav W. Wolff taken on as a personal assistant by Edward Harland.

1862   *January* Gustav W. Wolff taken on as a full partner and his name added to Harland's to create the shipyard of Harland & Wolff.
In the region of 150 men employed in the Harland & Wolff shipyard.
23 June William J. Pirrie engaged as a gentleman apprentice.
November Problems with the Belfast Harbour Commissioners and the location of the proposed Hamilton Dry Dock left Harland & Wolff considering a move to Liverpool.

1864   Rioting in Belfast between Catholics and Protestants spills into the shipyard of Harland & Wolff.

1867   Abercorn Basin & Hamilton Dry Dock completed.
MacIlwaine & Lewis have shipyard, known as Ulster Iron Works at Abercorn Basin.
William Dargan died.

1868   MacIlwaine & Lewis listed as Iron Shipbuilders. William J. Pirrie completes apprenticeship and is appointed draughtsman.
Walter H. Wilson promoted to Manager of the yard.

1869   *July* Thomas Ismay buys the failing White Star Line.

1870   *August* Harland & Wolff launch *Oceanic*, the first ship for the built for the White Star Line.
Alexander M. Carlisle engaged as a gentleman apprentice.
Robert Hickson died in the Liverpool area.

1872   Working hours in Harland & Wolff reduced from 57 to 51.
Street rioting in Belfast over Home Rule Bill, 500 men stopped work.

1873   *February* Thomas Andrews born in Comber. Gustav W. Wolff becomes a partner in the Belfast Rope Works.

1874   William J. Pirrie, Walter & Alexander Wilson offered a partnership in Harland & Wolff.
Alexander Wilson in charge of engine design and Chief Draughtsman.
April Edward Harland elected as Chairman of the Belfast Harbour Commissioners.

1875   Capital of Harland & Wolff £125,000. 1,000 men employed.
Alexander Wilson left shipyard, moving to John Rowan & Sons, marine engineers, as Managing Director.

1876   John MacIlwaine & Richard Lewis launch their first ship *Elizabeth Jane*.

1878   Alexander M. Carlisle appointed shipyard manager of Harland & Wolff.
Harland & Wolff acquire shipyard of Alexander McLaine for around £7,000.

1879   Workman & Clark open shipyard on Queen's Island.
William J. Pirrie marries Margaret Montgomery Carlisle.
Harland & Wolff expand Engine Works and

181

start building work on Main Office block.

1885	Edward Harland elected as Mayor of Belfast for the years 1885 & 1886. MacIlwaine & Lewis dissolve partnership. MacIlwaine takes Hector McColl as new partner.
1888	MacIlwaine with his new partner launch a 1,608 ton ship named *Titanic*.
1889	Thomas Andrews entered Harland & Wolff as a gentleman apprentice. Alexandra Dry Dock opened by Prince Albert Victor. *Teutonic* the first ship to enter the dock.
1892	Gustav W. Wolff elected as M.P. for East Belfast unopposed for five General Elections.
1893	Workman & Clark buy over MacIlwaine & McColl. Paul Rodgers Carrickfergus shipyard launches the *Result*.
1894	William J. Pirrie becomes Managing Director. Elected as Councillor to Belfast City Council and Commissioner to Belfast Harbour Commissioners. Harland & Wolff seriously considered relocating shipyard to England if the Home Rule Bill was successful.
1895	*December* Sir Edward Harland died. William J. Pirrie becomes Chairman of the shipyard.
1896	William J. Pirrie elevated to Lord Mayor of Belfast, starts campaign to have the Royal Victoria Hospital built.
1898	William J. Pirrie honoured as first Freeman of the City of Belfast.
1901	Walter H. Wilson retires from shipyard.
1902	Belfast Harbour Commissioners agree to construct the massive Thompson dry dock.
1904	*May* Walter H. Wilson died.
1906	Gustav W. Wolff retired from the shipyard, William J. Pirrie became controlling Chairman. *July* William J. Pirrie created Baron Pirrie.

■ 182

1907	William J. Pirrie agrees to build three ships in the new Olympic class for J. Bruce Ismay, Chairman of the White Star Line.
1908	Contract letter signed between Harland & Wolff and the White Star Line for the construction of the *Olympic, Titanic & Britannic*. *16 December* Keel for *Olympic*, shipyard No. 400, laid at new No. 1 slipway.
1909	*22 March* Keel for *Titanic*, shipyard No. 401, laid at new No. 2 slipway.
1910	*20 October Olympic* launched.
1911	*2 February* Gustav W. Wolff elected to Freedom of the City of Belfast. *31 May Titanic* launched, *Olympic* handed over to White Star Line. *21 October* Lady Rosa Harland died in Kent, England. *30 November* Keel of *Britannic*, shipyard No. 433, laid on No. 1 slip.
1912	*2 April* Following short and successful sea trials *Titanic* leaves Belfast. *10 April Titanic* commences maiden voyage from Southampton. *15 April* Thomas Andrews is lost on *Titanic*.
1913	*April* Gustav W. Wolff died.
1914	*1 January* Alexander M. Carlisle appointed as Managing Director. *26 February Britannic* launched.
1916	*21 November Britannic* sank in Aegean Sea while operating as a hospital ship in the First World War.
1920	*June Titanic* memorial unveiled and dedicated in Belfast.
1921	*July* William J. Pirrie created Viscount Pirrie of Belfast.
1924	*June* William J. Pirrie died.
1925	Alexander M. Carlisle died.
1935	*17 June* Lady Margaret Montgomery Pirrie died.
1937	*19 September Olympic* scrapped at Inverkeithing.

White Star Line vessels built by Harland and Wolff

Name: **OCEANIC**
Shipyard Number: 73
Type: Passenger ship
Tonnage: 3,808
Length: 420 ft
Rated Speed: 14 knots
Launched: 27 August 1870
Delivered: 24 February 1871
Engines: Compound 4 cylinder, single screw by Maudslay, Sons, & Field of London
Accommodation: 1st Class 166, 3rd Class 1,000

History of Vessel:
The first ship for the White Star Line, and often cited as the *Mother of Modern Liners*. The ship was the first to have promenade decks. *Oceanic* arrived in Mersey in late February 1871, and began preparing for her maiden voyage, sailing from Liverpool, bound for Queenstown and then on to New York, on 2 March 1871. During the voyage the ship had to return quite quickly to Liverpool for repairs to overheating bearings, with the maiden voyage recommencing on 14 March. For several years the vessel was chartered to the Occidental & Oriental Line engaged on the San Francisco–Hong Kong route. Returned to Belfast in 1895 for fitting new engines but this plan was cancelled and the *Oceanic*, was sold for scrap in London in 1896 after giving 26 years service.

Name: **ATLANTIC**
Shipyard Number: 74
Type: Passenger ship
Tonnage: 3,708
Length: 420 ft
Rated Speed: 14 knots
Launched: 26 November 1870
Delivered: 3 June 1871
Engines: Compound 4 cylinder, single screw by G. Forrester & Company, Liverpool
Accommodation: 1st Class 166, 3rd Class 1,000

History of Vessel:
Atlantic was taken over by the line on 3 June 1871 and sailed from Liverpool on her maiden voyage on 8 June. She left Liverpool for her 19th voyage on 20 March 1873, under the command of Captain J.H. Williams. In the early morning of 1 April while very low on coal to fuel her boilers, she ran aground at Meaghers Island, near Halifax, Nova Scotia. Passengers and crew tried to get ashore in the terrible weather, the hull of the ship failed, lifeboats were washed away and in the terrible commotion out of a total of 931 passengers and crew, 585 drowned, including 77 children.

Name: **BALTIC**
Shipyard Number: 75
Type: Passenger ship
Tonnage: 3,708
Length: 420 ft
Rated Speed: 14 knots
Launched: 8 March 1871
Delivered: 2 September 1871
Engines: Compound 4 cylinder, single screw by Maudslay, Sons, & Field of London
Accommodation: 1st Class 166, 3rd Class 1,000

History of Vessel:
Baltic sailed on her maiden voyage in September 1871, and set a new record by averaging better than 15 knots during an 1873 return journey from Liverpool to New York. On 7 May 1888, the ship had to return to Queenstown, for repairs to an engine, which lasted for over 10 hours when the low-pressure cylinders failed. In 1888 the ship was sold to the Holland-America Line, and renamed *Veendam*. In 1890 the ship had triple expansion engines fitted. On the 7 February 1898, the ship struck a submerged wreck in the North Atlantic and sank with no loss of life.

Name: **REPUBLIC**
Shipyard Number: 76
Type: Passenger ship
Tonnage: 3,708
Length: 420 ft
Rated Speed: 14 knots
Launched: 4 July 1871
Delivered: 21 January 1872
Engines: Compound 4 cylinder, single screw by G. Forrester & Company, Liverpool
Accommodation: 1st Class 166, 3rd Class 1,000

History of Vessel:
The maiden voyage of the ship was on 1 February 1872 on the Liverpool to New York route. On 20 September 1885 the ship collided with the Cunard vessel *Aurania* when in the Mersey casing slight damage to both vessels. She was sold to the Holland-American Line in 1889 and renamed *Maasdam*. Subsequently resold and named *Vittoria*, the ship was finally broken up in Genoa in 1910.

Name: **ADRIATIC**
Shipyard Number: 77
Type: Passenger ship
Tonnage: 3,868
Length: 437 ½ ft
Rated Speed: 14 knots
Launched: 17 October 1871
Delivered: 31 March 1872
Engines: Compound 4 cylinder, single screw by Maudslay, Sons, & Field of London
Accommodation: 1st Class 166, 3rd Class 1,000

History of Vessel:
The maiden voyage was on the 11 April 1872 from Liverpool to New York. *Adriatic* was more spacious than the *Oceanic*, with accommodation for of 1,150 passengers, 1,000 of them in steerage. The ship set a new Atlantic speed record of nearly 15 knots on a journey to New York in June 1872. In October 1874, while leaving New York, the ship collided with the *Parthia* owned by Cunard, as they were passing each other. In March of the following year while in heavy fog the ship hit and sank a schooner *Columbus* off New York and in December she again hit and sank another schooner *Harvest*

Queen off the east coast of Ireland. In 1878 the ship had another accident when she hit a brig *G.A. Pike* and caused the loss of five crew members. *Adriatic* was then sold for scrap and taken to the breakers' yard at Preston on 12 February 1899, after completing service of 26 years and 11 months, and quite a few accidents.

■ 184

Name: **CELTIC** — Shipyard Number: 79
Type: Passenger ship — Tonnage: 3,867
Length: 437 ½ ft — Rated Speed: 14 knots
Launched: 8 June 1872 — Delivered: 17 October 1872
Engines: Compound 4 cylinder, single screw by Maudslay, Sons, & Field of London
Accommodation: 1st Class 166, 3rd Class 1,000

History of Vessel:

Originally during construction named the *Arctic*, as another vessel of that name had sunk with over 300 persons being lost. The *Celtic*, ran aground in Belfast Lough when leaving the shipyard on her initial voyage on 18 October 1872. During her service she lost two propeller blades and on one occasion her propeller shaft snapped and the ship had to continue under sail. In May 1887 the ship in thick fog off New York hit the *Britannic* and caused considerable damage to both vessels *Celtic* made her maiden voyage for the White Star Line on the 24 October 1872 from Liverpool to New York. In 1893 was sold to the Danish Thingvalla Line, and renamed *Amerika*, The vessel was finally scrapped in 1898 in Brest.

Name: **GAELIC** — Shipyard Number: 80
Type: Cargo ship — Tonnage: 2,651
Length: 370 ft — Rated Speed: 14 knots
Launched: 21 September 1872 — Delivered: 7 January 1873
Engines: Compound 2 cylinder, single screw by J. Jack Rollo & Company, Liverpool
Accommodation: 1st Class 40

History of Vessel:

The ship was bought from J.J. Bibby during construction at Harland and Wolff. The maiden voyage was on 10 July 1873 from Liverpool to Valparaiso. She came to the assistance of the *Celtic* and had to tow her to Queenstown when the *Celtic* lost two propeller blades. In 1875 the ship was chartered to the Occidental & Oriental for use between San Francisco and Hong Kong. The vessel was sold in 1883 to a Spanish owner La Flecha and renamed *Hugo*. In 1896 the ship ran aground off Holland and was scrapped at Amsterdam.

Name: **BELGIC** — Shipyard Number: 81
Type: Cargo ship — Tonnage: 2,651
Length: 370 ft — Rated Speed: 12 knots
Launched: 17 January 1873 — Delivered: 29 March 1873
Engines: Compound 2 cylinder, single screw by J. Jack Rollo & Company, Liverpool

Accommodation: 1st Class 40

History of Vessel:

Similar to the *Gaelic* the ship was taken over from the Bibby Line during construction. The first voyage of the ship was on the 30 May 1874 from Liverpool to Valparaiso. In 1875 the ship was chartered to the Occidental & Oriental for use between San Francisco and Hong Kong. In 1883 the ship was sold to Spanish owners La Flecha, and renamed *Goefredo*. In January 1884 the *Belgic* ran aground outside Santiago and was refloated and sent to Liverpool for repair, while entering the Mersey for those repairs, a month later she was stranded on Burbo Bank, and broke her back being a total loss.

Name: **BRITANNIC** — Shipyard Number: 83
Type: Passenger ship — Tonnage: 5,004
Length: 455 ft — Rated Speed: 15 knots
Launched: 3 February 1874 — Delivered: 6 June 1874
Engines: Compound 4 Cylinder single screw by Maudslay, Sons & Field, London
Accommodation: 1st Class 220, 3rd Class 1,500

History of Vessel:

This next addition to the White Star Line was initially to be called *Hellenic* but the name was changed before she was handed over to the Line. Originally the vessel was fitted with an adjustable propeller shaft that could be raised or lowered but after a few voyages it was deemed not to be a success and was replaced with a standard design of shaft. The *Britannic* departed Liverpool on her maiden voyage to New York on the 25 June 1874, setting new speed records with an average speed of 15.7 knots. In May 1887 the ship collided with the *Celtic* off Sandy Hook, both ships were damaged. Three passengers were killed. The vessel was used as a troop transporter in 1899 for the Boer War, and on her return from Admiralty use the vessel was no longer required by the Line. After 25 years service, White Star decided that they would not stand the cost of a refit. The vessel, was taken to Hamburg in August 1903 where she was sold for £11,500 and then scrapped.

Name: **GERMANIC** — Shipyard Number: 85
Type: Passenger ship — Tonnage: 5,008
Length: 455 ft — Rated Speed: 15 knots
Launched: 15 July 1874 — Delivered: 24 April 1875
Engines: Compound 4 Cylinder single screw by Maudslay, Sons & Field, London
Accommodation: 1st Class 220, 3rd Class 1,500

History of Vessel:

The *Germanic* was to be the longest surviving ship constructed by Harland and Wolff. Her maiden voyage was on 20 May 1875 from Liverpool to New York. *Germanic* set a new record for an eastbound crossing of the North Atlantic in February 1876 when she completed the trip in 7 days, 15 hours and 17 minutes, at an average speed of 15.79 knots. During December 1894, the vessel returned to her builders to be modernised with the work taking around four months. New boilers and new Harland and Wolff designed triple-expansion engines and a new deck were fitted. On 13 February 1899 while refuelling with coal the ship capsized at New York, but rested against the quayside, allowing her to be salvaged. Her final voyage under the White Star flag was in September 1903. The vessel was then withdrawn from service and sold to the American Line. The ship was again sold to the Dominion Line who changed her name to *Ottawa*. She was later sold in 1911 to Turkish owners and renamed *Gul Djemal*. *Germanic* was demolished in Messina, Italy in 1950 having sailed for around 75 years.

Name: **WOODHOPPER** Shipyard Number: 140
Type: Hopper Barge Tonnage: unknown
Length: unknown
Launched: 18 June 1880 Delivered: 1880

History of Vessel:
Details of this vessel are unknown

Name: **ARABIC** Shipyard Number: 141
Type: Cargo ship Tonnage: 4,368
Length: 430 ft Rated Speed: 13 knots
Launched: 30 April 1881 Delivered: 12 August 1881
Engines: Compound 2 cylinder, single screw by J. Jack Rollo & Company, Liverpool

History of Vessel:
Initially to be called and launched as the *Asiatic*, the maiden voyage for *Arabic* was on 10 September 1881 from Liverpool to New York. The ship was chartered to Occidental & Oriental in 1887 for use in the Pacific. In 1890 the Arabic, sold to Holland-America, renamed *Spaarndam* and was scrapped at Preston in 1901.

Name: **COPTIC** Shipyard Number: 142
Type: Cargo ship Tonnage: 4,448
Length: 430 ft Rated Speed: 13 knots
Launched: 10 August 1881 Delivered: 9 November 1881
Engines: Compound 4 cylinder, single screw by J. Jack Rollo & Company, Liverpool

History of Vessel:
The maiden voyage was on 16 November 1881 from Liverpool to New York. In May 1884 the vessel was transferred to the New Zealand route after having a cargo refrigeration system added. The ship was then chartered to Occidental & Oriental in 1887 for use in the Pacific. The vessel was used on the Pacific route and new triple expansion engines were fitted by Harland and Wolff in 1894. She was sold in 1907 to the Pacific Mail Company and renamed *Persia* and then re-sold in 1915 to Toyo Kisen and renamed *Persia Maru*. She was scrapped in 1925 in Osaka, Japan.

Name: **IONIC** Shipyard Number: 152
Type: Cargo / Passenger ship Tonnage: 4,753
Length: 440 ft
Launched: 11 January 1883 Delivered: 28 March 1883

History of Vessel:
Ionic was placed on the London to New Zealand route in December 1884, under the joint management agreement between White Star and Shaw Savill. The ship took almost 44 days to complete the voyage. She underwent a major refit at Belfast in 1894 with new engines increasing her speed. The *Ionic* was used to transport cavalry horses for use in the Boer War. She was sold in August 1900 to the Aberdeen Line, and renamed *Sophocles*. The vessel was kept for eight years and then scrapped in Morecambe in 1908.

Name: **DORIC** Shipyard Number: 153
Type: Cargo / Passenger ship Tonnage: 4,744
Length: 440 ft
Launched: 10 March 1883 Delivered: 4 July 1883

History of Vessel:
Her maiden voyage was on the 26 July 1883 from London to Wellington. Apparently during this voyage a child was born on board the ship and named William Doric Jenkin. During 1896 the vessel was chartered to the Occidental & Oriental Steamship Company. In 1906, *Doric* was sold to the Pacific Mail Steamship Company and renamed *Asia*. The vessel was totally wrecked in fog close to Wenchau, near Shanghai, in South China in April 1911.

Name: **BELGIC (II)** Shipyard Number: 171
Type: Cargo ship Tonnage: 4,212
Length: 420 ft
Launched: 3 January 1885 Delivered: 7 July 1885

History of Vessel:
Belgic was the second ship to bear the name. She was virtually the same as the *Ionic*. The vessel was chartered to the Occidental & Oriental Steamship Company for use on their Pacific service. In 1899 the vessel was sold to the Atlantic Transport Liner and renamed *Mohawk*. The ship was then requisitioned by the UK Government for service in the Boer War. The ship was eventually scrapped at Garston in 1902.

Name: **GAELIC (II)** Shipyard Number: 172
Type: Cargo ship Tonnage: 4,205
Length: 420 ft
Launched: 28 February 1885 Delivered: 18 July 1885

History of Vessel:
As with the *Belgic*, the habit of reusing names was continued. After being charted to the Occidental & Oriental Steamship Company, the ship was sold to the Pacific Steam Navigation Company in 1905, and renamed *Callaco*. The vessel was broken up in France in 1907.

185

Name: **TEUTONIC** Shipyard Number: 208
Type: Passenger ship Tonnage: 9,685
Length: 565 ft Rated Speed: 19 knots
Launched: 19 January 1889 Delivered: 25 July 1889
Engines: 6 Cylinder Triple Expansion, Twin screw
Accommodation: 1st Class 300, 2nd Class 190, 3rd Class 1,000

■ 186

History of Vessel:
Teutonic was the first of the big liners constructed for the White Star Line, in some ways this ship was the *Titanic* of her day, and was placed on the Liverpool to New York route, with the maiden voyage taking place on 7 August 1889. Prior to this the ship had taken part in the naval review at Spithead. The ship was hailed by the press as a marvel and compared with the *Germanic* of 1875, the *Teutonic* was nearly double the size. In 1907 the ship was placed on the Southampton to New York route, in 1911 the ship was placed on the Liverpool to Montreal route. In 1915 the Admiralty commandeered the ship, for use as a troopship in the First World War. Following the war the ship was laid up at the Isle of Wight and in 1921 was broken up at Emden.

Name: **MAJESTIC** Shipyard Number: 209
Type: Passenger ship Tonnage: 9,861
Length: 565 ft Rated Speed: 19 knots
Launched: 29 June 1889 Delivered: 22 March 1890
Engines: 6 Cylinder Triple Expansion, Twin screw
Accommodation: 1st Class 300, 2nd Class 190, 3rd Class 1,000

History of Vessel:
Majestic, slightly larger than *Teutonic*, was also bound for the Liverpool to New York route, with her maiden voyage on 2 April 1890. In 1891 she gained the Blue Riband for the westward sailing with a top speed of 20.1 knots. This was lost to *Teutonic* a month later. In 1900 she was used as a troop carrier in the Boer War and after alterations and new boilers, funnels and being lengthened by 10 ft at Harland and Wolff in 1902, she returned to the North Atlantic route operating from Southampton. The ship was laid up in 1911 but brought back into service following the loss of *Titanic*. In 1913 she rescued the crew of the French schooner *Garonne*. *Majestic* was scrapped in Morecambe in 1914.

Name: **CUFIC** Shipyard Number: 210
Type: Livestock carrier Tonnage: 4,639
Length: 430 ft
Launched: 10 October 1888 Delivered: 1 December 1888

History of Vessel:
Cufic was the first of the White Star livestock carrier, with pens to transport up to 1,000 cattle. Within eight years the vessel was chartered to a Spanish company Cia Trasatlantica and renamed *Nueva Señora de Guadalupe*. In 1897, *Cufic* reverted to White Star Line ownership, while in 1900 she lost her propeller in the Atlantic and had to be towed to Queenstown. In 1901 the vessel was sold to the Dominion

Line and renamed *Manxman*, then being resold in 1915 to R. Lawrence Smith Ltd, of Montreal. In 1917 the *Cufic* was commandeered by the British Government for use as an armed merchant cruiser and a troopship. She was then sold to the Universal Transport Company of New York. The vessel sank in the North Atlantic on 18 December 1919 en route to Gibraltar, with the loss of around 40 souls.

Name: **RUNIC** Shipyard Number: 211
Type: Livestock carrier Tonnage: 4,639
Length: 430 ft
Launched: 1 January 1889 Delivered: 16 February 1889

History of Vessel:
After about six years service with the Line, the Runic was sold to the West India & Pacific Steamship Co., and renamed *Tampican*. She was resold in 1899 to Frederick Leyland & Co., resold again in 1912 to a Liverpool shipping line, and then almost immediately sold again to the South Pacific Whaling Company of Oslo and renamed *Imo*. The vessel collided with the *Mont Blanc* which was carrying explosives, very close to Halifax in early December 1917 resulting in the *Mont Blanc* exploding and killing about 1,500 people and injuring about another 8,000. A large part of the city of Halifax was destroyed in the blast. The *Imo* was badly damaged and had to be beached to prevent her from being lost. The vessel was sold once again in 1920 to Norwegian owners and renamed *Guvernoren*, running aground at Port Stanley in the Falkland Islands in thick fog in November 1921 and finally being declared a total loss.

Name: **NOMADIC** Shipyard Number: 236
Type: Livestock carrier Tonnage: 5,749
Length: 460 ft Rated Speed: 13 knots
Launched: 11 February 1891 Delivered: 14 April 1891
Engines: 6 Cylinder Triple Expansion, Twin screw

History of Vessel:
The maiden voyage from Liverpool to New York was on the 24 April 1891. The ship was the first White Star Line ship to be requisitioned for use in the Boer War and was used as a troop and horse carrier in that conflict. The *Nomadic* was sold to the Dominion Line in 1903 and renamed *Cornishman*. In 1921 the ship was resold to the Leyland Line. The vessel was broken up at Lelant, Cornwall in 1926.

Name: **TAURIC** Shipyard Number: 237
Type: Livestock carrier Tonnage: 5,749
Length: 460 ft Rated Speed: 13 knots
Launched: 12 March 1891 Delivered: 16 May 1891
Engines: 6 Cylinder Triple Expansion, Twin screw

History of Vessel:
The maiden voyage of the ship was on the 22 May 1891 from Liverpool to New York. The *Tauric* was sold to the Dominion

Line in 1903, and renamed *Welshman*, and sold again to the Leyland Line in 1921. The vessel was eventually broken up at Bowness in December 1929.

Name: NARONIC Shipyard Number: 251
Type: Livestock carrier Tonnage: 6,594
Length: 470 ft Rated Speed: 13 knots
Launched: 26 May 1892 Delivered: 11 July 1892
Engines: 6 Cylinder Triple Expansion, Twin screw

History of Vessel:
The ship's maiden voyage was on 15 July 1892 from Liverpool to New York. On the ships seventh voyage on 11 February the following year the ship set sail under the control of Captain William Roberts with 74 persons on board along with cattle and cargo. The pilot was dropped of at Point Lynas on the North Wales coast. *Naronic* continued on her voyage and was never heard from again. Sometime later four messages in bottles were washed up stating that the ship was sinking. Two were washed up on the east coast of America and two on both sides of the Irish Sea. A court of Enquiry was held in Liverpool, which put doubt on the messages and felt that the ship sank off the coast of Nova Scotia.

Name: BOVIC Shipyard Number: 252
Type: Livestock carrier Tonnage: 6,583
Length: 470 ft Rated Speed: 19 knots
Launched: 28 June 1892 Delivered: 22 August 1892
Engines: 6 Cylinder Triple Expansion, Twin screw

History of Vessel:
The maiden voyage from Liverpool to New York was on 26 August 1892. In 1917 the ship was requisitioned for service in the First World War. In 1922 the vessel was sold to the Leyland Line, becoming the *Colonian*. She was eventually scrapped at Rotterdam in 1928, after sailing for 36 years.

Name: GOTHIC Shipyard Number: 267
Type: Passenger ship Tonnage: 7,669
Length: 490 ft
Launched: 28 June 1893 Delivered: 28 Nov 1893
Laid down on slipway No. 8

History of Vessel:
Gothic was deployed on the London to New Zealand route and her maiden voyage to Wellington was on 30 December 1893. The vessel was requisitioned by the UK Government for service in the Boer war. Off the coast of Lands End in 1906, the ship's cargo of wool caught fire and she had to be grounded near Plymouth. Repairs would take nearly nine months. In 1907 the ship was sold to the Red Star Line after an extensive refit and renamed *Gothland*, being fitted out for single class. The vessel was bought back by White Star in 1911, renamed *Gothic*. On a return crossing from Canada the vessel ran onto the Gunner Rocks off the Scilly Isles in

June 1914, causing serious damage. The ship was towed off to Southampton for months of repairs. *Gothic* was eventually scrapped at Bowness in England in 1926.

Name: MAGNETIC Shipyard Number: 269
Type: Passenger Tender Tonnage: 619
Length: 170 ft
Launched: 28 March 1891 Delivered: 6 June 1891

History of Vessel:
Magnetic was commissioned to serve the *Teutonic* and the *Majestic* in the river Mersey. In June 1897 the ship was used as *Teutonic's* tender at the Spithead review to celebrate the diamond Jubilee of Queen Victoria. The vessel was withdrawn from service in 1932, and sold the following year being renamed *Ryde*. The *Ryde* was then moved to Llandudno in North Wales and used as an excursion steamer, before finally being broken up at Port Glasgow in August 1935.

Name: CEVIC Shipyard Number: 270
Type: Livestock Carrier Tonnage: 8,301
Length: 500 ft Rated Speed: 19 knots
Launched: 23 September 1893 Delivered: 6 January 1894
Engines: 6 Cylinder Triple Expansion, Twin screw
Laid down on slipway No. 6

History of Vessel:
The maiden voyage from Liverpool to New York was on 12 January 1894. In 1908 the ship was transferred to the Australia route. The *Cevic* was requisitioned by the Admiralty in 1914 and converted into a dummy battle cruiser, the *Queen Mary*. The vessel after the war was sold to Lane & McAndrew and named *Bayleaf*, then being resold in 1920 to Anglo Saxon Petroleum and being renamed *Pyrula*. She was broken up in Genoa, Italy in 1933.

Name: PONTIC Shipyard Number: 283
Type: Baggage Tender Tonnage: 395
Length: 150 ft
Launched: 3 February 1894 Delivered: 13 April 1894
Laid down on slipway No. 10

History of Vessel:
The *Pontic* was specifically designed for use as a tender for shipping on the River Mersey. The vessel was sold in 1919 to Rea Tugs of Liverpool who continued using her as a tender. *Pontic* was again sold to John Donaldson of the Clyde who used the ship as a sand ballast carrier until she broken up on the Clyde in 1930.

Name: VICTORIAN Shipyard Number: 291
Type: Passenger / Cargo Ship Tonnage: 8,767
Length: 512 ft Rated Speed: 13 knots
Launched: 6 July 1895 Delivered: 31 August 1895

187

Engines: 3 Cylinder Triple Expansion, Single screw
Accommodation: 1st Class 60
Laid down on slipway No. 9

History of Vessel:

The ship was launched for F. Leyland & Co. Ltd. and taken over by White Star, with the maiden voyage from Liverpool to New York on 7 July 1903. By the following year the vessel was used primarily for transporting cargo. In 1914 the ship was sold to the Leyland Line and renamed *Russian*. On 14 December 1916 the ship was torpedoed and sank by a German submarine near Malta.

Name: **ARMENIAN**	Shipyard Number: 292
Type: Passenger / Cargo Ship	Tonnage: 12,551
Length: 585 ft	Rated Speed: 13 knots
Launched: 25 July 1895	Delivered: 19 September 1895

Engines: 3 Cylinder Triple Expansion, Single screw
Accommodation: 1st Class 60
Laid down on slipway No. 6

History of Vessel:

The ship was originally constructed and launched for F. Leyland & Co. but was taken over by the White Star Line with the maiden voyage from Liverpool to New York on 20 March 1903. On 25 June 1915 the ship was torpedoed and sunk by a German submarine, *U38*, off Cornwall, with the loss of 20 lives.

Name: **GEORGIC**	Shipyard Number: 293
Type: Livestock Carrier	Tonnage: 10,077
Length: 558 ½ ft	Rated Speed: 13 knots
Launched: 22 June 1895	Delivered: 8 August 1895

Engines: 6 Cylinder Triple Expansion, Twin screw
Laid down on slipway No. 8

History of Vessel:

The maiden voyage from Liverpool to New York was on 16 August 1895. On 10 December 1916, during the First World War, while en route from Philadelphia to Liverpool, about 500 miles south of Cape Race, the *Georgic* was captured and finally sunk by a German raider *Moewe*.

Name: **CUFIC (II)**	Shipyard Number: 294
Type: Cargo Ship	Tonnage: 8,196
Length: 475 ft	
Launched: 8 August 1895	Delivered: 8 October 1895

Laid down on slipway No. 10

History of Vessel:

The *Cufic* originated as the *American* built by Harland & Wolff for the West India & Pacific Steam Navigation Co., but was bought by White Star Line in 1904 and renamed *Cufic*. The vessel was later sold for scrap in 1923 to Italian owners

and resold the following year to new Italian owners who decided to use the vessel rather than scrap her and changed the name to *Antartico*, and later to *Marie Guilie*. *Cufic* was finally sold for scrap in 1932 and broken up in Italy.

Name: **TROPIC**	Shipyard Number: 303
Type: Cargo Ship	Tonnage: 8,196
Length: 475 ft	
Launched: 9 July 1896	Delivered: 3 December 1896

Laid down on slipway No. 10

History of Vessel:

The *Tropic* similar to the *Cufic (II)* was built for the West India & Pacific Steam Navigation Co., and initially named *European*. The vessel was purchased by White Star Line in 1904 and remained in service until 1923. In that year, *Tropic* was sold to an Italian company and her name changed to *Artico*. The vessel was then resold in 1927, she was renamed *Transylvania*, being scrapped in Italy in 1933.

Name: **DELPHIC**	Shipyard Number: 309
Type: Passenger / Cargo Ship	Tonnage: 8,196
Length: 475 ft	
Launched: 9 July 1896	Delivered: 3 December 1896

Laid down on slipway No. 7

History of Vessel:

Initially the ship was to be used on the American route but after her maiden voyage the ship was moved to the Australia route. The vessel was requisitioned for use in the Boer War, and also in February 1917, during the First World War, she was fired on by a German submarine, which missed, however the *Delphic* was not so lucky when she was torpedoed off Bishop Rock in the Scilly Isles on 16 August 1917 while en route from Cardiff to Montevideo with a cargo of coal and sunk. Five lives were lost.

Name: **ROMANIC**	Shipyard Number: 315
Type: Passenger Ship	Tonnage: 11,394
Length: 550 ft	
Launched: 7 April 1898	Delivered: 30 June 1898

Laid down on slipway No. 6

History of Vessel:

The *Romanic* was originally built for Richard Mills and Co., and named *New England*, then in 1903 the vessel was acquired by White Star Line. *Romanic* was sold to the Canadian Pacific Line in 1912, and renamed *Scandinavian*. The vessel was scrapped in Germany in 1923.

Name: **CYMRIC**	Shipyard Number: 316
Type: Passenger Ship	Tonnage: 12,551
Length: 585 ft	Rated Speed: 15 knots

Launched: 12 October 1897   Delivered: 5 February 1898
Engines: 8 Cylinder Triple Expansion, Twin screw
Accommodation: 1st Class 150, 3rd Class 1,160

History of Vessel:
The maiden voyage was on 11 February 1898 on the Liverpool to New York Route. In 1900, during the Boer War, the ship was requisitioned and used as a troopship. In 1903 she returned to the Line and the Liverpool to New York route. In 1913 the passenger accommodation was altered and in 1915 the ship was once again placed on the Liverpool to New York route. On 8 May 1916, while on her way to Liverpool from New York and 140 miles north west of Fastnet, she was hit by three torpedoes from German submarine *U20*, and sank the following day. Five of the 110 man crew died.

Name: **OCEANIC (II)**   Shipyard Number: 317
Type: Passenger Ship   Tonnage: 17,274
Length: 685 ½ ft   Rated Speed: 19 knots
Launched: 14 January 1899   Delivered: 26 August 1899
Engines: 6 Cylinder Triple Expansion, Twin screw
Accommodation: 1st Class 300, 2nd Class 190, 3rd Class 1,000
Laid down on slipway No. 2

History of Vessel:
When the *Oceanic (II)* was delivered she was the largest vessel in the world, being the first ship to exceed the length of the *Great Eastern*. Her maiden voyage was on 6 September from Liverpool to New York, with an average speed of 19.57 knots. In September 1901 the vessel ran down the coaster *Kincora* in fog, the coaster sank with the loss of seven souls. In 1907 the vessel was transferred to the Southampton to New York route. In 1914 she was fitted out as an Auxiliary Cruiser attached to the Royal Navy. The Naval Captain, W.F. Slater had little experience in controlling such a large vessel so the *Oceanic's* own Captain Henry Smith was also in charge. This was to lead to confusion over command orders, and in September of the same year the ship was wrecked in fog of the rocks at Foula in the Shetlands and declared a total loss. She was broken up where she sat with work not being completed until 1924.

Name: **AFRIC**   Shipyard Number: 322
Type: Passenger / Cargo Ship   Tonnage: 11,948
Length: 550 ft
Launched: 16 November 1898   Delivered: 2 February 1899
Laid down on slipway No. 3

History of Vessel:
The maiden voyage was on the 8 February 1899 on the Liverpool to New York route. In September of the same year the ship was transferred to the Liverpool to Sydney route. During the Boer War the ship was used as a troop carrier. On 12 February 1917,whilst en route from London to Sydney, the *Afric* was torpedoed by German submarine *U66* whilst 12 miles southwest off Eddystone and sank with the loss of 22 souls.

Name: **MEDIC**   Shipyard Number: 323
Type: Passenger / Cargo Ship   Tonnage: 11,985
Length: 550 ft
Launched: 15 December 1898   Delivered: 6 July 1899
Laid down on slipway No. 1

History of Vessel:
The maiden voyage was on 3 August 1899 on the Liverpool to Sydney route. Later in that year the *Medic* was used as a troop transporter for the Boer War, returning to service in 1900. Again the ship was requisitioned into the war service during the First World War, returning to the White Star Line in 1919. In 1928 the ship was sold to N. Bugge of Tonsberg and converted into a whale factory ship, being renamed *Hectoria*. During the conversion the ship was to be one of the first to have an aft ramp fitted, which allowed for whales to be dragged onto the ship. The vessel was resold in 1932 to Hektoria Ltd., of London. On 11 September 1942 she was torpedoed and sunk in the North Atlantic by German submarine *U608*.

Name: **PERSIC**   Shipyard Number: 325
Type: Passenger / Cargo Ship   Tonnage: 11,973
Length: 550 ft
Launched: 7 September 1899   Delivered: 16 Nov 1899
Laid down on slipway No. 7

History of Vessel:
Her maiden voyage on the Liverpool to Sydney route was on 7 December 1899 and on that voyage, whilst off Cape Town, her rudder stock broke and she had to wait while a new one was shipped out from Harland & Wolff in Belfast. The ship was requisitioned during the First World war and in September 1918 was torpedoed by submarine *UB87* off Sicily but the ship managed to reach port for repair. The vessel was returned to the White Star Line in 1920 and underwent a refit at Harland & Wolff's yard on the Clyde. On the 7 July 1927, the ship sailed to Holland to be scrapped.

Name: **CANOPIC**   Shipyard Number: 330
Type: Passenger Ship   Tonnage: 12,096
Length: 550 ft
Launched: 31 May 1900   Delivered: 7 July 1900
Laid down on slipway No. 1

History of Vessel:
The *Canopic* was originally constructed for Richard Mills & Co., and named *Commonwealth*. In 1927, *Canopic* was sold for scrap.

Name: **RUNIC (II)**   Shipyard Number: 332
Type: Passenger Ship   Tonnage: 12,482
Length: 550 ft
Launched: 25 October 1900   Delivered: 22 December 1900
Laid down on slipway No. 7

189

History of Vessel:

The vessel was engaged on the Australian route. Runic was called up for service in the First World War. In 1928 she collided with *HMS London* and suffered damage to her stern. In July 1930 she was sold to the Sevilla Whaling Company of London and renamed *New Sevilla*. On 20 October 1940, while en route from Liverpool to the Antarctica, the ship was torpedoed off Malin Head in Ireland and sank with the loss two lives, fortunately the Runic stayed afloat for nearly 20 hours allowing over 400 people to be saved.

Name: **SUEVIC** Shipyard Number: 333
Type: Passenger Ship Tonnage: 12,531
Length: 550 ft
Launched: 8 December 1900 Delivered: 9 March 1901
Laid down on slipway No. 8

History of Vessel:

Once the ship was completed she was requisitioned by the British Government for use as a troopship, and was seriously damaged when she ran aground near the Lizard in 1907. The forward section of the ship had to be removed due to the damage, and once the ship was watertight it sailed to Southampton. Meanwhile a new 212 ft forward section was constructed in Belfast and eventually floated to Southampton. The ship was out of service nearly a year. The *Suevic* was also called up for service in the First World War. In 1928 the ship was sold to Norwegian owners and converted for use as a whaling factory ship, and renamed *Skytteren*. The ship was scuttled by her crew in April 1942 after being cut off by the German navy while trying to escape internment and reach Britain.

Name: **CELTIC (II)** Shipyard Number: 335
Type: Passenger Ship Tonnage: 20,904
Length: 680 ft Rated Speed: 16 knots
Launched: 4 April 1901 Delivered: 11 July 1901
Engines: 8 cylinder Quadruple Expansion Twin Screw
Accommodation: 1st Class 347, 2nd Class 160, 3rd Class 2,350
Laid down on slipway No. 2

History of Vessel:

Celtic (II) was the final ship to be ordered by T.H. Ismay prior to his death, and when launched was the biggest ship in the world. Her maiden voyage was on 26 July 1901 on the Liverpool to New York route. The *Celtic* was called for service under the 10th Cruiser Squadron and was fitted with 8 by 6 inch guns. For the second part of the war she was used as a troop carrier. The ship was struck by a mine off the Isle of Man on 15 February 1917 and had to be towed back to Liverpool, and then repaired at Belfast. She was again involved in another war incident when she was torpedoed soon after leaving Liverpool on 31 March 1918. *Celtic* ran aground off Roches Point lighthouse near Queenstown, on 10 December 1928. Stuck fast, she was bought by Danish ship

breakers Petersen & Albeck, and dismantled where she lay taking up to 1933 to complete the work.

Name: **CEDRIC** Shipyard Number: 337
Type: Passenger Ship Tonnage: 21,073
Length: 680 ft Rated speed: 16 knots
Launched: 21 August 1902 Delivered: 31 January 1903
Engines: 8 cylinder Quadruple Expansion Twin Screw
Accommodation: 1st Class 365, 2nd Class 160, 3rd Class 2,352
Laid down on slipway No. 3

History of Vessel:

The maiden voyage from Liverpool - New York was on 11 February 1903. In November 1904 the ship was requisitioned by the Navy and fitted out as an armed merchant cruiser. She returned to full service for the Line in December 1916. In January 1918 near the Mersey Bar, she collided with and sank the vessel *Montreal*. In 1920 alterations were made to reduce the passenger accommodation, while in 1923 the ship collided with the *Scythia* off the coast of Ireland Her last voyage was on the 5 September 1931, she was then sold for scrap and was broken up at Inverkeithing.

Name: **ARABIC (II)** Shipyard Number: 340
Type: Passenger Ship Tonnage: 15,801
Length: 600 ft Rated speed: 16 knots
Launched: 18 December 1902 Delivered: 21 June 1903
Engines: 8 cylinder Quadruple Expansion Twin Screw
Laid down on slipway No. 4

History of Vessel:

The ship was originally laid down in Belfast as the *Minnewaska* for the Atlantic Transport Company, but was taken over by White Star while the vessel was still under construction. The maiden voyage from Liverpool to New York was on 26 June 1903. For a while the ship was placed on the Liverpool to Boston route. On the 19 August 1915 the ship was torpedoed by German submarine *U24* of the Old Head of Kinsale, Ireland, the ship sank with the loss of 44 souls.

Name: **ATHENIC** Shipyard Number: 341
Type: Passenger Ship Tonnage: 12,234
Length: 500 ft
Launched: 17 August 1901 Delivered: 23 January 1902
Laid down on slipway No. 7

History of Vessel:

The *Athenic* was engaged on the New Zealand route. During the First World War the ship was used for carrying frozen meat from Australia and New Zealand. In May 1920 she rescued 80 passengers and crew from *Minamar*, which had run aground at the Bahamas. The vessel was sold in May 1928 to the Tonsberg Line, and renamed *Pelagos*. During the Second World War the vessel was captured by the Germans and was reportedly used as a refuelling ship for German submarines. In 1944 the vessel was sunk but refloated and put back into service. She was reputed to still be afloat in 1961.

Name: **CORINTHIC**   Shipyard Number: 343
Type: Passenger Ship   Tonnage: 12,231
Length: 500 ft
Launched: 10 April 1902   Delivered: 14 July 1902
Laid down on slipway No. 8

History of Vessel:
The *Corinthic* was engaged on the New Zealand route. During the First World War the ship was used like the *Athenic* for transporting frozen meat to the United Kingdom. The ship was sold for scrap to Hughes Bolckow of Blyth in 1931, and then broken up by Swan Hunter at Wallsend in 1932.

Name: **REPUBLIC (II)**   Shipyard Number: 345
Type: Passenger Ship   Tonnage: 15,378
Length: 570 ft   Rated speed: 16 knots
Launched: 26 February 1903   Delivered: 12 Sep 1903
Engines: 8 cylinder Quadruple Expansion Twin Screw
Laid down on slipway No. 6

History of Vessel:
The *Republic (II)* was launched as the *Columbus* for Richard Mills & Company The maiden voyage was from Liverpool to Boston, on 1 October 1903. The ship was purchased in December 1903 by the White Star Line, and then renamed *Republic*. The maiden voyage for White Star was on 17 December from Liverpool to Boston. The ship was also engaged on the Boston to Genoa route for a period of time. On 23 January 1909 the *Republic* collided with the *Florida* near the Nantucket Lighthouse. The *Republic* sank the following day with the loss of four souls. This was the first occasion that the new Marconi radio was used to transmit the SOS distress call. The *Baltic (II)*, another White Star Line vessel, came to the rescue. At the time it was rumoured that included in the ship's cargo were millions of US dollars in Naval pay which were being transported to Gibraltar. In the hold there were also supposed to be newly minted Gold Eagle Coins worth hundreds of millions of dollars.

Name: **IONIC (II)**   Shipyard Number: 346
Type: Passenger Ship   Tonnage: 12,232
Length: 500 ft
Launched: 22 May 1902   Delivered: 15 December 1902
Laid down on slipway No. 2

History of Vessel:
The *Ionic (II)* joined *Gothic, Athenic* and *Corinthic* on the New Zealand route. Her maiden voyage was to Wellington on 16 January 1903. She was called up for service in the First World War and returned to the White Star Line in 1919. In 1927 she rescued the crew of a fishing vessel *Daisy. Ionic* was eventually sold to Japanese ship-breakers in 1934.

Name: **BALTIC (II)**   Shipyard Number: 352
Type: Passenger Ship   Tonnage: 23,875
Length: 708 ft   Rated speed: 17 knots
Launched: 21 November 1903   Delivered: 23 June 1904
Engines: 8 cylinder Quadruple Expansion Twin Screw
Accommodation: 1st Class 425, 2nd Class 500, 3rd Class 2,000
Laid down on slipway No. 2

History of Vessel:
When delivered in 1904 the *Baltic (II)* was the largest ship in the world. The maiden voyage was on 29 June 1904 from Liverpool to New York. On 23 January 1909 the ship came to the rescue when the *Republic (II)* and *Florida* collided in fog near the Nantucket Lighthouse taking on board all the survivors. In 1914 the ship was used occasionally as a troop transporter. In 1921 the 3rd Class accommodation was reduced to around 1,000. In December 1929 she rescued the crew of a sinking schooner *Northern Light*. The ship was laid up in 1923 and on 17 February 1933 the ship sailed from Liverpool to Osaka, Japan for final breaking up.

Name: **ADRIATIC (II)**   Shipyard Number: 358
Type: Passenger Ship   Tonnage: 24,540
Length: 709 ft   Rated speed: 17 knots
Launched: 20 September 1906   Delivered: 25 April 1907
Engines: 8 cylinder Quadruple Expansion Twin Screw
Accommodation: 1st Class 425, 2nd Class 500, 3rd Class 2,000
Laid down on slipway No. 3

History of Vessel:
The maiden voyage was on 8 May 1907 from Liverpool to New York. In June of that year the ship was transferred to the Southampton route but in 1911 was transferred back to Liverpool. In 1919 the accommodation was altered to 1st Class 400, 2nd Class 465, 3rd Class 1,320, and for the next three years was transferred back to Southampton before returning in May 1922 to Liverpool. In that same year, five men were killed and four hurt after an explosion in a coal bunker on board the ship. In 1928 the accommodation was altered again to Cabin Class 506, Tourist Class 560 and 3rd Class 404. In 1933 the ship was laid up and the following year after the merger with Cunard and White Star the ship was used for seven months. On 5 March 1935 the ship was sold for scrapping and sailed to Osaka for breaking up.

Name: **CERIC**   Shipyard Number: 391
Order cancelled on 25 November 1906
Laid down on slipway No. 1 (provisionally booked)

Name: **LAPLAND**   Shipyard Number: 393
Type: Passenger Ship   Tonnage: 18,565
Length: 605 ft   Rated speed: 17 knots
Launched: 27 June 1908   Delivered: 27 March 1909
Engines: 8 cylinder Quadruple Expansion Twin Screw

Accommodation: 1st Class 450, 2nd Class 400, 3rd Class 150
Laid down on slipway No. 1

History of Vessel:

The ship was built and launched for the Red Star Line but taken over by White Star with the maiden voyage for the Line on the 29 October 1914 from Liverpool to New York. In 1917 the ship was mined off the Mersey but managed to reach Liverpool. During the war the ship was converted as a troop carrier with a capacity for 3,000 troops and their equipment. In 1919 the ship was placed on the Southampton to New York route and later that year transferred back to the Red Star Line. The ship was broken up in Osaka, Japan in 1933.

Name: **LAURENTIC**   Shipyard Number: 394
Type: Passenger Ship   Tonnage: 14,892
Length: 550 ft   Rated speed: 16 knots
Launched: 10 September 1908 Delivered: 15 April 1909
Engines: 8 cylinder Quadruple Expansion Triple Screw
Accommodation: 1st Class 230, 2nd Class 430, 3rd Class 1,000
Laid down on slipway No. 6

History of Vessel:

The ship was originally constructed as the *Alberta* for the Dominion Line but was launched for White Star as the *Laurentic*. The maiden voyage from Liverpool to Quebec and Montreal was on 29 May 1909. In 1910 the ship was used by Inspector Dew of Scotland Yard to out pace the *Montrose*, which was carrying Dr Crippen. Dew arrested Crippen on board the *Montrose*. In 1914 the vessel was used as a troop transporter. On 25 January 1917 the ship ran into minefields laid by German submarines off Malin Head, Northern Ireland. The ship sank quickly with the loss of 354 lives. Among the cargo was gold worth £5 million. The gold was recovered by 1924.

Name: **MEGANTIC**   Shipyard Number: 399
Type: Passenger Ship   Tonnage: 14,877
Length: 550 ft   Rated speed: 16 knots
Launched: 10 December 1908   Delivered: 3 June 1909
Engines: 8 cylinder Quadruple Expansion Twin Screw
Accommodation: 1st Class 230, 2nd Class 430, 3rd Class 1,000
Laid down on slipway No. 7

History of Vessel:

The ship was initially laid down as the *Albany* for the Dominion Line, but was transferred to White Star prior to launch. The maiden voyage from Liverpool to Quebec and Montreal was on 17 June 1909. The ship would bring Dr Crippen and Ethel Le Neve along with Inspector Dew back to the United Kingdom where Crippen would stand trial for murder. In 1914 the vessel was used as a troop transporter. In 1918 the ship returned to the Liverpool to New York route. In 1919 the accommodation was altered to 1st Class 325, 2nd Class 260, 3rd Class 550 and was placed on the Liverpool to Montreal route. In 1928 the ship was transferred to the

London to New York route. In July 1931 the ship was laid up in Rothesay Bay and taken to Osaka, Japan the following year to be broken up.

Name: **OLYMPIC**   Shipyard Number: 400
Type: Passenger Ship   Tonnage: 45,324
Length: 860 ft   Rated speed: 21 knots
Launched: 20 October 1910   Delivered: 31 May 1911
Engines: 8 cylinder Triple Expansion Triple Screw
Accommodation: 1st Class 735, 2nd Class 674, 3rd Class 1,026
Laid down on slipway No. 2

History of Vessel:

The maiden voyage from Southampton to New York was on 14 June 1911. In August 1911 the ship collided with *HMS Hawke* in Southampton water and was returned to Belfast for repairs. In November she returned to Southampton. Following the loss of *Titanic* in 1912 the ship returned to Belfast for work to her bulkheads and the addition of extra lifeboats. In 1914 the ship unsuccessfully tried to tow a British battleship after striking a mine in the Irish Sea. From 1915 to 1917 the ship was used as a troop transporter, under the White Ensign. In May 1918 the ship was attacked by German submarine *U103*. The submarine ran under *Olympic* and was badly damaged and sank. In 1919 the ship was converted in Belfast to oil firing and accommodation was slightly altered. In 1920 the ship returned to the Southampton to New York route. In 1928 the accommodation was reduced. On 16 May 1934 the ship in heavy fog rammed the Nantucket Lighthouse, which sank, with the loss of seven lives. In April 1935 the ship was laid up at Southampton and sold for scrap, the ship was taken to Jarrow for partial breaking up and in 1937 the hull was towed to Inverkeithing for final scrapping.

Name: **TITANIC**   Shipyard Number: 401
Type: Passenger Ship   Tonnage: 46,328
Length: 860 ft   Rated speed: 21 knots
Launched: 31 May 1911   Delivered: 2 April 1912
Engines: 8 cylinder Triple Expansion Triple Screw
Accommodation: 1st Class 1,034, 2nd Class 510, 3rd Class 1,022
Laid down on slipway No. 3

History of Vessel:

The maiden voyage from Southampton to New York was on 10 April 1912. The ship struck an iceberg in the North Atlantic on the evening of 14 April and sank on a few hours later on 15 April with the loss of approx. 1,503 lives.

Name: **ZEALANDIC**   Shipyard Number: 421
Type: Passenger / Cargo Ship Tonnage: 10,897
Length: 500 ft   Rated speed: 13 knots
Launched: 29 June 1911   Delivered: 12 October 1911
Engines: Quadruple Expansion Twin Screw

Accommodation: 1st Class 6, 3rd Class 1,000
Laid down on slipway No. 7

History of Vessel:
The maiden voyage from Liverpool to Wellington was on 30 October 1911. In 1926 the ship was chartered to the Aberdeen Line, renamed *Mamilius* and used on the London to Australia route. In 1923 the ship was sold to Shaw Savill & Albion and renamed *Mamari*. In 1939 the Admiralty bought the ship and had her altered to resemble the aircraft carrier *HMS Hermes*. In 1941 while off Crome the ship was attacked by German aircraft and was a total loss.

Name: **NOMADIC (II)**   Shipyard Number: 422
Type: Passenger Tender   Tonnage: 1,260
Launched: 25 April 1911   Delivered: 27 May 1911
Laid down on slipway No. 1

History of Vessel:
The vessel had sea trials on 27 May 1911 and was handed over to the White Star Line on 31 May along with *Olympic* and *Traffic* the sister tender. They were built to transport passengers from Cherbourg harbour out to the Olympic Class Liners, which were too large to dock in the harbour. The tender was at one stage used as a floating restaurant on the river Seine. Since then it has been laid up, unused and is the last White Star vessel still afloat. The vessel was bought at auction by the Northern Ireland Office in 2006 and returned to Belfast later that year, where a Charitable Trust was established to act on the vessel's future.

Name: **TRAFFIC**   Shipyard Number: 423
Type: Passenger Tender   Tonnage: 639
Launched: 27 April 1911   Delivered: 27 May 1911
Laid down on slipway No. 7

History of Vessel:
The vessel was built to operate along side the *Nomadic* at Cherbourg. In 1934, *Traffic* was sold, and renamed *Ingénieur Riebell*. Scuttled by the French in June 1940, and latter raised and used by the German Navy. *Traffic* was attacked and sunk by British motor torpedo boats in the English Channel on 17 January 1941.

Name: **CERAMIC**   Shipyard Number: 432
Type: Passenger Ship   Tonnage: 18,481
Length: 679 ft   Rated speed: 16 knots
Launched: 11 December 1912   Delivered: 5 July 1913
Engines: Triple Expansion Triple Screw
Accommodation: 3rd Class: 600
Laid down on slipway No. 1

History of Vessel:
The maiden voyage from Liverpool to Sydney was on 24 July 1913. From 1914 to 1917 the ship was used for troop transport. In 1920 the vessel returned to the Liverpool to Sydney route. In 1934 the ship was sold to Shaw Savill & Albion and placed on the Liverpool to Brisbane route. In 1936 the ship was reconstructed by Harland & Wolff at the Govan works, accommodation was reduced to 480 and then in 1938 to 340. From 1940 to 1942 the vessel was again used for troop transport. On 7 December 1942 the ship, while en route to Australia, was torpedoed west of the Azores by German submarine *U515*, no distress call could be sent and only one man survived.

Name: **BRITANNIC (II)**   Shipyard Number: 433
Type: Passenger Ship   Tonnage: 48,158
Length: 860 ft   Rated speed: 21 knots
Launched: 26 February 1914   Delivered: 8 December 1915
Engines: Triple Expansion Triple Screw
Accommodation: 1st Class 790, 2nd Class 830, 3rd Class 1,000
Laid down on slipway No. 2

History of Vessel:
The ship was handed over to the Admiralty on 8 December 1915 and fitted out as a hospital ship. On 21 November 1916 the ship sank four miles off Port St. Nikolo in the Aegean sea. After striking a mine, which had been laid by German submarine *U73*, the vessel sank with the loss of 21 lives.

Name: **JUSTICIA**   Shipyard Number: 436
Type: Passenger Ship   Tonnage: 32,234
Length: 740 ft   Rated speed: 18 knots
Launched: 9 July 1914   Delivered: 7 April 1917
Engines: 8 cylinder Triple Expansion Triple Screw
Laid down on slipway No. 3

History of Vessel:
The vessel was launched as the *Statendam* for the Holland-America Line. The vessel was requisitioned by the Admiralty before completion. On 7 April 1917, the ship was handed over as a troop ship under White Star Line management for the duration of the war. On 19 July 1918, the ship was torpedoed by German submarine *U64* while of the north west coast of Ireland, but remained afloat, being taken undertow. The following day she was torpedoed again by submarine *UB124* and sank with the loss of 10 lives.

Name: **CALGARIC**   Shipyard Number: 442
Type: Passenger / Cargo Ship   Tonnage: 15,120
Length: 550 ft   Rated speed: 18 knots
Launched: 5 April 1917   Delivered: 25 May 1918
Engines: 8 cylinder Triple Expansion Triple Screw
Accommodation: Cabin Class, Tourist Class, 3rd Class
Laid down on slipway No. 7

History of Vessel:
The ship was laid down as the *Orca* for the Pacific Steam

Navigation Company and was acquired by the White Star Line in 1927 when they renamed the ship *Calgaric*. The maiden voyage for the Line was from Liverpool to Montreal on 4 May 1927, it was also engaged on the Southampton to Montreal route. In 1933 the ship was laid up in Milford Haven and in December 1934 the *Calgaric* sailed to Inverkeithing where she was scrapped.

Name: **REGINA** Shipyard Number: 454
Type: Passenger Ship Tonnage: 16,313
Length: 574 ft Rated speed: 15 knots
Launched: 19 April 1917 Delivered: 26 October 1918
Engines: 8 cylinder Triple Expansion Triple Screw
Accommodation: Cabin Class 631, 3rd Class 1,824
Laid down on slipway No. 1

History of Vessel:
The ship was built by Harland and Wolff at Govan for the Dominion Line and had her engineering work carried out at the Belfast shipyard. The White Star Line took the vessel over after it had been used as a troop carrier in the last period of the war and its maiden voyage from Liverpool to New York was on 12 December 1925. The ship was sold in 1930 to the Red Star Line, and renamed *Westernland*. She was sold again the Holland-America Line in 1935 and sold again to the Admiralty in 1943 before being scrapped at Blyth in 1947.

Name: **PITTSBURGH** Shipyard Number: 457
Type: Passenger Ship Tonnage: 16,322
Length: 574 ft Rated speed: 15 knots
Launched: 11 November 1920 Delivered: 25 May 1922
Engines: 8 cylinder Triple Expansion Triple Screw
Accommodation: Cabin Class 600, 3rd Class 1,500
Laid down on slipway No. 1

History of Vessel:
The ship was originally laid down for the American Line, taken over by the White Star Line and had its maiden voyage for the Line on 6 June 1922 from Liverpool to Boston. In November 1922 the ship rescued the crew of the *Monte Grappa*. The vessel was transferred to the Red Star Line in 1923, and was renamed in 1926 as *Pennland*. In 1939 the vessel was transferred to the Holland-America Line. In 1940 the ship was acquired by the Ministry of War and served as a troop ship. In 1941 the ship was bombed and sank by German aircraft in the Gulf of Athens

Name: **VEDIC** Shipyard Number: 461
Type: Cargo Ship Tonnage: 9,332
Length: 460 ft Rated speed: 14 knots
Launched: 18 December 1918 Delivered: 10 July 1918
Engines: Steam Turbine Twin Screw
Laid down on slipway No. 9

History of Vessel:
The vessel was built and launched at Harland & Wolff's yard at Govan, and engineering work carried out in Belfast. The maiden voyage was on 11 July 1918 from Belfast to Glasgow and Boston as a troopship. In September the ship repatriated British troops from Russia. In 1920 the ship was refitted and placed on the Liverpool to Montreal route. In 1925 the vessel was refitted in Belfast for the Australian emigrant service. In 1934 the ship was scrapped at Rosyth.

Name: **GERMANIC (II)** Shipyard Number: 470
 HOMERIC
 LAURENTIC (II)
Type: Passenger Ship Tonnage: 18,724
Length: 578 ft Rated speed: 16 knots
Launched: 16 June 1927 Delivered: 1 November 1927
Engines: 8 cylinder Triple Expansion Triple
Accommodation: Cabin Class 594, Tourist Class 406, 3rd
 Class 500
Laid down on slipway No. 3

History of Vessel:
The vessel was ordered from Harland and Wolff in 1914 as *Germanic (II)*, the name was changed to *Homeric* and then *Laurentic (II)*. The maiden voyage was on 11 July 1918 from Liverpool to Quebec and Montreal. On 3 October 1932 the ship collided in the Belle Isle Strait with the *SS Lurigethan*, both were damaged above the waterline. On 18 August 1935 the ship again collided in the Irish Sea with the *Napier Star*. In 1936 the ship was used to transport troops to Palestine. In 1939 the ship was converted to an armed merchant cruiser and on 3 November the ship was torpedoed by German submarine *U99* off Bloody Foreland and sank with the loss of 49 lives.

Name: **CALGARY** Shipyard Number: 573
 DORIC (II)
Type: Passenger Ship Tonnage: 16,484
Length: 575 ft Rated speed: 15 knots
Launched: 8 August 1922 Delivered: 29 May 1923
Engines: Steam Turbine Twin Screw
Accommodation: Cabin Class 600, 3rd Class 1,700

History of Vessel:
The maiden voyage was on 8 June 1923 on the Liverpool to Montreal route. In May 1923 the ship was used for cruising. On 5 September 1935 the ship collided with the *SS Formigny* off Cape Finisterre. The vessel was scrapped at Newport in 1935.

Name: **LAURENTIC (III)** Shipyard Number: 615
Type: Passenger Ship

History of Vessel:
The order for this vessel was cancelled.

Name: **BRITANNIC (III)**   Shipyard Number: 807
Type: Passenger Ship   Tonnage: 26,943
Length: 711 ft   Rated speed: 18 knots
Launched: 6 August 1929   Delivered: 21 June 1930
Engines: 4 Stroke Single Acting, Twin Screw
Accommodation: Cabin Class 504, Tourist Class 551, 3rd
     Class 506

History of Vessel:
The maiden voyage was on 28 June 1930 on the Liverpool
to New York route. In 1935 the ship was transferred to
the London to New York route. In 1939 the ship was
requisitioned as a troop carrier. In 1948, after a refit and
reduced accommodation, the ship returned to the Liverpool
to New York route. On 1 June 1950 the ship collided with the
SS Pioneer Land, causing little damage. On 16 December 1960
the ship sailed to Inverkeithing where she was scrapped.

Name: **OCEANIC (III)**   Shipyard Number: 844
Type: Passenger Ship   Tonnage: 60,000
Length: 1,000 ft   Rated speed: 30 knots
Engines: Diesel Electric, Quadruple Screw

History of Vessel:
The keel for this gigantic new *Oceanic (III)* was laid in June
1928 but the order was soon to be cancelled.

Name: **GEORGIC (II)**   Shipyard Number: 896
Type: Passenger Ship   Tonnage: 27,267
Length: 711 ft   Rated speed: 18 knots
Launched: 12 November 1931   Delivered: 10 June 1932
Engines: 4 Stroke Single Acting, Twin Screw
Accommodation: Cabin Class 479, Tourist Class 557, 3rd
     Class 506

History of Vessel:
The maiden voyage for this, the last White Star Line ship
built at Harland and Wolff, was on 25 June 1932 on the
Liverpool to New York route. The following year the ship was
transferred to the Southampton to New York route, while in
1935 after the merger with Cunard the ship was placed on the
London to New York route. In 1940 the ship was converted
to a troop ship at the Clyde. On 14 July 1941 she was bombed
and burnt out at the Gulf of Suez and towed to Port Sudan for
temporary repairs. She was towed back to Belfast and rebuilt
as a troop ship. In 1948 the vessel was refitted at Tyneside for
the Australian emigrant trade. The ship was finally scrapped
at Garelough in February 1956.

195

Other Selected Ships built by Belfast Shipyards

This list is a purely personal choice to show the diversity of the output of the Belfast shipyards in the various types of vessels that they constructed.

Name: **KHERSONESE**   Built by: Robert Hickson
Initially built for F. Lewis & E. Geoghegan, Belfast
Type: Cargo Ship   Tonnage: 1409
Length: 246 ft   Max. Rated Speed: 9 knots
Launched: 4 October 1855   Rated A1 at LLoyds
Engines: Sail and 2 cylinder simple steam engine by
    Randolph, Elder & Company, Glasgow

History of Vessel:
The maiden voyage under Captain Thompson was in April 1856 when she sailed from Liverpool to the Black Sea. The ship was engaged in repatriating troops from the Crimean War. In 1856, while on a return trip from America, the ship lost a propeller and had to continue under sail. The ship was sold to the North Atlantic Steam Navigation Company in 1857 and two years later was again sold to Weir & Cochrane of Liverpool who placed the ship on the Liverpool to New York route. In 1866 her engines were removed and the ship re-rigged as a barque. In 1889 the ship was sold to Dutch owners and in 1891 the ship was destroyed by fire while tied up at Montevideo.

Name: **CIRCASSION**   Built by: Robert Hickson
Initially built for North Atlantic Steam Navigation Co.
Type: Passenger / Cargo Ship   Tonnage: 1,387
Length: 255 ft   Max. Rated Speed: 9 knots
Launched: 18 July 1856
Engines: Sail and 2 cylinder simple steam engine by
    Randolph, Elder & Company, Glasgow
Accommodation: Cabin Class, Intermediate Class & 3rd Class

History of Vessel:
The Maiden voyage with Captain Powell in charge, was on 7 March 1857 from Liverpool to St. John's with 200 passengers, but due to heavy gales had to put back to Liverpool, finally setting sail on 19 March. In September 1857 the ship was taken over for use as transport in the Indian Mutiny. In 1858 the ship was charted to the Galway Line sailing from Galway to New York. The ship was captured by the American Navy while blockade running, and taken over by the Americans. Sailed for Ruger Bros. From New York to Southampton. And sailed for some years on the North Atlantic. In 1874 her engines were removed and in 1876 the vessel was wrecked off Long Island.

Name: **VENETIAN**   Built by: Harland & Wolff
Initially built for J. Bibby & Sons (The Bibby Line)
Type: Cargo Ship   Tonnage: 1,508
Length 270 ft   Rated Speed: Steam 6–7
                    knots, sail 10–12 knots
Launched: 30 July 1859   Delivered: 14 August 1859
Engines: Sail and 2 cylinder simple steam engine
Accommodation: 1st Class & 2nd Class

History of Vessel:
Originally engaged by the Bibby Line on the Mediterranean route. The ship was sold in 1873 to Leyland & Co. and then sold again in 1870 to the African Steamship Co. when she was renamed *Landana*. In 1891 the ship was sold to Gerard of South America and the name changed again to *Tarpaca*. The ship was wrecked off the coast of Chile in 1894.

Name: **JANE PORTER**   Built by: Harland & Wolff
Initially built for J. P. Corry & Co.
Type: Sailing Ship   Tonnage: 952
Length: 200 ft
Launched: 1 September 1860   Delivered: 15 Sep 1860
Engines: Sail

History of Vessel:
The ship was the first iron hulled sailing vessel built by the shipyard. It was constructed for the local Belfast Timber importers, and named after the wife of one of the firm's Directors, William Corry. The *Jane Porter* was engaged on the Calcutta route. In 1889 the ship was sold to the Liverpool firm of William Ross & Co., and in 1896 the ship was transferred to German owners and renamed *Nanny*.

Name: **DALMATIAN**   Built by: Harland & Wolff
Initially built for J. Bibby & Sons (The Bibby Line)
Type: Cargo Ship   Tonnage: 1,989
Length: 331 ft
Launched: 19 November 1861   Delivered: December 1861
Engines: 2 cylinder simple steam engine

History of Vessel:
The *Dalmatian* was the first ship in which Harland altered the standardised design of the ship by increasing the length of the vessel and not increasing the breadth. Due to this unusual design the ships were referred to as 'Bibby Coffins'. The design of the masts was changed and resulted in improved handling of the square set sails. Steam winches were also provided to assist with cargo loading and discharging. Changes were also made in the design of the boilers, allowing

seawater to be used as a coolant, without seeping into the boilers. The Bibby Line set a precedent by ending all their ships in *ian*.

Name: **BRITISH EMPIRE**   Built by: Harland & Wolff
Initially built for British Shipowners Ltd
Type: Passenger / Cargo Ship   Tonnage: 3,361
Length: 392 ft   Rated Speed: 12 knots
Launched: 18 May 1878   Delivered: 10 August 1878
Engines: 4 cylinder compound steam engine
Accommodation: 1st Class 70, Steerage Class 800

History of Vessel:
The ship prior to entering service was sold to the Holland-America Line and renamed *Rotterdam*, and engaged on the Rotterdam to New York Route. The vessel was an iron hulled four masted barque. The ship was chartered to the American Line and used between Liverpool and Philadelphia. The vessel was renamed *Edam* and was sold for scrap in Italy in 1899.

Name: **OCEANA**   Built by: Harland & Wolff
Initially built for Peninsular & Oriental Steam Navigation Co. (The P. & O. Line)
Type: Passenger Ship   Tonnage: 6,610
Length: 468 ft   Rated Speed: 16 knots
Launched: 17 September 1887   Delivered: 26 February 1888
Engines: Triple expansion steam
Accommodation: 1st Class 250, 3rd Class 160

History of Vessel:
The ship cost £200,000 to construct. The vessel was also fitted with four masts, and there was a cargo capacity of 4,000 tons. Coal consumption in the ship was around 110 tons per day. In March 1912 the *Oceana* was in collision with a German barque in the Straits of Dover. The ship sank in the English Channel. In her hold was bullion valued at £700,000, which was recovered at a later stage.

Name: **TITANIC**   Built by: McIlwaine & McColl
Initially built for H & J Scott
Type: Schooner   Tonnage: 1,608
Length: 280 ft
Launched: 4 May 1888
Engines: Triple expansion with 3 cylinders operating at 160 psi

History of Vessel:
The vessel was acquired by Smith & Service of Glasgow before being fully completed and its maiden voyage, under Captain S.S. Nelson, was from Belfast to Glasgow. The ship was later sold to the Ulidan Steam Navigation Co. who sold the *Titanic* in 1903 to a company in Chile who renamed the ship the *Luis Alberto*, its name was later changed in 1915 to *Don Alberto*. There is no further record of the ship after 1928.

Name: **RESULT**   Built by: Paul Rodgers/ Robert Kent & Co. at Carrickfergus
Initially built for Thomas Ashburner & Co.
Type: 3 masted steel Schooner   Tonnage: 122
Length: 102 ft
Launched: 6 January 1893

History of Vessel:
Paul Rodgers in his Carrickfergus shipyard started to construct the *Result*, but was forced to sell the yard to Robert Kent & Co. who continued with the building of the ship. In 1909 the ship was sold at auction to G.C. Clark of Devon. Captain S.J. Ingledon was placed in charge. In 1914 a single cylinder 45 hp engine was fitted, while in 1916 the Admiralty had the ship rigged out as a Q ship. She was rigged with double topsails and a quick firing gun on was placed aft. In 1917 the *Result* engaged with a German submarine *U45* and damaged it. After the war the ship was returned to her owners. The ship was laid up in 1967 and three years later it was bought by the Ulster Folk & Transport Museum at Cultra.

Name: **OROPESA**   Built by: Harland & Wolff
Initially built for Pacific Steam Navigation Co.
Type: Passenger Ship   Tonnage: 5,317
Length: 421 ft   Rated Speed: 15½ knots
Launched: 29 November 1894   Delivered: 9 February 1895
Engines: Triple expansion steam
Accommodation: 1st Class & 2nd Class

History of Vessel:
The *Oropesa* was the ship of this Line to be fitted with twin propellers. The ship was engaged on the Liverpool to South America route and sailing into the Pacific via the Straits of Magellan. During the First World War the ship was fitted out as an armed merchant cruiser with six six-inch guns and two six-pounder guns. She was attached to the 10th Cruiser Squadron and sank a German U Boat. In December 1915 the ship was transferred to the French Navy and renamed *Champagne*, she was torpedoed in the Irish Sea in 1917 and was lost.

Name: **CHINA**   Built by: Harland & Wolff
Initially built for Peninsular & Oriental Steam Navigation Co. (The P. & O. Line)
Type: Passenger Ship   Tonnage: 7,899
Length: 500 ft   Rated Speed: 16 knots
Launched: 13 June 1896   Delivered: 26 February 1888
Engines: Triple expansion steam
Accommodation: 1st Class 320, 3rd Class 160

History of Vessel:
The maiden voyage of the ship was on 18 December 1896 from the UK to Australia. Two years later the ship suffered

197

damage and for a while was stranded on Perim Island near the Yemen. The ship was repaired and had a long and successful career on both the Australian and Indian routes. The ship was scrapped in May 1928 with a Japanese shipyard buying the ship for £24,000.

198

Name: **STAR OF AUSTRALIA** Built by: Workman Clark
Initially built for J.P. Corry (Belfast)

Type: Cargo Ship   Tonnage: 7,200
Length: 440 ft   Rated Speed: 12 knots
Entered Service 1899

History of Vessel:

The ship was initially square rigged on the foremost but this was removed quite quickly. In 1904 she rescued the crew of a sinking Canadian ship during a voyage to South America. In 1912 whist 600 miles east of Aden the propeller shaft snapped, which resulted in the ship drifting. There was no radio fitted to the ship, so two officers and four crewmen took to a lifeboat in an attempt to get to Aden and raise the alarm. Within two days they managed to contact a ship the *Glenlochy* which came to their assistance and towed the disabled ship to Aden. The ship was towed back to England for repairs. The ship changed ownership to the Commonwealth & Dominion Line in 1916 and was renamed *Port Stephens*. In 1918 she collided with and sank the *North Cambria*. In 1920 she assisted in the rescue of the steamship *Tashnoo* and was awarded salvage to the value of £9,500. The ship was broken up in Italy in May 1924.

Name: **DEVONIAN**   Built by: Harland & Wolff
Initially built for Frederick Leyland & Co. (The Leyland Line)

Type: Passenger Ship   Tonnage: 10,417
Length: 570 ft   Rated Speed: 14 knots
Launched: 28 June 1900   Delivered: 6 September 1900
Engines: Triple expansion steam
Accommodation: 1st Class 135

History of Vessel:

The maiden voyage of the ship was on the Liverpool to Boston route on which she was engaged. On 21 August 1917 the *Devonian* was torpedoed by a German U boat 20 miles of Tory Island, the ship sank and two people were lost.

Name: **IROQUOIS**   Built by: Harland and Wolff
Initially built for Anglo American Oil Company

Type: Oil Tanker   Tonnage: 9,201
Length: 476 ft   Rated Speed: 16 knots
Launched: 27 June 1907   Delivered: 19 October 1907
Engines: Quad expansion steam
Accommodation: nil

History of Vessel:

The *Iroquois* was the first oil tanker to be built by Harland &

Wolff, and was, when it entered service, the largest such vessel of her time. The ship was designed to take under permanent tow the *Navahoe* (Yard No. 389) an oil barge of 7,718 tons.

Name: **DESEADO**   Built by: Harland & Wolff
Initially built for Royal Mail Steam Packet Company

Type: Passenger / Cargo Ship   Tonnage: 11,471
Length: 500 ft   Rated Speed: 13½ knots
Launched: 26 October 1911   Delivered: 27 June 1912
Engines: Quad expansion steam
Accommodation: 1st Class 95, 2nd Class 38 & 3rd Class 860

History of Vessel:

The maiden voyage of the ship was on 5 July 1912 when the ship left Liverpool sailing to Buenos Aires. The ship was one of the largest meat carriers afloat and could carry up to 41,500 carcasses of Argentinean beef. The *Deseado* was sold for scrap in 1934.

Name: **APPAM**   Built by: Harland &Wolff
Initially built for British & African Steamship Company

Type: Passenger / Cargo Ship   Tonnage: 7781
Length: 426 ft   Rated Speed: 14 knots
Launched: 10 October 1912   Delivered: 27 February 1913
Engines: Quad expansion steam
Accommodation: 400 in three Classes

History of Vessel:

The maiden voyage of the ship was on 12 March 1913 sailing from Liverpool to West Africa. The ship was requisitioned as a troop carrier during the First World War and was captured in January 1916 by a German ship the *Moewe*. The ship was taken to America with crew and passengers on board and finally released. The vessel was renamed *Mandingo* for the rest of the war and after the war returned to the West Africa route on which she was engaged until she was sold for scrap in 1936.

Name: **KATOOMBA**   Built by Harland & Wolff
Initially built for McIlwraith, McEacharn & Co. of Australia

Type: Passenger Ship   Tonnage: 9,424
Length: 450 ft   Rated Speed: 16 knots
Launched: 10 April 1913   Delivered: 10 July 1913
Engines: Triple expansion steam
Accommodation: 1st class 150, 2nd class 250, 3rd Class 300

History of Vessel:

The vessel was called for service in the First World War as a troop carrier. Following the War she was the first ship to pass through the Dardanelles. The ship was used on the Australian route and also used for cruising the Pacific Islands. The ship was again requisitioned as a troop carrier in the Second World War and was shelled by a Japanese submarine but escaped. In 1946 the ship was transferred to Italian owners and was used on the Marseilles to French Africa routes. In 1949 the vessel was converted to oil burning and renamed *Columbia*, she was again sold to South African owners, the ship was finally broken up in Japan in 1959.

Name: **CARDIGANSHIRE**   Built by: Workman Clark
Initially built for Royal mail S.P. Company
Type: Cargo Ship   Tonnage: 9,426
Length: 520 ft   Rated Speed: 14 knots
Entered Service 1913

History of Vessel:
On entering service the ship was placed on the Far East route. In September 1914 the ship was used to ferry troops across the channel to France and was commandeered by the Admiralty in 1915. At one stage, while entering the harbour at Zeebruge, the Belgian pilot ordered full speed ahead and steered the vessel into the stone breakwater causing damage to the bow. He was later arrested and finally shot for an act of sabotage. In April 1915 the ship was at the Dardenelles, and was chased by a German submarine but escaped. The ship also transported US troops to the United Kingdom. In 1929 the ship was sold to Christian Salvesen & Co. and converted into a whaling ship. On 27 July 1940, while approaching Rosyth, the ship struck a mine and sank in the Firth of Forth.

Name: **MINNEKAHDA**   Built by: Harland & Wolff
Initially built for Atlantic Transport Co.
Type: Passenger Ship   Tonnage: 17,220
Length: 620 ft   Rated Speed: 16½ knots
Launched: 8 March 1917   Delivered: 21 March 1918
Engines: Triple expansion steam
Accommodation: 3rd Class 2,150

History of Vessel:
The ship was engaged on the Hamburg to New York route primarily carrying emigrants. In 1924 the ship was transferred to the London to New York route and was refitted to accommodate all classes of passengers. In 1926 the ship was refitted again as a 'Tourist' Class carrying 750 passengers. The ship was broken up in Scotland in 1936.

Name: **MAYOLA**   Built by: Harland & Wolff
Initially built for Peninsular & Oriental Steam Navigation Co. (The P. & O. Line)
Type: Passenger Ship   Tonnage: 20,837
Length: 600 ft   Rated Speed: 17½ knots
Launched: 19 April 1923   Delivered: 25 October 1923
Engines: Quad expansion steam
Accommodation: 1st Class 327, 2nd Class 329

History of Vessel:
The maiden voyage was from London to Bombay, and then

engaged on the London to Australia route. During the Second World War the ship served as an auxiliary cruiser armed with eight six-inch guns during this conversion. The ships aft dummy funnel was removed as well as her main mast. Following the war the ship returned to the Australian route and continued in service until she was sold for scrap in 1954 for £100,000.

Name: **ULSTER MONARCH**   Built by: Harland & Wolff
Initially built for Belfast Steamship Company
Type: Cross Channel Passenger Ship   Tonnage: 3,851
Length: 358 ft   Rated Speed: 17 knots
Launched: 24 January 1929   Delivered: 10 June 1929
Engines: 10-cylinder diesel
Accommodation: 1st Class 418, 3rd Class 86

History of Vessel:
The ship was the first motorship to be built for the Belfast to Liverpool route. During the Second World War the ship was used as a troop carrier and was used at the evacuation from Dunkirk. She was fitted out as a landing craft and was used in the North African campaign, as well as Tripoli. She was hit by a torpedo, which passed straight through her without exploding. She returned to the Belfast to Liverpool route after the war and in 1966 was sold for scrapping at Ghent.

Name: **HMS BELFAST**   Built by: Harland & Wolff
Initially built for The Admiralty
Type: 'Southampton' Class Cruiser   Tonnage: 10,173
Length: 613 ft   Rated Speed: 32 knots
Launched: 17 March 1938   Delivered: 3 August 1939
Engines: Four Admiralty Drum Boilers
Accommodation: Compliment of 750–850 officers and men

History of Vessel:
The ship, which was launched on St. Patrick's Day, cost in the region of £2.1 million. She played an important role in the Second World War and was involved in the sinking of the German Cruiser *Scharnhorst*. She was also used as part of the naval bombardment of the French coast and especially the Gold and Juno beachheads during the D-Day landings. Following the War the ship was used in support of the United Nations in the Korean War. *HMS Belfast* was finally decommissioned in 1965 and in 1971 the ship was saved and placed on the Thames in London.

Name: **HMS FORMIDABLE**   Built by: Harland & Wolff
Initially built for The Admiralty
Type: 'Illustrious' Class Aircraft Carrier   Tonnage: 28,094
Length: 781 ft   Rated Speed: 32 knots
Launched: 17 August 1939   Delivered: 24 Nov 1940
Engines: Admiralty Drum Boilers
Accommodation: Compliment of 2,200 officers and men

History of Vessel:

On launch day the wooden props supporting the keel at the bow of the ship collapsed allowing *HMS Formidable* to slide down the slipway before the launching ceremony. A woman who was present was hit by flying metal and was killed. The ship took part in the battle of Cape Matapan in March 1941. In May 1941 *HMS Formidable* suffered serious damage following an air attack by 1,000 kg bombs. The vessel was out of commission for six months and was repaired in the USA. While serving in the Far East the ship was attacked in a Kamikaze attack. She was placed on the reserve list in 1947 and finally scrapped in November 1956 at Inverkeithing.

Name: **PARTHIA**   Built by: Harland & Wolff
Initially built for Cunard-White Star Line
Type: Passenger Ship   Tonnage: 13,362
Length: 531 ft   Rated Speed: 17 knots
Launched: 25 February 1947   Delivered: 7 April 1948
Engines: Steam Turbine
Accommodation: 1st Class 251

History of Vessel:

The *Parthia* was the only vessel ever built for the Cunard Line at the Harland & Wolff shipyard. The maiden voyage was on 10 April 1948 from Liverpool to New York. She was equipped with motion stabilisers and all public rooms were air-conditioned. In November 1961 the ship was sold to the New Zealand Shipping Company and renamed *Remura*. In January 1965 the vessel again changed hands, being bought by the Australian Steamship Company and renamed *Aramac*. The vessel was scrapped in Taiwan, the contract being completed on 31 May 1970.

Name: **JUAN PERON**   Built by Harland & Wolff
Initially built for Compania Argentina de Pesca S.A.
Type: Whale Factory Ship   Tonnage: 24,569
Launched: 4 April 1950   Delivered: 15 October 1951
Engines: Diesel

History of Vessel:

The *Juan Peron* cost in the region of £3 million to construct and was named after the Argentinean dictator. It appears to have been a somewhat jinxed ship. Eva Peron was due to visit Belfast to launch the ship, but due to political unrest in Argentina, her visit was cancelled. A Harland & Wolff secretary, who was considered to have a 'latin look' about her, was given the honour of launching the ship. During fitting out a gangplank collapsed while workmen were leaving the ship after a days work. Nineteen men were killed and 59 were injured in the accident. It was rumoured that the gangplank had originally been used during the construction of the *Titanic* in 1912. After the fall of Peron the ship was renamed the *Cruz Del Sur,* and was not a very successful whaling ship. During her history a woman was murdered on board and her body thrown overboard. The ship was later used to carry bulk oil. No further details of the ships final fate could be found.

Name: **SOUTHERN CROSS**   Built by: Harland & Wolff
Initially built for Shaw Savill & Albion Co.
Type: Passenger Ship   Tonnage: 20,204
Length: 531 ft   Rated Speed: 17 knots
Launched: 17 August 1954   Delivered: 28 February 1955
Engines: Steam Turbine
Accommodation: 1st Class 251

History of Vessel:

The Southern Cross cost around £3.5 million to construct. H.M. Queen Elizabeth II launched the ship, becoming the first Monarch to launch a passenger ship. During construction the owners requested that the propelling machinery be placed aft in the ship. This had the effect of increasing the available space for passengers. The ship was engaged on the emigrant run between the UK and Australia and New Zealand. In 1973 the ship was sold to the Ulysses Line and renamed *Calypso*.

Name: **CANBERRA**   Built by: Harland & Wolff
Initially built for Peninsular & Oriental Steam Navigation Co. (The P. & O. Line)
Type: Passenger Ship   Tonnage: 45,270
Length: 818 ft   Rated Speed: 29 knots
Launched: 16 March 1960   Delivered: 19 May 1961
Engines: Oil fired superheated boilers
Accommodation: 1st Class 548, Tourist Class 1,690

History of Vessel:

When the *Canberra* left Belfast, the shipyard had lost around £2 million on the contract. The ship was engaged on the Southampton to Sydney emigrant or assisted passage route. In January 1963 the ship suffered from a serious fire, while approximately 150 miles from Malta. *Canberra* had to be towed back to Belfast for repair work. The ship was then used for cruising and in 1974 the accommodation was changed to one class for 1,737 passengers. The vessel was about to be sold when the British Government requisitioned her to serve as a troop carrier in the Falklands War. While in San Carlos Bay she was attacked by Argentinean aircraft but survived. Following that conflict, *Canberra* was used to repatriate around 5,000 Argentinean POWs. She returned to cruising and was broken up in 1997.

Name: **SEA QUEST**   Built by: Harland & Wolff
Initially built for B.P. Clyde Tanker Co.
Type: Sedco Oil Drilling Rig   Tonnage: 7,900
Length: 818 ft   Rated Speed: 29 knots
Launched: 7 January 1966   Delivered: 5 July 1966

History of Vessel:

The Sea Quest was not allocated a yard number but rather

given an order number. When launched the three-legged platform was the largest oil rig built in the United Kingdom. The three bottle shaped legs were each 35 ft in diameter and because of the size of the rig it had to be constructed on adjoining slipways. Various shipyards around the world doubted that it would be possible to launch the platform, but it carried out, taking over an hour to slide down the slipway. The *Sea Quest* was used for oil exploration drilling in the North Sea, and was the first oil rig to discover oil.

Name: **MYRINA**   Built by: Harland & Wolff
Initially built for Deutsche Shell A.G.
Type: VLCC Oil Tanker   Tonnage: 95,450
Length: Unknown   Rated Speed: 29 knots
Launched: 6 September 1967   Delivered: 24 April 1968
Engines: Steam Turbine

History of Vessel:
The *Myrina* was the first Very Large Crude Carrier (V.L.C.C.) to be built in the United Kingdom, and the largest such vessel at that time in Europe. With the *Myrina* being so large the ship had to have her aft section constructed first, this was then pulled under control down the slipway so that there would be room to complete the forward section. This problem was to eventually be overcome by the construction of the Building Dock.

Name: **GALLOWAY PRINCESS**   Built by: Harland & Wolff
Initially built for Sealink UK Ltd.
Type: Passenger / Car Ferry   Tonnage: 6268
Length: 818 ft   Rated Speed: 29 knots
Launched: 24 May 1979   Delivered: 22 April 1980
Engines: Diesel

History of Vessel:
The vessel was used on the Larne to Stranraer route. In 1991 the ship was renamed *Stena Galloway*.

Name: **ANVIL POINT**   Built by: Harland & Wolff
Initially built for The Ministry of Defence
Type: Roll on Roll Off Ferry   Tonnage: 45,270
Length: 818 ft   Rated Speed: 29 knots
Launched: 1 April 2003   Delivered: 23 June 2003
Engines: Oil fired superheated boilers

History of Vessel:
The *Anvil Point* was the last ship to be built at the Harland & Wolff shipyard.

Shipyard Trades

Trades engaged in the Shipyard

Blacksmiths
Blacksmiths Strickers
Blacksmiths Helpers
Boatbuilders
Boilermakers
Brassmoulders
Bull Runty
Cabinetmakers
Caulkers
Coppersmiths
Crane Drivers
Drillers
Electricians
Fitters
Hole cutters
Ironmen
Iron sorters
Joiners
Joiners in ships
Labourers
Loftsmen
Minute men
Painters
Patternmakers
Platers & Helpers
Polishers
Plumbers
Red leaders
Riggers & Helpers
Riveters (Heater Boy, Catch Boy & Holderup)
Rivet Counters
Sawers
Sheetmetal workers
Shipwrights
Stablemen
Stagers
Storemen
Tinsmith
Woodturners
Works Fireman (with fire engine)

Trades engaged in the Offices

Accountants
Bookkeepers
Cooks and ancillary staff
Cleaners
Draughtsmen
Message Boys
Naval Architects
Secretaries
Tracers
Telephonists
Time keepers
Managers

Notes to Chapters

Chapter 1
1 Irwin, D., Tides and Times in the 'Port, Groomsport: Groomsport Presbyterian Church, 1991, p. 13
2 Millin S., *Sidelights on Belfast History*, Belfast: 1932
3 Moss, M. & Hume, J. R., *Shipbuilders to the World*, Belfast: Blackstaff Press, 1986
4 *Bible Christian*, February 1834

Chapter 2
1 *Northern Whig*, June 1831
2 Interview with V. Dargan January 2009

Chapter 3
1 *Belfast Newsletter*, November 1853
2 *Belfast Newsletter*, August 1854

Chapter 4
1 Harland, E.J., 'Shipbuilding in Belfast – its origin and progress' in Smiles, S. (ed.), *Men of Invention and Industry*, London: John Murray, 1884
2 *Belfast Newsletter*, July 1855
3 Rebbeck, D., *The history of iron shipbuilding on the Queen's Island up to July 1874*, unpublished Ph.D. Thesis, dated 1950 and held at Queens University Belfast
4 *Belfast Newsletter*, July 1859
5 Harland, E.J., 'Shipbuilding in Belfast – its origin and progress' in Smiles, S. (ed.), *Men of Invention and Industry*, London: John Murray, 1884
6 Public Record Office in Northern Ireland, Harland and Wolff Records, document number D/2805
7 Harland, E.J., 'Shipbuilding in Belfast – its origin and progress' in Smiles, S. (ed.), *Men of Invention and Industry*, London: John Murray, 1884
8 *Ibid*

Chapter 6
1 Interview with T. McBride July 1994

Chapter 7
1 *Belfast Telegraph*, 17 August 1939

Chapter 9
1 Harland, E.J., 'Shipbuilding in Belfast – its origin and progress' in Smiles, S. (ed.), *Men of Invention and Industry*, London: John Murray, 1884

Chapter 10
1 Anderson, E.B., *Sailing Ships of Ireland*, Dublin: Morris & Co., 1951

Chapter 11
1 *Belfast Newsletter*, December 1895
2 Jefferson, H., *Viscount Pirrie of Belfast,* Belfast: Wm. Mullan & Son Ltd., 1948
3 *Ibid*

Chapter 13
1 Interview with Sarah Agnew, September 2010

Chapter 14
1 Jefferson, H., *Viscount Pirrie of Belfast,* Belfast: Wm. Mullan & Son Ltd., 1948, p. 69
2 British Board of Trade Inquiry 1912. Evidence from A.M. Carlisle
3 *Belfast Newsletter*, 10 October 1910
4 Public Record Office in Northern Ireland, Harland and Wolff Records, document number D/2805/MIN/A1
5 Public Record Office in Northern Ireland, Harland and Wolff Records, document number D2805/C1/1
6 Public Record Office in Northern Ireland, Harland and Wolff Records, document number D2805/C1/1
7 Letter in Andrews family collection
8 *Belfast Telegraph*, December 1912
9 Public Record Office in Northern Ireland, Harland and Wolff Records, document number D2805/TUR/44

Chapter 15
1 Johnstone, R., *Belfast, Portraits of a City,* London: Barrie & Jenkins Ltd., 1990, p. 113
2 *Ibid*
3 National Electoral Results, 1892
4 Wolff Obituary, *The Times*, London, April 1913
5 Johnstone, R., *Belfast, Portraits of a City,* London: Barrie & Jenkins Ltd., 1990, p. 114
6 *Belfast Newsletter*, 21 April 1911
7 Johnstone, R., *Belfast, Portraits of a City,* London: Barrie & Jenkins Ltd., 1990, p. 113
8 Millin S., *Sidelights on Belfast History*, Belfast: 1932, p. 129
9 *Ibid*
10 Jefferson, H., *Viscount Pirrie of Belfast,* Belfast: Wm. Mullan & Son Ltd., 1948
11 Public Record Office in Northern Ireland, Andrews Papers, document number D3655/A/2/6
12 Letter from Thomas Andrews to Helen R. Barbour 1905, Morrison collection

Chapter 16

1 Jefferson, H., *Viscount Pirrie of Belfast,* Belfast: Wm. Mullan & Son Ltd., 1948
2 Jefferson, H., *Viscount Pirrie of Belfast,* Belfast: Wm. Mullan & Son Ltd., 1948
4 *Belfast Telegraph,* 21 July 1898
5 Public Record Office in Northern Ireland, Andrews Papers, document number D3655/A/6/1

6 Jefferson, H., *Viscount Pirrie of Belfast,* Belfast: Wm. Mullan & Son Ltd., 1948

Chapter 17

1 Pirrie Obituary, *Belfast Newsletter,* June 1924
2 Letter from Saxon Payne to Helen Andrews, May 1912, Andrews family collection

Owen, D.J., *A Short History of the Port of Belfast,* Belfast: 1912

Owen, D.J., *History of Belfast,* Belfast: W.G. Baird, 1921

Stewart, A.T.Q., *The Ulster Crisis,* London: Faber & Faber Ltd., 1979

Sweetnam, R., & Nimmons, C., *Port of Belfast 1785–1985,* Belfast: Belfast Harbour Commissioners, 1985

Newspapers and Periodicals

Belfast Evening Telegraph

Belfast Newsletter

Belfast Telegraph

Bible Christian Magazine

Causeway Journal, Belfast: Autumn 1997

CQD Titanic, Official Journal of the Belfast Titanic Society, Various editions

Northern Life, Vol. 2, January 1981–June 1981

Northern Whig

Belfast Natural History and Philosophical Society Report and Proceedings of for Session 1915–1916, published 1917

Maritime Wales, No.7, 1983

The Signal, BT N.Ireland magazine, Issue No 12, August 1988

Unpublished Manuscripts

Rebbeck, D., *The history of iron shipbuilding on the Queen's Island up to July 1874,* unpublished Ph.D. Thesis, dated 1950 and held at Queens University Belfast.

Internet Web Sites Consulted

Hickson, A, *Hickson Genealogy on the Internet,* www.hickson.org

www.manfamily.org/Schwabe_Family.htm

www.lennonwylie.co.uk

1911 Irish Census online, www.census.nationalarchives.ie

Picture Credits

Index

Index of Ships